MW01711898

SECURE AND UNCERTAIN

Secure and Uncertain

A Father's Story

Raymond F. Currie

Front cover image: Brazilian soapstone sculpture, *Things We Share*, 2001, by Abraham Anghik Ruben, Canadian, b. 1951; 58.0 x 53.7 x 31.5 cm; collection of The Winnipeg Art Gallery; gift of Tradition Fine Foods Ltd.; accession # 2004-30; photograph by Ernest Mayer, The Winnipeg Art Gallery

Cover and text design: Rachelle Painchaud-Nash

Photograph of Raymond Currie on page ii courtesy of Frank Nolan

Unless otherwise noted, all photographs are courtesy of the author

Library and Archives Canada Cataloguing in Publication

Currie, Raymond F., 1934-
Secure and uncertain : a father's story / Raymond F. Currie.

ISBN 978-0-9736071-2-3

1. Currie, Raymond F., 1934- 2. Catholic ex-priests—Manitoba—Biography. 3. Deans (Education)—Manitoba—Winnipeg—Biography. 4. University of Manitoba—Faculty—Biography. 5. Parents of children with disabilities—Manitoba—Biography. I. Title.

LE3.M38318C87 2008 378.7127'43 C2008-902451-6

Dedicated to
the Currie family, a supportive and safe haven,
my kissing cousins, the Sturleys,
their ancestors and progeny, and the Thackers,
especially Charlene, the third family I call my own.

Bohr: A curious sort of diary memory is.
Heisenberg: You open the pages, and all the neat headings and tidy jottings dissolve around you.

—Michael Frayn, *Copenhagen*

Dad, the trouble with you is that you think everyone is nice!

—Catherine, our daughter

One day I gathered my four sons around me and gave them each a stick, asking them to break it. It was easy for them. I then asked them to put the sticks all together in a bundle and try again. Of course they could not break it. The bundle, that's the family.

—Alvin Straight, *The Straight Story*

We must never be afraid to speculate—and never, never be afraid of those who urge us to contemplate the seemingly impossible, to examine ancient formulae for new meanings. Believe me, we are more readily betrayed by our certainties than by our doubts and curiosities.

—Morris West, *Lazarus*

We do not teach so that our students know all the answers, but rather to lead them to examine their own faith, morals, assumptions, as well as the consensuses by which they are surrounded.

—Walter Kauffman, *The Future of the Humanities*

Contents

FOREWORD

Secure and Uncertain is an amazing book; it is at once an autobiography, a confession, an apologia, a case history of a father written by that father, a love story.

The author, Raymond Currie, at the beginning of Chapter 3, asks himself a question that gives shape to his book: "How did I get from my life as a Franciscan friar and priest to that of a married man with two children?"

Raymond Currie, twice a father, first in the Catholic Church, then as the father of a family, begins to answer his own question by continuing, "As any social scientist might expect, it was not the result of a momentous decision following a conversion experience in the tradition of St. Paul. Rather, it resulted from a series of small choices made over a period of about 10 years. That is also the best way to describe how I decided to enter the Franciscans in the first place."

The story of that series of small choices becomes a book that is grand in its design, daring to portray and interpret a private life, a public life, a secular life, a spiritual life. Raymond Currie grew up in a Catholic family in the secular prairie city that is Winnipeg. He aspired to the priesthood, an aspiration that took him at the age of 14 to study at St. Anthony's College in Edmonton, a place where he was to discover, along with his deep spiritual concerns, the pleasures and pain of youthful sexual desire. He came early in life to know the conflict between security and uncertainty.

The road to a life as a Franciscan friar took him to study in Quebec and in New York City. In New York he was to meet Charlene, a nun from Kentucky, a fellow student who was to become his companion and support and wife, the mother to their two adopted children. That relationship with Charlene was to lead back, by a series of small choices, to Winnipeg.

Raymond Currie is a sociologist with a novelist's impulse to render the world as story. His accounts of the lives of his parents are models of anecdotal story-telling. Models of the homily, one is tempted to add. Raymond Currie as a child was fascinated by oratory, a fascination that years later led to his preaching retreats across western Canada. It helped lead him to classrooms and a deanship at the University of Manitoba. It gave him the skills that allowed him to engage in the debates that are part of current society and part of the shape of the self.

Secure and Uncertain, in its larger intention, is just that: a debate we engage in with our various selves, with our children, with ideas of learning, with the community, with versions of the spiritual. How and why do we come to choose, or receive, the lives we live? Where do we choose to live our lives? What is our relationship and our responsibility to our fellow human beings?

Raymond Currie is a philosopher of the lived life. He is a thinker and a story-maker. He tells a prairie story that engages and entertains us, and all the while he guides us through a contest for his soul that echoes St. Augustine's courageous and heartfelt autobiography, *Confessions*.

—Robert Kroetsch
Winnipeg, March 2008

Acknowledgements

I want to express my deep appreciation to Abraham Anghik Ruben, a friend, and an outstanding Inuit sculptor who has graciously permitted me to reprint a photograph of one of his remarkable art pieces on the cover of this book. (Charlene and I cherish a large sculpture of his, which stands inside the entrance to our home.) The Winnipeg Art Gallery generously provided the photograph, which was on the cover of the catalogue describing Abraham's solo exhibition at the Gallery in 2001–2002.

My large network of family, relatives, friends, colleagues, university administrators, doctors, social workers, secretaries, neighbours, and politicians all deserve my deep appreciation for their support, affection, advice, and tolerance.

The contribution of my wife, Charlene, to my life cannot be summarized in a few sentences. In the context of this book, she gently urged me to reconsider certain interpretations when they did not strike her as accurate.

Our children have taught me not only my shortcomings but also the meaning of unconditional love, which, obviously, they both deserve.

For their helpful feedback, my cousins Sheila Sturley and Esmé Peterkin deserve special mention. I have benefited greatly from the editorial work of Carol Dahlstrom, who pushed me to write with greater precision and led me to clarify my thoughts especially for readers, like herself, not brought up in the Roman Catholic tradition.

Sylvia Anderson Koshyk has expertly handled a myriad of details essential to a smooth publication process.

Marjorie Anderson has taken an intense interest in this project. Her advice and editorial guidance expanded my thinking in a number of areas. In fact, I could have not completed this manuscript without her encouragement.

Don McCarthy, a colleague at the University of Manitoba and a demanding critic, offered his helpful advice. Bob and Dawn Galston, friends and neighbours, read and commented on the manuscript with great care. And many others have offered me strong encouragement to write this story.

Robert Kroetsch read the first two chapters of my manuscript as we shared a plane trip to Chicago. His encouragement was the first sign I received that the story might be of interest beyond my family. For this I am most grateful, as well as for his foreword to this book.

I first met Senator Sharon Carstairs when she was finishing her term as the leader of the Liberal Party in Manitoba and the first woman to lead the Official Opposition in a Canadian legislative assembly. As dean of the Faculty of Arts, I invited her to teach a course on women in politics at the University of Manitoba, which she graciously accepted. Her leadership as a woman in politics, her commitment to ending domestic violence, and her work in extending palliative care are just a few of her enormous contributions to our Canadian way of life. I truly appreciate her willingness to comment on my book.

Gregory Baum has been one of the most respected Catholic theologians in Canada and internationally since the Vatican II Council (1962–1965), where he served on committees that prepared the Council documents on ecumenism, religious liberty, and non-Christian religions. I have always valued his insights on theology and social justice and thank him for his willingness to review the book.

Introduction

The beginning of what has become the first chapter of this memoir occurred in November of 1999. I didn't know that a particular memory on that day would lead to such an extensive project. I often wrote pages of reflection, frequently while sitting on the dock at our cottage in the early mornings, with my fishing pole inserted into one of the hollow iron guide posts. For years I simply filed these reflections in a binder.

On that November day in 1999, I was home from work, recovering from a virus. Charlene, my wife, was in Kentucky caring for her mother, who was dying of cancer. It was late afternoon, just before I was scheduled to make my regular phone call to Kentucky, and I was lounging before the television watching Oprah, the popular talk show that Charlene often finds insightful. That day, the show focussed on 10 teenage girls, each telling her own story about having lost her boyfriend. The common thread in all the stories was how devastated these young women were; they thought their lives were over. Sustained depression, even thoughts of suicide, was not uncommon among them. Oprah and her guest concluded that parents should never tell their daughters that what they had experienced was just "puppy" love. In fact, Oprah added that breakups during their teens could be harder for these girls to understand and accept than a divorce might be later in their lives.

That program brought back memories of a comparable

experience I'd had when I was a teenager, vivid memories that were still with me the next day while I was flying to Queen's University in Kingston for a meeting. As the plane levelled off at flying altitude, I set up my laptop and began to write. Images of my first love experience flooded back, and I wrote a complete draft of what is now Chapter 1 of this book.

Highly positive reactions from family members who read that first chapter encouraged me to write about other aspects of my life—first, about my parents, my loving Catholic family, and the love I received from my whole extended family, especially my cousins. As I wrote down these memories, I realized that I was embarking on a much larger project, which has become this book, a most surprising and wonderful experience. It has sharpened my focus and allowed me to discover things about myself that I might not otherwise have. This feature—explaining myself to myself—has been, without question, the most satisfying aspect of this enterprise.

One amazing discovery is to have found just how prominent my Catholicity has been in my life. It may appear naïve of me not to have realized this earlier, given that I spent 20 years in the Franciscans,* almost 13 of them as a priest. I also did graduate studies at a Catholic University (Fordham, in New York) and later resigned from the priesthood and the Franciscans and married Charlene, who was a religious* of the Sisters of Charity of Nazareth, Kentucky. What I had not consciously contemplated and what this memoir has brought into sharp focus is that my approach to my work as an academic during the 35 years I spent at the University of Manitoba, including eight years in post-retirement appointments, has been influenced by my Catholic experience, especially by the rituals that I have taken part in since childhood.

For example, soon after I became head* of the Department of Sociology, one of my colleagues, who knew of my life in the ministry, told me, jokingly, that I would have to stop "celebrating" everything that was happening in the Department. Equally as significant is what I'd call my Catholic interpretation of reality. I feel that this memoir has articulated the underpinnings of my pastoral approach to administration, be it in the Church or at the University of Manitoba—an outcome I certainly did not set out to achieve when I began writing.

The very title of the book illustrates another aspect of my life that has come into sharper focus through this writing. While I have always felt secure in life, primarily because of the incredible love that has enveloped me, I have been led to reflect even more on the sources of uncertainty in my life. What do I believe? Why do I behave the way I do? What motivates me? Most people (likely all people) delve into these matters at some point in their lives, but I believe that the hours of meditation that were part of monastic life gave me greater opportunities to reflect upon these questions than most people have. This dichotomy—the competing realities of security and uncertainty—followed me from the priesthood into academic life.

Associated with these uncertainties have been the complex realities of addressing the most appropriate ways of supporting our children in their disabilities. While I am sure that many parents are uncertain about their parenting skills and approaches, I do believe that disabilities complicate the matter, especially when the professionals are at times unsure themselves about the origins and treatments of these disabilities. At times, that has made the writing of my story an extremely difficult process. Our daughter, Catherine, now 30, has also recalled events of the past with vivid clarity, which has forced me to rethink some of the unhappy years when she was a child. We did not know at that time that she was suffering from Asperger syndrome,* a variation of autism. She can recall events and names of people with remarkable accuracy. I cannot ignore her interpretation of events as I try to recall my own. Our son, Vincent, now 31, also suffers from disabilities—attention-deficit hyperactivity disorder (ADHD) as well as foetal alcohol spectrum disorder (FASD). In the art world we know that a frame can enhance or weaken the effect of a picture. We are also all aware of the derogatory expression "I've been framed." This latter interpretation is certainly not my goal. To choose the appropriate frame to tell the story of my relationship with Vincent has not been an easy task. Yet I have felt the need to reflect on the realities associated with the suffering of our children.

I must say that, as this writing project morphed into a book, I began to reflect seriously on my audience. At first, I wrote only for myself, which remains central if these reflections are to be honest and authentic. However, for any audience other than my immediate family, it was necessary for me to have clarified some of the relationships among the people I mention (see page 26). As well, for readers who do not have a Catholic background or an association with a university, I have added a glossary. A term referenced in the glossary is accompanied by an asterisk the first time the term is used.

Research in cognitive psychology has documented well the reconstructive nature of human memory. This is more than a simple annoyance for a historian trying to interpret the events of the past. In rereading what I've written, I realize that events often were either better or worse than I've described. I am aware that "memory is a strange diary." The most we can hope for is external verification of facts and internal integrity in interpreting them. That is what I offer.

Chapter 1

Noranne

With Father Oswald Fuchs, picking potatoes, 1951

I remember vividly the first time I spoke to Noranne. I was working in the potato fields one Saturday just outside Edmonton when I saw her coming toward me, stepping through the rows of potatoes lying exposed in the field. I'd been stooping for hours, placing the newly unearthed potatoes into bags, to be stored for winter. I took out my handkerchief and tried to rub off the dirt that was caked on the edges of my mouth. It was late in the afternoon of a beautiful, crisp, fall day, warm enough so that all I needed was a light jacket. The aspen and birch trees in the distance were golden in the fall light, some of their leaves wafting gently to the ground. The black earth and the new potatoes made for a distinctive musty aroma, one that I will always associate with falling in love with Noranne.

Noranne was 16, just slightly younger than I, and, at that moment in the potato field as she walked toward me, she was the most beautiful girl in the world. Her auburn hair framed her face in tiny waves, and she wore an outfit of some soft material, perhaps angora, that hugged her body and added to her appeal. I was filled with a mixture of excitement, surprise, and apprehension. I remember the wave of heat rising in me, and the racing of my thoughts: *Is she coming to talk to me? What will I say?* I stood up as she approached and let go of my potato bag.

"I lost my horse today," she began. She quietly explained that her horse, Silent Honour, had been sold that afternoon at a race track in Toronto. Her eyes glistened with tears, and she looked down, clearly devastated. It was a completely new experience to have a girl share such deep feelings with me. I didn't know what to do or say. My heart raced but at the same time burst with affection. I looked away and saw the other potato pickers, my classmates from St. Anthony's, stand up and stare. I felt a rush of pride, then a quick jolt of shame at the realization that I was thinking only of myself and not her pain. I said I was sorry but, in my state of giddy panic, my voice came out flat and low, I'm sure not conveying anything like the emotion I felt. We talked some more, I don't remember about what, but, by the time she left, I knew that I was in love. This was a profound experience for me, one that was more pervasive and all-consuming than I ever could have imagined.

Her formal name was Honora Ann, but she was called Noranne, a beautiful name that later I repeated to myself over and over again. She was the daughter of a cabinet minister in the Alberta legislature and lived with her parents and her younger brother and sister on their family farm about six miles outside Edmonton. Her mother and father were great supporters of St. Anthony's College. I had met her several times before but always as part of a group that got together just after we were finishing up at the farm. We had never really spoken to each other. I didn't know if she had ever even noticed me.

St. Anthony's College was run by the Franciscans and located in the northeast corner of Edmonton. It was a minor seminary* —that is, a residential school for about 80 Roman Catholic boys who were thinking of becoming priests. I had come from Winnipeg to attend the school for grades 10 to 12 because I was interested in entering the Franciscan religious order when I was older. About five or six of us from the school would go out to the farm on Saturday afternoons to earn a bit of money planting or harvesting potatoes, according to the season. It was a nice break from residence life; normally we got out only one Saturday afternoon a month, when we went downtown for a movie or some other acceptable entertainment.

I loved being at the College, which was an intellectual, cultured, and sports-minded beehive, but I wasn't always happy with its strict rules. With the licence that youth provides, I found ways to bypass the regulations that I didn't want to follow: heading down to the pantry at night for extra food, sneaking out into the neighbourhood in the evening walking "The Avenue" (118th) admiring girls, and even meeting some, despite the prohibition against such encounters. All these adventures made life at such a strict boarding school bearable and indeed thoroughly enjoyable.†

---

† *I want to mention one other aspect of my life at St. Anthony's College. In the light of the Mount Cashel scandal and the stories of abuse in residential schools, I have reflected on why I did not hear of a single such incident at St. Anthony's. I have concluded that, first, the students were older than the children in the Native residential schools and were therefore much less vulnerable to abuse. Second, the school was in an urban environment, and therefore neither*

I have always been a romantic. I lean to romantic comedies and weep easily at sad scenes in plays, books, and movies. At St. Anthony's I found an outlet for this tendency. I would go for walks around the College property with Rod Banks and listen to the hit parade on his portable radio, dreaming of and talking about the mystery of girls. I still know all the words to the love song "Because of You," my favourite in those years.

Yet I wanted above all to be a priest. This was a desire that had been with me for years. As a youngster when I helped Mom clean St. Ann's Church back in Winnipeg, I would often pause while dusting the pulpit and give a silent but highly gesticulated sermon to the imagined congregation. I also loved public speaking and took advantage of any opportunity to develop this skill; in Grade 8, I was elected to the Catholic School Parliament and also won the right to represent our school in the city-wide oratorical contest. The priesthood seemed a special way of blending my oratorical skills and my interest in helping people; even as a child I could imagine myself mobilizing people around a cause. A natural progression of these inclinations was that, after spending a year at St. Paul's High School in Winnipeg for Grade 9, I asked if I could go to St. Anthony's in Edmonton for grades 10 to 12, a move my parents permitted only reluctantly; they had wanted me to stay home until I was older.

Like any other boy of that age, I was aware of the attraction of girls, but until I met Noranne I had been too shy to pursue my interest. I'd never had much luck with members of the opposite sex, starting back in Grade 8 at our small, three-room school, St. Ann's,

---

the staff nor the students were isolated from the rest of society (it is in isolated situations where abuse is more likely to occur). We did not have permission to go out often, but the school was open to the "outside" society in important ways. We not only played both home and away games in hockey, basketball, and baseball leagues, but also had drama, public-speaking, and music clubs, and a school newspaper, as well as the opportunity to attend plays and musicals downtown. We were being trained to be leaders, and I think the environment was a healthy one—that is, not conducive to abuse.

on Hampton Street in Winnipeg. The school was on the main floor, the church upstairs. We had a class of perhaps 15, and we were a tight group. Some of us wrote little love notes to one another, which we passed back and forth in class until our teacher, a very strict nun, caught us and read some of the notes out loud, to our extreme embarrassment. In the spring of my Grade-8 year, our class was to have a dance, the first one that we were allowed. I wanted to invite one of my classmates, Cecilia. I remember that Mom and I were home alone when I told her I wanted to ask Cecilia to go with me, and she encouraged me to call. She intentionally went out into the backyard with some sheets to hang on the line to give me privacy when I made the call. My palms were sweating as I picked up the phone.

No, Cecilia would not come to the dance with me next Friday; she had to study. *Had to study! On a Friday evening?* I was humiliated. It was the first time I had asked a girl for a date, and it was also the last for several years. Much later I heard that she had entered a convent, and, with the sting of her refusal still with me, I thought, *Good riddance!*

Back at St. Anthony's in Edmonton, when I had fallen in love with Noranne in the potato field on that golden day, I was in Grade 11, a veteran there. As such, I was awarded the prestigious job of walking three blocks every afternoon after classes to pick up the college mail at the local drugstore. Noranne had been much on my mind since I'd talked to her in the field, but I hadn't expected to see her again. However, a week after our pototo-field encounter, who should I run into in the drugstore, picking up her family's mail, but Noranne! "Hi," I said, my heart beating wildly. "Hi," she answered. She was as shy as I was. Our eyes met, she paused briefly, and then she went on about her business. Nothing more was said. But I walked back to college with my imagination totally out of control. I was just conscious enough to remember the exact time she had come into the drugstore.

Day after day, I arranged to be at the store at that same time, playing over and over in my mind what I would say to Noranne when I saw her next. Often I would linger longer than necessary to pick up the mail, hoping for a moment with her, but my outings were time-limited, so I could risk only a slight delay. Nevertheless, we met at the drugstore about half a dozen times over the course of the term. I would try to prolong the greeting a little more each time, perhaps inquiring about her horses, and then go on my way, basking in her beautiful smile. Little did she know the state of my mind.

I could hardly wait for the call the next spring to go to the farm on Saturdays to plant potatoes. Sitting 12 inches off the ground on a potato planter being pulled by a tractor, eating dust for four or five hours a day was worth the chance that she might come out to the field to say hello. More often than not, I didn't see her at all, and, when I did, it was only from a distance.

Summer came, school closed, and I headed back to Winnipeg for the holidays. In the fall, I returned to Edmonton for Grade 12. My close friend, Rod Banks, did not return to the College, so I lost my companion for walking and listening to popular music. My mailbox duties continued, and I was able to see Noranne at the drugstore from time to time. Our meetings were still short, but now at least we had real conversations, not just simple greetings. I looked forward to Saturday afternoons at the farm, where she might come out to the field and see me for a more extended period of time.

A new opportunity presented itself later in the fall when I was in Grade 12. The Winnipeg Blue Bombers were to be in town for a Saturday evening football game with the Edmonton Eskimos, and rumour had it that we students would be allowed to go. I went to the phone booth outside the prefect's office, but not until after hours, when I knew he would not be in his office. I called Rod, who lived in the city, and suggested a double date, using Rod's car for transportation. I called Noranne and invited her to go to the game with me, Rod, and Rod's girlfriend. This was the first time I had ever called her, and I did so with great trepidation, afraid that she might turn me down the way Cecelia had in Grade 8. However, Noranne not only agreed but also suggested that her dad might supply the tickets. I was on top of the world. It was the first real sign I had that perhaps she cared for me. Sure enough, she came up with four tickets, and they turned out to be right at mid-field. Her father must have thought it important that he give his daughter these special tickets.

As we were walking into the stadium, Noranne told me that her dad normally gave those particular tickets to the priests who ran St. Anthony's. On this occasion, he offered the priests some other tickets, down near the 10-yard line. This presented a problem I had not foreseen. While we students had permission to attend the game, we certainly did not have permission to have dates. So, as the four of us sat high up in the stands on the 55-yard line, Rod and I kept our eyes peeled for the priests, and when half-time came we hid under our blanket as they walked past us. I was sure they would glance up toward the seats they usually had, and I was relieved when it appeared that they hadn't seen us.

At the end of the game, Noranne and I got into the back seat of Rod's car, and we headed out of the parking lot with some ten thousand other cars. We inched forward slowly and suddenly noticed that beside us was the College car, which had two priests and two students in it. "Hi, Father," I said sheepishly through the open car window. I was in agony, squirming in the back seat as I anxiously waited for the traffic to move, not wanting Noranne to know the trouble I was in.

I felt sure I'd be expelled from the College, so I made the most of my stolen opportunity and stayed out late after the game, thus committing another misdemeanor. The four of us went back to Noranne's home. Her shyness seemed to melt as the evening progressed and we talked and danced to music in the kitchen.

I crept back into the College well past 1:00 a.m. through a window that I'd had the foresight to unlock before the game. As I quietly headed toward the dorm area, I passed the bulletin board. A new cartoon there caught my eye. *Incredible!* It was a picture of a male teenager peering out from under a blanket that he shared with his girlfriend at a football game. The caption read, "Anyone know the score?" Scrawled in pen, below that caption was another, this one handwritten: "Currie." I immediately ripped down the cartoon, but I still assumed that there would be a public flagellation ritual in the morning, including derisive laughter from the other students, right by the bulletin board where we tended to gather before classes. The formal consequence would take place in the prefect's office. As luck would have it, the prefect had had to take an early-morning train to Regina, and, by the time he returned a week later, my punishment was less severe than it might have been. I was simply hauled in for a lecture and told that if I did that again I would be out on my ear. I also lost my privilege to go to the drugstore to pick up the mail.

The year progressed, and I immersed myself in my studies, the College basketball team, drama, and the school paper. Several of us started the 3M Club (Music in the Modern Mood). But Noranne was "always on my mind," as the Elvis Presley song goes. I did not see her during this half year, nor did I try to call her. Neither did she call me; she knew that a phone call from a girl would have been extremely difficult for me, given the College rules against dating, or even talking to girls, during the school year. During my last day in Grade 12, before returning to Winnipeg, when I knew I was beyond the control of the College, I got up my courage to phone Noranne and ask her out again. Rod and I were planning another night to remember. Travelling in his flashy Thunderbird, we picked up Noranne and Rod's nurse friend for a night on the town: a movie, then dinner at the Seven Seas, the nicest restaurant in Edmonton, followed by dancing at the Trocadero.

It was a full evening. I remember how lovely it was to hold Noranne as we danced, how our physical closeness seemed a natural expression of my tender feelings for her. I felt much more relaxed than I had at the football game in the fall, and on that night I was simply trying to show her a good time, not dodging priests from the College. By the end of the evening, all my potato earnings were gone. I got on the train at 6:00 the next morning for the 20-hour trip back to Winnipeg with less than a dollar in my pocket, but it had been worth it. As the train sped on, away from Edmonton, away from Noranne, I could not stop thinking of the kiss we'd shared at the end of the evening. It was a chaste kiss, not long, but beautiful in its simplicity, enduring in its memory.

It was the last time I ever saw Noranne. But she stayed on in my thoughts. In fact, I became physically ill—*lovesick* I think would be a more accurate term—and was unable to focus on my studies or think about my future. I had returned to St. Anthony's in the fall of 1952 to begin studies in philosophy, but my heart was not in it, and I did not complete the year. I returned home to Winnipeg in late October. I lived with Mom and Dad and took a job in an auto repair shop in the city.

There was no one in Winnipeg with whom I could talk about my experience. I certainly couldn't talk to Mom and Dad, for I recognized that I was not supposed to have developed an interest in a girl while at a minor seminary. And they did not press me about my relationships or my future plans. The romantic part of my nature understood that early encounter with love as a Romeo-and-Juliet relationship with all the characteristics of forbidden love. But, in reality, our two evenings together and our occasional conversations in the drugstore or the potato field did not provide enough time to develop a lasting bond. I did occasionally think of returning to Edmonton to pursue my relationship with Noranne, but at 18, without resources or a clear plan, I couldn't convince myself that this was realistic, and I did not try to contact her. As the year progressed, some of the intensity of my feelings for her faded, and by March of 1953 I had reached my decision to prepare for the priesthood. I decided to cherish the experience of loving Noranne but not let it deter me from my original and long-term goal. And so, in August of 1953, I entered the Franciscans with a new-found peace in my heart.

While I went on with my life, I did not consciously try to forget about Noranne, and the occasional memory did surface. That first year in the friary,* with no television, radio, or daily newspaper, I still managed to know which Saturday was Grey Cup day, to find out the score, and to entertain fond memories of the football game I went to with Noranne. I was even able to talk and laugh about the experience with several other young Franciscans who had been students with me at St. Anthony's and knew the story. But I don't remember talking about any girlfriends they had had.

To this day, I have no idea if Noranne knew how much I cared for her, and I have no idea how she felt about me. But our brief friendship was important to me. During the last year that I knew her, those of us thinking of the priesthood were expected to take a course on relations between men and women, on sexuality and reproduction. It was taught by one of the priests. I remember thinking about the beauty of the sexual union explicitly as it related to the miracle of conception. I wept as I thought of the pain that my mother endured giving birth to us children and resolved that I would never show disrespect to any woman.

I look back on the time of falling in love with Noranne not with regret but rather with great fondness. And, because of my experience with her, I was more compassionate as a priest than I would otherwise have been when I later gave high-school retreats all over western Canada. I could always empathize with the teenagers I listened to who were in love or who were experiencing the agonies of lost love. I understood that these experiences were about discovering the sensual, sexual aspect of being human. Losing the person associated with that awakening was like a "death" of a part of themselves, and almost impossible to bear.

I will forever be grateful to Noranne. My experience with her gave me the awareness of sensual attraction without the pain and humiliation of rejection or betrayal. She gently, unknowingly left me with a sense of the beauty and power of the attraction between men and women.

CHAPTER 2

Our Catholic Family

On our property on the Assiniboine River, 1950. Standing: Robin, John, me. Sitting: Claude (Dad), Maureen, Eileen (Mom)

"Who lives in your home with you?" About 20 years ago, two close friends of ours told Charlene and me that a psychiatrist had once asked them this question. We all thought it was a profoundly insightful query, and the four of us spent an evening answering it. All of us had come from healthy families and had enjoyed happy childhoods. We discussed our attitudes, our likes and dislikes, and we even laughed about specific behaviours that we recognized as carryovers from our parents. Now, more than 50 years after my father's death and 17 years after my mother's, I recognize how much the life I've lived and the choices I've made came from the influences of my loving parents and their approaches to life. Indeed, their examples still "live in my home" with me.

My father, Claude Francis Currie, was a little over six feet tall, a trim man with a full head of prematurely grey hair and a moustache. We have a black-and-white photograph of him in the house, standing erect in his military uniform and wearing a black arm band in memory of the death of Queen Victoria. (Both Dad's father, Mark Robert, and his mother, Ella, were from Bath, England.) There is no doubt that my dad's life was "marked" by his father, although my grandfather died when Dad was about six. Mark Robert was educated at Eton, Cambridge, and at the famous military college at Sandhurst. He and his wife came to Canada in the early 1880s, first to Winnipeg and then to Moosomin, Saskatchewan, where he was an agent for the Canada North West Land Company. Connie, their eldest daughter, was born there. When Mark Robert heard of a mining boom in Superior, Wisconsin, he moved the family there, only to find that the stories of the boom were exaggerated. That is where Dad was born in 1894, and later his other siblings —Agnes, Margaret, and a set of twins, Edward and Katherine.

Dad's father returned to England shortly thereafter and apparently sent five telegrams to his wife, each asking her permission to fight in the Boer War to raise money for the family. She refused four times but finally consented; perhaps she was finally just worn down. The account of his death, which we heard many times over the years, does not match what we've discovered more recently. We were told that he was killed when a roof collapsed in the army quarters in South Africa the day after the war ended, and, precisely because the war was over, his wife did not receive any compensation for his death. However, according to my cousin Ellen, who recently travelled to Pretoria, South Africa, where our grandfather is buried, he was discharged from the army before the war was over because of a mental illness. (Today his condition would probably have been identified as post-traumatic stress disorder.) Ellen had discovered a brief article in a British newspaper of the time that reported his death as a suicide. He had bought some arsenic from a veterinarian, ostensibly to kill a dog, and had consumed it himself.

I rather doubt that Dad knew how his father really died. If he had known, I think he would have told us, for it's unlikely that he would have harboured a sense of shame or had a need to hide the story. We certainly knew of a cousin of my mother who was mentally ill, and the attitude in our home was that mental illness is a tragic reality that many families face.

Our connection to the Franciscans on his side of the family has an interesting history. Dad's mother sent him from Wisconsin to Trois Rivières, Quebec, when Dad was about 14, to study in French at a minor seminary run by Franciscans. The fact that Dad was singled out to go to a French school in Canada always struck us as odd since, according to family history, his mother had placed great value on the British system of education. Religion had certainly been an important part of Dad's early family life. His grandmother had been converted from Anglicanism to Roman Catholicism by a Franciscan. In fact, the event was in some sense tragic. Her husband was an Anglican priest, and the conversion of his wife, facilitated by one of his own friends, was a terrible embarrassment to him. He consequently felt he had to resign from his position as pastor. He died not too long afterward, according to family stories, of a broken heart. So it is noteworthy that Dad, some 30 years later, was sent off to a school run by Franciscans.

At the end of Dad's year in Quebec, he was sent home because, as he told me in a matter-of-fact way years later, he "did not have a vocation to the priesthood." Given his own decision about the priesthood, I've wondered over the years what he thought about his two sons becoming priests. Did he feel that we were more suited to this vocation than he was? While I certainly sensed pride in him, I never once felt pressured by him, either to enter the priesthood or to scrutinize whether that was my true vocation.

After returning from Quebec, Dad spent some time in the United States and a year at le Collège Universitaire de Saint Boniface in Winnipeg. Then, in 1914, at the age of 20, he enlisted in the 28th Infantry Battalion, which was part of the 105th Regiment (Saskatoon Fusiliers). Less than a year later, while on a military move to Winnipeg, for reasons he never told us, he switched to the Canadian Army Medical Corps. He was assigned Quartermaster at No. 1 Canadian General Hospital in England at Neveravon base, Wiltshire County, with the rank of honorary captain. He was responsible for ordering and maintaining all the supplies in the hospital. In May of 1915, he sailed for France, where he served at Etaples until 1919. In 1917, he was assigned to the 11th Canadian Field Ambulance. This unit was made up of predominantly prairie boys, and a number of them would have graduated from the University of Manitoba in 1917. These soldiers wrote a moving history of their war service simply entitled *The 11th Canadian Field Ambulance.* In it they described holding a mock graduation convocation in their barracks one day, complete with a chancellor and a president of the University and including humorous awards for a number of the soldiers. (When I brought this to the attention of others at the University of Manitoba several years ago, the text was read on campus at the Remembrance Day ceremony the following year.) Etaples is close to Vimy Ridge, where Canadians forces fought so bravely and effectively. Dad's war records reveal that he had undergone an operation for appendicitis at a military hospital in England the week of the Vimy Ridge attack, so he could not have been in this battle, but he did return to Etaples two weeks later. He certainly would have been part of the many other battles, including The Battle of the Somme, where Canadian casualties totalled 24,029 between July and November 1916.

Dad returned to Winnipeg in 1919, the year after the war ended. He talked very little to us children about his war experience, so I never had a concrete image of his life of service during those years. Perhaps that accounts for my strong emotional response to the vivid paintings that were part of the 2004 touring National Art Gallery art exhibit entitled Canvas of War. One of the paintings, *The Stretcher-Bearer Party* by Cyril Barraud, was particularly poignant given Dad's service in the 11th Canadian Field Ambulance. In fact, I was so moved that I visited that same exhibit in three different locations—Toronto, Fredericton, and Winnipeg.

After the war ended, he worked for several grain companies, and then in 1926 he met my mother while she was working as a secretary in Brandon, Manitoba, where her family lived. Dad proposed to Mom in February of 1927, just three weeks after meeting her. They were married in Brandon in August.

My mother, Eileen Mary Margaret Bradshaw-Fullard, was born in Toronto in 1901. She spent her childhood there and in Halifax, and she spent her early adult life in Brandon, where she moved with her parents.

Mom's father (Richard Bradshaw-Fullard) did not do well in business in Halifax. As my cousin Esmé put it, "Gramps was never trained to work, but to be a gentleman." He was a quiet man, who was more demanding of himself than of others. Esmé reminded me that he lost money twice, the first time when his own father displeased Gramps's grandfather by enlisting in the army instead of buying a commission, as gentlemen did at that time. However, Gramps still inherited enough money to live comfortably all his life. But he lost it all by 1914. The story we heard was that he lent a good deal of money to people early in his career as an insurance agent, and few paid him back. He was too kind and gentle a man to press for repayment. His marriage to Nanno (Elizabeth Leahy) was clearly one of convenience and not a particularly happy one. Nanno would never let him talk about his early life or his background, even to his daughters, Mary and Mom. We think it was partly related to the unverified family story that one of his ancestors may have been an illegitimate child of the Duke of Kent, the Father of Queen Victoria. (Pictures of Mom in her 50s and 60s show a stunning resemblance to Queen Elizabeth II; they might have been sisters. Once, when Mom was about to leave a restaurant in Vancouver, the pianist began playing "God Save the Queen"!) Gramps died at a St. Boniface nursing home, where the Grey Nuns always raved about what a gentleman he was.

Nanno's family was prominent in Halifax. Her father, Edward Leahy, served as a city councillor. "Leahyville" or Leahy Villa, was a name popularly used in Halifax to designate a range of buildings erected in 1868. Some of the buildings were one-and-a-half-storey, pitched-roof cottages for workers, a few of which survived until 1997. His brother, Thomas, was also a well-known Halifax personality. Together with Andrew Downs, these two created in Halifax North America's first zoological gardens.

Nanno took pride in the status of her family and insisted on "cultured" behaviour. That led to far too much concern, in my opinion, about "what the neighbours will think," an emphasis I was never comfortable with even as a youngster. The story is told of Nanno getting off a bus about two blocks from where she was going to tea and getting into a taxi to arrive "properly." Proper table manners were also important to her. In his indomitable way, when my brother Robin was young, he announced at dinner one evening to Katherine Leahy, a middle-aged Irish American cousin visiting from Quincy, Massachusetts, "I wish I could eat wrong like you do!" She was a great sport, however, and howled with delight; she even wrote about it in her "bread-and-butter letter" after her return home.

Nanno was a wonderful story-teller and wrote short stories that were published in the *North West Review*, a prairie Catholic newspaper. But my memories of her are clouded by the stories I heard of the nasty way in which she would speak about Dad when she and Gramps lived with us. The strange thing, though, was that her favour shifted. When they lived in Flin Flon, with Mom's sister Mary and her husband, Jack, then Jack was the villain and Dad was the hero. Another typical Nanno moment occurred when she threatened to go to the archbishop and tell him that my brother John should not be ordained a priest because he scolded her once for the way she was talking about Mom and Dad. Because Nanno was so difficult, it was hard for Mom to have the same degree of affection for her as she had for her father. As well, when my mother was young, I think she felt that her sister Mary received more attention. One time in Brandon, when Mom was out with her mother, someone stopped Nanno and inquired about her daughter. The story goes that Nanno said, "You mean the pretty one," referring to Mary.

At the time (I was only three or four), Mom felt that the conflict that Nanno caused was having a negative effect her and Dad's marriage. When I was older, Mom told us that she had felt it necessary to ask her mother and father to leave. She added that it had been an extremely difficult thing to do, yet she felt it was her responsibility—not Dad's—to take the step. Her marriage was too important for her to allow it to be jeopardized. I remember several other similar conversations with Mom, which together instilled in me a sense that marriage required careful nurturing.

Less than a year after their marriage in Brandon, Mom and Dad moved to Winnipeg. They lived in apartments in what is now called Osborne Village and then in a house on MacMillan Avenue, close to Stafford Street, where I was born. In 1939, when I was five, we moved to Assiniboine Avenue in Woodhaven, an area in the far west end of the city. It was a small house, almost a cottage, on a large property, with the lawn stretching 400 feet down from the street to the banks of the Assiniboine River. The setting was idyllic. With so many trees on the property, Mary, Mom's sister, had suggested we call it Eighty Oaks, an affectionate name we often used informally.

When I think back to my parents and what has "lived" with me since my growing-up years, I often think of how they demonstrated ways of being, ways of caring. One vivid memory I have relates to my father's thoughtfulness.

Early one evening in the spring of 1953, Mom, Dad, and I were in the living room. John, the oldest, was studying to be a priest at St. Peter's Seminary in London, Ontario. Robin, the next oldest, was working for the Bank of Montreal in a small Manitoba town, Bissett. Maureen had entered the Religious of the Sacred Heart,* just over a year previously and was in the convent in Albany, New York. I had just returned from St. Anthony's in Edmonton for Christmas and was the only one of the four children living at home.

Mom was sitting, feet up on the couch, reading a novel, while Dad was finishing reading *The Winnipeg Tribune.* I was feeling restless, so I stood up, headed through the kitchen and stepped out the back door, planning on a short walk. Our property allowed for a nice little stroll, or simply a quiet time watching the water round the riverbank to the west of us on its way to the heart of the city. The evening was warm for December. I was hardly out the door when Dad appeared, paper in hand at the window, opened it and asked, "Would you like to have a game of chess?" "Thanks, Dad, but I really don't feel like it," I replied, too quickly. I was touched by his thoughtfulness, his sense of my mood, and I remember regretting that I had not said yes anyway. I'm sure he never realized how much I felt his love right then. He died the next year.

Thoughtfulness, such as he showed me that evening, was to me the most dominant characteristic of my father's personality. I was 30 or so before I came to realize just how important he had been in my life, how much I missed him. He was the perfect gentleman and consciously taught us to think of the needs of others. Mom, of course, was the principal object of his consideration. I remember as a youngster running into the house one day and slamming the door. He made me go back out and come in again quietly. "Don't you realize your mother could be resting?" he asked. Mom used to love to take a nap in the afternoons, lying on the couch in the living room. Another time, he picked me up from school, and we stopped at Harman's Drug Store, at Sherbrook and Portage, because he wanted to surprise Mom with peanut brittle, her favourite sweet. It was not a birthday or any other special occasion; it was simply an opportunity for him to show his caring.

Even strangers benefited from Dad's generosity. When we moved to Woodhaven, a trolley car ran from Deer Lodge to St. Charles and returned on the same track, so the wait between trolleys was at least 45 minutes. One bitterly cold winter day, again driving me home from school, Dad noticed a young woman carrying a baby huddled against the punishing prairie wind waiting in the open for the trolley. "She must be frozen," he said, and immediately turned the car around, stopped in front of her and offered her a ride to the next stop, where she could wait in a warm shelter.

After Dad died, when Mom and I were sharing some memories of him, she confided to me that Dad had taught her to be thoughtful. I remember thinking what a beautiful thing—married couples learning in that way from each another. There are many examples of their generosity to each other and, together, to others. After the war, as one example, they took in an English woman who had married a Canadian soldier and, with her child, was trying to get settled in Canada. And on Sundays, they would often take the three members of the Sisters of St. Joseph who taught in St. Ann's, our three-room grade school on Hampton Street, out for a drive just so they could "get out." They lived in a cubby hole on the second floor of an apartment behind the church. And, as another example, at the request of Father Bedford, a Jesuit who was chaplain at Stony Mountain Penitentiary, for years Mom and Dad took on the task of driving wives and girlfriends the 20 miles to visit their husbands or boyfriends. I don't have the sense that they did these things to teach us a lesson; it was simply the way they lived their lives. After Dad died, Robin and his wife, Irene, took on the task of driving visitors to the prison.

Dad's thoughtfulness and generosity were complemented by his honesty and principled behaviour. One evening when I was about 11, I invited my friend and neighbour, Barry Thorndycraft, for a sleepover. It was late in the summer, and our neighbour's very large garden was full of row upon row of ripe corn. We had a devious plan. Before heading for bed, I had managed to get a pot of water, some butter, some salt, and a knife from the kitchen, and I placed them on the porch of the Annex where we were sleeping. As dusk settled, Dad was putting away the lawn tools, and, much to my surprise, he came onto the porch and went around the side. "What's this all about?" he asked when he spotted my poorly hidden kitchen accoutrements. I was required to spell out our plan in great detail, even though I knew it had been obvious to him what we were planning. That was the end of our proposed corn feast. But I remember that the next day I was expected to apologize to Mr. Meurer for even thinking of stealing his corn.

I remember an earlier time when I had had to apologize with great embarrassment. I had been collecting stamps from an early age, and I once delayed giving a neighbour, Mr. Whitehead, the money for the stamps that I had sold for him, offering excuses one upon the other when, in fact, I had simply spent it. When Dad found out, I had to commit my allowance for the next month and, as well, drive over to Mr. Whitehead's home with Dad to ask for forgiveness. (True to my father's teachings, I remember taking our young son, Vincent, to meet the manager of a drugstore so that he could apologize and return some small items he had taken.)

I was simply learning about Dad's moral integrity and the importance of living by one's word. He was a man of his word in all things, and my brothers and I joked over the years that, if we ever decided to meet at Portage and Main on a specific date, we would all be there, and within a minute of the appointed time.

Dad was also a practical man. One year during the war, he bought Mom a carton of toilet paper as her Christmas present, because that rationed item was on sale. She teased him for years after that. Another example: my cousin Esmé's friend Norma was over for dinner one evening. Dad always sat at the end of the table with his back to the river, but, after the main course was finished, he would push his chair back, cross his legs and enjoy a cup of coffee, a practice I consciously imitate. He glanced out the window, got up suddenly and picked up a .22 rifle that he had placed in the corner of the room that evening, opened the door, and shot a squirrel from the front porch. He came back in, sat down, and continued the meal as if nothing had happened. Poor Norma was appalled. But the squirrels were getting into the attic and Dad felt they just had to be dealt with.

There is one significant example of Dad's practical nature that had a great influence on my life. As a youngster, Maureen was an unusually spiritual girl. Unless special permission was secured to do otherwise, it was considered mandatory by the Church in those days for Catholic children to attend a Catholic school, and Maureen was keen to do so. But Dad judged that her health could not stand the day-long absence that included the lunch hour, so he arranged for her to attend Woodhaven, a public school much closer to our home. This was an important lesson to me: while living a religious life was important, it had to be done within the context of one's whole life.

Early in Grade 9, I asked Mom and Dad if I could attend St. Anthony's College in Edmonton the following year and stay for the rest of my high school years. I was thinking seriously about becoming a Franciscan priest, and St. Anthony's was a minor seminary run by the Franciscans. At the same time, I hated going to St. Paul's High School because I was being bullied by a boy there. The boy had tripped me intentionally on the basketball court, and, while the coach expelled him from the team, a number of other students felt that I was at fault and shunned me for the rest of the year. I could hardly wait to leave that school. A friend of our family heard of my interest in the priesthood and anonymously gave the necessary money to Mom and Dad so that I could attend St. Anthony's. Only much later did we find out who our benefactor was. I wonder if he has any idea of the huge effect he had on my life. That gesture has been a model for my own life. Real generosity does not require repayment, but it sets up a chain reaction; as a recipient of an act of generosity, I have always felt the urge to seize opportunities to help others when I'm able.

Once it was agreed that I could go to St. Anthony's, Dad and I drove the 800 miles to Edmonton. When we arrived, I remember him taking me to one end of the High Level Bridge, letting me out of the car so that I could take the street car across, and then picking me up on the other side. Again, it was his thoughtfulness that led him to perceive what would give me a thrill. I can't recall all the events of that trip, but the emotional bonds that resulted are vivid in my memory. As we drove, we would stop on the way at various grain facilities so that Dad could conduct his business as a sales representative for Woods Manufacturing Company. In Saskatoon, we stayed at the Bessborough, the nicest hotel in town, then owned by the Canadian National Railway. At dinner, as Dad pulled out a cigarette, I saw the maître d' quickly cross the room and produce a lighter. At 14, I was extremely impressed. My Dad was an important person, I concluded.

I did not forget that experience at the Bessborough. Several years later, on the 20-hour train trip back to Winnipeg after the night of dinner and dancing with Noranne, I missed my connection in Saskatoon for the train to Winnipeg. With no money left, I headed to the Bessborough and told them I was the son of Mr. Claude Currie. I was convinced that they would allow me to stay the night on the promise that I would send a cheque back to them when I arrived in Winnipeg. They did! After checking into my room, I headed out for a walk, quite dazzled that a doorman would hold the door for me as if I were an honoured guest. I know that Dad was not pleased that I ran out of money, but he was impressed with my resourcefulness and the fact that I wrote a note of thanks with the cheque I sent.

~

If thoughtfulness was Dad's pearl, Mom's was the way in which she gave praise to her children. She instilled in us a pride in accomplishment that was strong and balanced. For example, during my early teen years, I was responsible for cutting the lawn. It was a big job and would take me the better part of a day. At noon, Mom would come out with sandwiches and a glass of milk. She'd

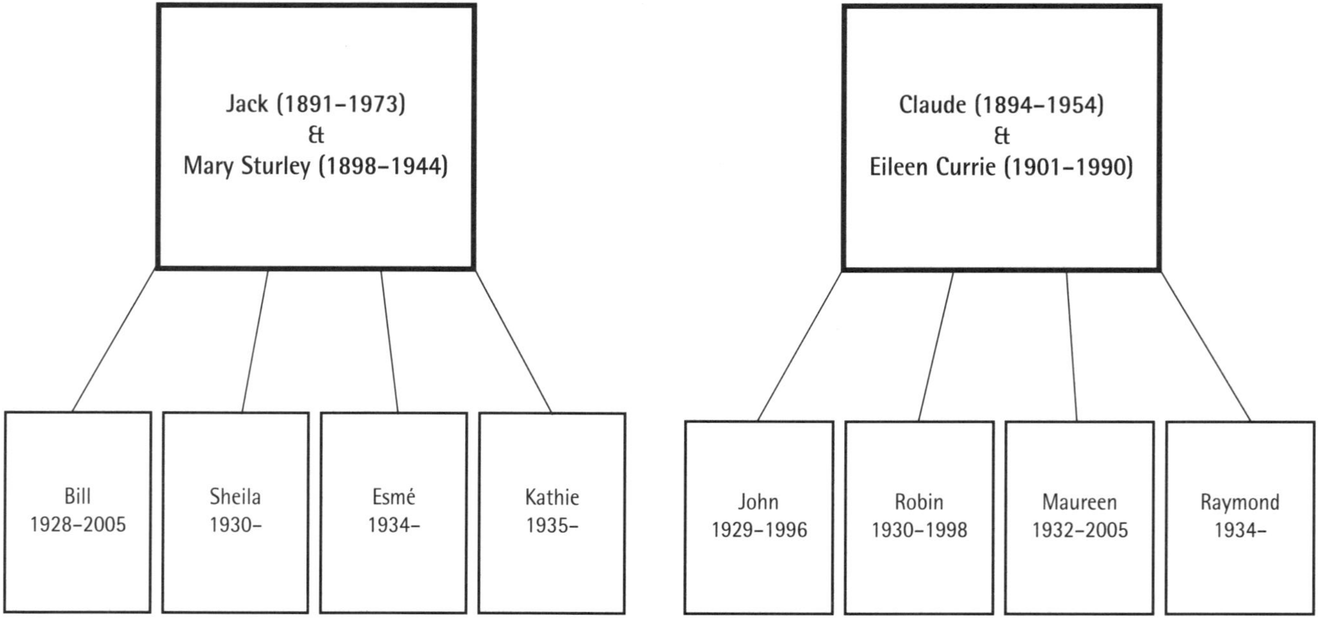

Children of sisters Mary and Eileen Bradshaw-Fullard and their husbands

put the food down and immediately take a tour of the lawn. She would always be astounded that I had done so much mowing and done it so well. Her obvious pleasure motivated me to work even harder in the last hour before lunch. Once, I built her a rock garden, hauling stones from near the water, again to abundant praise. She made it a thrill for me to do anything to surprise or please her. From her, I learned that it is effective (and costs little) to acknowledge the good things people have done.

My family story cannot be told without including reference to the Sturleys. I remember that in one day we went from a family with four children to a family with eight. In December of 1944, Mom's sister and only sibling, Mary, died of breast cancer at the age of 46 in Flin Flon, 500 miles northwest of Winnipeg. She left her husband, Jack, and four children—Bill, Sheila, Esmé, and Kathie—their ages ranging from 9 to 16, which almost paralleled the ages of the four of us. In fact, Esmé is two weeks younger than I. For the two years that Mary was sick prior to her death, Sheila already lived with us and went to the Convent of the Sacred Heart School on West Gate with my sister Maureen. And Mary had come down from Flin Flon often for treatments, so our families were already tightly blended. After Mary died, Esmé and Kathie also came to Winnipeg for school. They were enrolled as resident students at St. Charles Academy and later at St. Mary's Academy, and they came to our place on weekends. Bill went to Montreal to live with other family members, the Goughs, but he was now considered a member of our family. Uncle Jack came to Winnipeg for a time to help Dad build what we called the Annex. They had the garage at the top of our property on Assiniboine Avenue moved down beside the house, leaving about 10 metres between the two buildings. They insulated the garage, built a veranda on two sides, and put beds in the four corners. They installed a pot-bellied stove near one of the walls. The pipes rose up from the stove and extended to the far end of the building so that the length of pipe would help keep the room cozy. The boys of the two families slept in the Annex, and the girls slept in the house. For the boys, trips to the bathroom in the middle of the night, especially in winter, meant going across to the house and so were to be avoided at all costs.

I was too young to understand the effect on the Sturley children of all their losses. In addition to losing their mother, they had to leave their father and their friends in Flin Flon for the school year. They had to leave the beauty of the North, with its festival of stars and the dazzling display of northern lights. The three sisters were separated from their brother, who was in Montreal, and they had to adjust to life in the city, an adjustment not without its hardships. Esmé and Kathie hated the rigid discipline of St. Charles Academy, and Uncle Jack was deeply in debt for years, until he paid off the medical bills associated with Mary's cancer.

With little thought at the time about how difficult these adjustments were for all of the Sturleys, I perceived the whole situation simply as a gain. We were now a family of eight. However, Mom not only felt a loss for herself in Mary's death but also said over and over how hard it was for Mary's four children and for Jack.

Our lives have been intertwined ever since. The two families are the centre of our social lives. Christmas and Thanksgiving dinners have almost always included everyone in the family who is in Winnipeg, usually over 20 of us. What is most precious of all is that all of Bill's, Esmé's, and Kathie's children call Charlene and me aunt and uncle. I had the privilege of toasting the bride at Esmé's marriage to John Peterkin, as well as at four of the children's weddings. Uncle Jack was very much a part of this network. Later in his life, he was hit by a car in a parking lot in Burnaby while visiting Kathie. He never fully recovered, and Mom invited him to live with her in her apartment at Wellington Crescent and Hugo Street until he died in 1973 while visiting Robin and Irene at their cottage.

In many ways, we were the stereotypical happy family, with a strict father and a compassionate, interceding mother, which translated for me into a family life that was wonderfully safe and secure. It was not that I consciously thought, *I feel secure.* One either is or isn't. I reflect on this now because I serve on the board of Prairie*action* Foundation, which supports research that seeks to find solutions to domestic violence and abuse. I realize that as a child I never witnessed my parents disrespect or mistreat one another and that, in retrospect, was the most important source of our emotional security. There is a frequently quoted saying: "The best gift a man can give to his children is to love his wife." We received that gift.

I am aware of research on the effect on siblings of their birth order, with the oldest generally coming out the luckiest. As the youngest of four, I don't find this a fruitful avenue to explore. I see that our relatively close ages (four of us born between 1929 and 1934) facilitated a closeness that only grew stronger as we became adults.

My memories of us as children are of contented times together, punctuated periodically with misadventure. John, as the eldest, was often busy with school, but I do remember us three boys taking our rowboat and our dog across the Assiniboine River and camping in a tent in the woods right across from our home. It was Robin who was more often my play companion. One clear memory I have is of him chopping wood behind the Annex while I rode around on my fictitious horse and battled all the foes, coming back to get his advice on which outlaw to capture next. He would help me pile logs up to form "the jail" that I needed in which to hold the dangerous criminals. He could also lead us into some trouble. One day after school, he took Maureen and me on a detour to the airport, where we climbed in and out of small planes. We arrived home after dark, and, of course, Mom and Dad had been extremely worried. Maureen was in

Grade 3, Robin in Grade 5, and I in Grade 1—all of us much too young to be out alone after dark. While Maureen and I were sent to bed without dinner, I think Robin had to go to the woodpile to pick out the stick with which Dad was going to spank him! This is the only time I remember Dad ever spanking any of us.

As both John and Robin got older and started going to dances, before heading off to bed, Dad would set the alarm clock at the hour that they were to be home. Mom would lie awake and, if it looked as if they might be late, she would shut off the alarm and be sure she was at the door to let them in as quietly as possible. There were other times when it was Dad's support that was featured. I remember vividly the time when, as a young teenager, Robin carved a nude woman from a small piece of wood, and together we brought it to show Dad. I thought Robin might get a real lecture and, being the self-designated moral watchdog of my older siblings in those days, I was quite looking forward to it. Much to my surprise, Dad told him it was an excellent piece of art and encouraged him to continue on with his artistic expression. Dad surprised me further when he commented on what a good figure Mom had, and I think it was the next day that he invited me for a walk up and down our property and asked me what I wanted to know about sexuality. I remember asking questions related to how babies were made and his answering them in a straightforward manner.

When we were in our early teens, my sister Maureen and I formed a deep emotional bond that never weakened. During the summer when I was 15, we would sit on the lawn while she read to me an incredibly romantic teen novel, *Seventeenth Summer,*[1] as well as the writings of St. Francis of Assisi[2] (apt readings for both my teenage and our family inclinations). Recalling this leads me to realize that our bond has really been the sharing of values and feelings, culminating in more recent years in sharing the spiritual journeys of our lives. This aspect of my relationship with Maureen, and to an extent with Robin and John, was a source of great comfort to me. Sharing values and a common faith with my siblings provided me with a deeper understanding of their personal lives and also, as I came to discover, allowed me to call on a shared comfort when they were facing their deaths.

Another aspect of our lives that contributed to our closeness as adults was our love of water, born of growing up on the Assiniboine River and nourished by spending time at our cottage at Netley Creek. The cottage was first owned by Robin, then John, then Charlene and me, and it offered opportunities for us all to spend important bonding time together.

As a sociologist, I have often reflected on our family's attitudes toward ethnic, racial, and religious groups, and toward social-class differences. There is no question that Dad was English to the core, both in his values and in his mannerisms. The only time we children ever remember a heated conversation between our parents was when Mom, with her Irish background, disagreed with Dad over England's treatment of India. Maureen came into the living room during this discussion and asked Mom if she wanted to put her feet in a pan of cool water so she could calm down. We learned a great deal of ethnic and racial tolerance in our youth. We drove to Minneapolis many times at Easter week to visit Dad's mother, and later his brother and sisters and "Young" Connie, our cousin who is our age. Sitting kitty-corner across the living room in the house in Minneapolis, "Big" Connie and her brother Edward would hold forth about their careers as social workers. Connie was the director of Neighborhood House in St. Paul, which served recent, usually poor, immigrants. Edward had started Pillsbury Settlement House in Minneapolis and looked after poor and delinquent boys. They were both prominent in their respective cities, and even today there are memorials of their contributions in Currie Park, Currie Avenue, and in Neighborhood House. As well, there is a fellowship for students named after

Connie, and the St. Paul Museum has an exhibit that celebrates her as a prominent woman of Minnesota. Connie had once entertained and opened her home to Marion Anderson, the prominent African American singer; in those days African Americans were not allowed to stay in downtown hotels. We were very proud of Dad's family, and I think they strengthened our sense of service to others, no matter what their ethnic, racial, or religious backgrounds were.

Our parents were more preoccupied with social-class differences than with ethnic or racial differences. In fact, while there was a clear willingness in them to help the poor and at the same time to associate with the middle class and upper class of all groups, I sensed less tolerance for the working classes. (Of course the categories are not always neatly distributed.) When Robin went out with a policeman's daughter, I remember Mom telling him that this girl might be nice to date but certainly wouldn't be a good choice for marriage. As well, there seemed to be a sense in our family that, while we could be comfortable in Woodhaven (which was definitely White-Anglo-Saxon-Protestant) and Dad could work easily with members of the Jewish community, we would not be comfortable living in the diversity of North Winnipeg. There was a certain sense of the superiority of our Anglo Saxon roots. I don't remember at what age I determined that I did not concur with these attitudes, but I certainly know that I made a conscious decision not try to model this one attitude, and to this day I love to celebrate the diversity of Winnipeg.

While we didn't have much money, we children did not feel deprived. I grew up with a sense that we were extraordinarily fortunate. Mom in particular spoke often of the Depression, and we knew that our parents were very careful with money because they had lived through it. But I didn't ever experience hunger or a lack of proper clothing, nor did I worry that we might. I remember the rationing of butter, sugar, and meat during the Second

World War, and the sense that we had to accept limitations because of the war, but my memory is that the sacrifices were not onerous and that they even provided a certain challenge.

Our religious beliefs were the foundation of our social life as well as of our attitudes about other ethnic groups and races. But, if religion was central to our lives, we were not pious. "Poor Protestants," Mom lamented one day. "They don't have anywhere near as much fun as we do." Religion did not seem forced, contrived, or burdensome. It was woven into our lives in the same way that a pattern is knitted into a sweater. I don't remember any of us going through teenage rebellion about attending church; it was not even a topic of discussion. We were in fact both culturally and socially a Catholic family. We had numerous dinner parties at home, and it was not unusual to have Jesuits or Franciscans for dinner. (Ironically, though, most of our friends were not Catholic, partly because almost none of our neighbours was Catholic, and because the Catholics we did know through our parish, St. Ann's, were mostly working-class.)

The Eaton's department store downtown had a room available for community groups to use, and Mom would often serve at teas there in support of Catholic charities. Dad was a fourth-degree Knight of Columbus and actively worked to promote cooperation with the Shriners. Mom cleaned the church, an all-day task once a week, and I often helped by washing the floors and dusting. Dad served as a financial advisor, or syndic, for the Franciscans in Winnipeg, a role that Robin later took on. Mom gathered clothes for people in poor missions in the North. I didn't ever think of these activities as religious acts. When, in 1951, Dad had his first heart attack and was in hospital for two months (the common treatment in those days), Mom sat beside the bed every day and spent her time preparing four large scrapbooks, one for each of us children. Interspersed with personal and family pictures in our scrapbooks were newspaper clippings about such events as the

Winnipeg Flood and the papal Proclamation of the Assumption of the Blessed Virgin, both of which took place in 1950. Mom's message was that our lives were integrated as part of a larger world in both its temporal and spiritual dimensions.

Prayer was part of our daily lives but wasn't engulfing. We went to Mass on Sundays and on special feast days. But, while Sunday Mass was important, my memories focus more on the family breakfasts after Mass when we often discussed the sermon. Even at Mass itself, Father MacCauley, our parish priest during my entire youth, was such a character that he would have us in fits of quiet laughter during Mass. As we knelt in the second pew from the front, we prayed for the sick, "whether or not they were in hospital," Father insisted. We prayed "for our families, for our friends, and our friends' friends." Mom and Dad always knelt for a short prayer before bed, a time we were not permitted to interrupt. We often listened to Right Reverend Monsignor Fulton J. Sheen on the radio, and it was woe to us if we talked during that half hour. He was the Catholic equivalent of Billy Graham in his enormous popularity. But, when we said the rosary as a family, I remember more giggling than anything else. We prayed the rosary for only a couple of years. It had been at Maureen's insistence following the visit of Father Patrick Payton to the Winnipeg Stadium; his motto was "The family that prays together stays together." On the other hand, I think Mom personally said the rosary every day of her life, until her last year when she was too ill. When items were lost, we prayed for their recovery. Mrs. Bennett, a non-Catholic neighbour down the street (note, others were simply "non"-Catholic), lost an earring when the grandson she was holding in her arms pulled it off and threw it into the dense garden. Several days later, after some fruitless searches, Mom told her to pray to "Tony" (St. Anthony of Padua), the patron of those seeking lost articles. Mom added that if she found the earring she should give a small donation to a charity in honour of St. Anthony. "Of course," Mrs. Bennett agreed. Mom then went over to the garden, looked down, and observed, "There it is!" This caused great laughter and a sense of awe on the part of Mrs. Bennett. And it simply confirmed our Catholic view that that was how the world operated.

I had personal experience with what I believed at the time was the power of prayer. Shortly before Mom's birthday, I think it was when I was in Grade 6, Dad and all of us children were standing in the living room in a circle quietly planning what we should get for her. I felt somewhat left out, as I did not have much of an allowance. But I asked for a nickel to take part in a draw at school for a sewing basket. When I arrived at school that morning, I went upstairs, where the church was located, knelt before the statue of St. Ann on the side altar and prayed to her that I would win the basket. I went upstairs to pray again at recess, at noon, and at the afternoon recess. As Sister was about to draw the winner at the end of the school day, I distinctly remember standing up beside my seat near the back of the room and starting to go forward to claim my prize. I was sure I would win—and I did! Mom treasured that gift for some 30 years. It was always around the house. I don't have such a simplistic view of prayer now, of course, but the experience left an indelible mark on me: perhaps prayers *can* be answered.

Another prominent aspect of prayer taught to me by Mom was its role in seeking guidance on what to do in complex situations. In the late 1950s, when my cousin Bill decided to marry Chieko, a Canadian of Japanese descent from Pincher Creek, there was serious consternation in the family. She was not a Catholic. Dad had already died by then, but I remember Mom kneeling to pray to the Holy Spirit and then getting up to write Bill and congratulate him. What carried the day was Mom's fantasy that perhaps they might have children who would grow up and go to Japan and convert some of the population. Years later, when

Charlene and I adopted Vincent, whom we later found out has Cree treaty rights as a member of the Peguis Reserve, there was not even a hint of disapproval. On the contrary, Mom was totally supportive, loving, and affectionate with him. I also remember her praying and expressing the hope that one day he would be a good leader of his people.

Charlene imagines the Church as a giant snowball rolling along and picking up not only snow but also dirt, twigs, and debris. This strikes me as a powerful, accurate image for understanding how my mom also saw it. While I don't think she ever used the term *community of sinners*, Mom certainly understood that none of us, including the clergy, was free of human frailty. This view is well illustrated in one of my favourite novels, Graham Greene's *The Power and the Glory*,[3] which is set in Mexico. In this novel, the State is trying to rid the country of all clergy. The last known Catholic priest is an alcoholic who has had an affair with a woman in the village. Yet he continues to carry out his ministry, even going to hear the confession of a dying man when he knows that he is walking into a government trap and will be caught by the police and executed. Mom understood this mixture of sin and goodness in people and, at the time that both John and I were studying for the priesthood, she told us she prayed daily that we would be good and faithful priests in spite of our flaws.

When I left home at 14 to go to Edmonton for high school, I had no idea that I would have so few years left with my father. Those four years at St. Anthony's included most of one summer, when I worked as a waiter in the dining room at the Franciscan Retreat house at Cochrane, Alberta. During those years, I certainly got into my share of mischief. (As I mentioned earlier, I frequently sneaked out of St. Anthony's at night, I dated Noranne against the rules of the school, and, on one occasion, several of us convinced the local taxi dispatch office that we had been sent by one of the priests to pick up a case of beer, which we proceeded to drink.) Had I been at home, my relationship with Dad might have been tense because of this mischief. I was not living up to his ideals. I am the first to admit that this period of separation favourably affected my relations with him. Our relationship was not forged and tempered by fire, as was Robin's, for example. Still, I so wish I had known him beyond my 19 years. He was only 60 when he died. I believe we would have been true friends in adulthood, as I have been with Charlene's mom and dad.

I came home for Dad's funeral in mid-March of 1954 from Sherbrooke, Quebec, where I was in my novitiate* year as a Franciscan. Dad had died suddenly and quickly from his second heart attack, in the early evening, as he and Mom were getting ready to go out for dinner. I was heartbroken when I heard the news; my worst fears had become a reality. In those days, after someone had a first heart attack, loved ones always lived in fear of the inevitable next one, which was often fatal. I had especially longed for him to live to see me in my Franciscan robes because of his own history and love of the friars, but it was not to be. After Dad's burial service, I took Mom's arm as we went down the steps of the church. I felt her pull away and I was momentarily hurt. But I later realized that she was asserting her strength and her ability to carry on by herself. She was now a widow, after only 27 years of marriage. She lived another 36 years.

Because Dad's pension was modest at best, Mom went to work fairly soon after he died. She had not been employed since before her marriage in Brandon, where she had worked as a secretary. She had left school after Grade 6 because the family lacked the finances for her school books and other related expenses. But during her whole life, she devoured books and newspapers and was extremely articulate in discussing world affairs and literary works.

Mom's work life revolved around the Church. At first, she worked for Catholic Welfare and then spent several years in charge of the office at the Rectory of St. Mary's Cathedral. These were difficult years. Archbishop Sinnott was thought to have been an alcoholic, and an auxiliary bishop was appointed to assist him. The office assistant to the bishop, the chancellor of the diocese, had left his post rather suddenly, and the office was in shambles. The records of baptisms for those years were incomplete, and as young adults came in for proof of their baptism in order to be married in the Church, they often had to provide family witnesses of their baptisms before Mom could prepare a certificate.

Mom moved on to manage Camp Morton, at that time a Catholic summer camp just north of Gimli owned by the Winnipeg Archdiocese. She loved this job. She lived on the site in the smallest cottage possible, which she nicknamed the Bird Cage. She ran the camp on a shoe-string budget and was in charge of every aspect. In fact, it was her dream job; in the 1940s she had begged Dad to open up a motel, a very new idea in those days. But he was too conservative in his financial affairs to take such a risk.

In the late 1950s, Mom accepted a position as housekeeper for Archbishop Phillip Pocock. He had a beautiful home on the Assiniboine River in Tuxedo, on a street later named Bishop's Lane. It was almost directly across the river from where we lived when I was growing up. Although Archbishop Pocock was not tall, he had an imposing presence. I think he truly appreciated Mom's ability to host elaborate dinners and events for prominent people in the community. The reception after my ordination was held at his home, and several times I stayed there with Mom during my holidays. The house had a beautiful sunroom overlooking the Assiniboine River where she and I would have breakfast and wonderful conversations.

Several years later, Archbishop Pocock was appointed archbishop of Toronto, and he asked Mom to go there ahead of him and supervise the decorating of the house that he had purchased. The interior designer Mom hired was a real character, an alcoholic for whom Mom also served as a counsellor. But together they did a job that was most satisfactory to the archbishop. Because she'd always had to be so careful with money, this challenge of decorating with high-quality fabrics and furniture without being extravagant was satisfying to her, and she delighted in showing me the result when I visited Toronto. When the archbishop arrived in Toronto, he asked her to stay on, but after a short period she was anxious to return to Winnipeg.

Archbishop Flahiff, who had replaced Archbishop Pocock and who was later appointed cardinal, was delighted when she agreed to move back to the residence that he had inherited in Winnipeg. The salary was very low. I used to threaten to go to the archbishop and ask for a raise for her, but she was horrified at the idea. I have at other times also felt that the Church paid unjust salaries. When I was chair of the Development and Peace Committee for the Diocese, we had decided to hire Fran Molero as the educational officer. When I submitted the budget, the reaction of the Chancery Office was: "We can't pay her that much, she would be earning more than a priest!" My answer was that the committee could not be asked to hire a person to work on social-justice issues and pay an unjust salary. We did not change our budget. It is interesting that later my brother John also had to insist on a decent salary for a secretary before he would take on the directorship of the Renew Program in the archdiocese. Mom's salary should have been twice what it was. When she told the cardinal that she was going to resign from the position, he urged her not to on the grounds that he would have to hire two people to replace her. And, when she left, that is exactly what he did.

My sense of Mom's expectations of me were truly tested in 1973 when I decided to take a leave of absence from the Franciscans and the priesthood, and three months later to request laicization.* Even a year earlier, when several of us in the priesthood were discussing the issue, I remember stating very emphatically that if I ever left the priesthood I would have to get out of town. Our family had such a high-profile Catholic presence that I felt I would be ostracized; it would just be too embarrassing for Mom if I continued to live in Winnipeg. I had known and counselled a young priest in another western Canadian city who had decided to resign. I knew his reasons, how conscientiously he had come to the decision, and felt that he was making the right decision. But I also knew that, after his resignation, his parents walked down back alleys and refused to go to any social events in that city because they were so ashamed. It was the bishop of the city who told them how wrong they were to behave in that manner. When I finally came to my decision after much agony and counselling, I went to Mom's apartment to tell her. I was in tears and felt I was about to let her down in probably the worst possible way. "I knew you were unhappy, but I didn't know why," she said very calmly. And just a very few moments later, she added, "Would you like to come and stay with me until you get settled?" This was an extraordinary gesture on her part, for my circumstances must have been extremely painful for her. I say this because several times over the ensuing years I tried to explain to her why I had come to the decision to resign. She would always stop me; she never did let me raise this issue with her, even though we had discussed many personal issues over the years. Over time, I came to respect her reluctance on this matter and to understand that she likely viewed my resignation, as others did, as a serious betrayal of a commitment I had made. Yet, her action clearly trumped every other emotion she might have felt, and she was obviously determined to focus on giving me the support I needed.

Recently I have reflected on how supportive Mom was of all

my major life choices. When I left home for St. Anthony's College in Edmonton in September of 1948, I was only 14. While I sensed reluctance from Mom and Dad about my going away at such an early age, I knew that their concern was about my well-being, not about any agenda they had for my life. When I returned home in the middle of the school year in 1952 ("because I was sick," I said, but not telling them about my confusion over Noranne), there was never a word said about my having let them down, having wasted theirs and other people's money, or anything of the sort. I think their restraint was remarkable. Father Godfrey, a Franciscan in Winnipeg, later said to me, "You told us you were sick; but we knew otherwise," so I assume that my parents knew too. Finally, when I resigned from the priesthood in 1973, it was Mom to whom I turned first. Again, there was not a word of reproach, judgement, or complaint about any embarrassment she might have felt. My siblings were as supportive. My brother John invited me to live with him at his rectory at St. Vital Parish on Pembina Highway, where I stayed for a year. My sister, Maureen, told me several times in the ensuing years that I had simply continued my ministry in a different form. For several months, I also discussed my decision with people at various convents and rectories in the city, which helped me greatly to understand that I no longer needed to shed tears; I was at peace about my decision and wanted to get on with my life.

In May of 1975, two years after my resignation, when Charlene and I were married, Mom found some reason (which I don't remember) not to come to the wedding in Louisville, Kentucky. I knew that the event would have been just too difficult emotionally for her. In fact, I was grateful that she made that decision. She seemed to understand that it was a time of celebration for us, and if she had been present, my concern for her comfort would have impeded my ability to fully enjoy the celebration. Other family members did attend; Robin, who served as my best man, added a great deal to our wedding day, as did my cousin Connie and her family. As soon as the wedding was over, we called Mom in Winnipeg. She was entirely gracious, and I was relieved and thankful. Charlene and I headed off for six weeks in South America.

Shortly after we arrived in Winnipeg in July, Mom held a party to introduce Charlene, to which all her women friends were invited. I, of course, was not invited. Charlene admired Mom right from the beginning, but I wanted much more than just admiration and courtesy between them. I wanted them to love each other. For several years I kept gently prodding Mom to tell me how wonderful Charlene was. But both these women were as honest as they could be, and neither was about to express feelings they did not have. A resignation from the priesthood is a traumatic event in a Catholic family, and, even though Mom accepted and supported my decision, it took time for her to attain real comfort with it. Eventually, however, Mom and Charlene developed a wonderful relationship, and Mom could not say enough about how gracious, thoughtful, and *dear* (a term she used often) Charlene was to her. The love was truly mutual. Their approach to the development of their relationship taught me an important lesson: particularly while I was dean of the Faculty of Arts, I was always careful not to say things to people if I did not really mean them. Being honest within relationships was something I learned from watching Mom and Charlene sort out theirs.

The last 10 years of Mom's life was a difficult time for her. The difficulties were precipitated by an incident one Sunday evening in winter. We received a call from Irene that Robin had just taken Mom to Grace General Hospital. She had left the dining table at their home on Strathmillan Road and headed toward the bathroom. She fell down 13 stairs, landing on the concrete basement floor. Perhaps she'd had a stroke. While holding vigil in her hospital room the next morning, I suddenly thought she stopped breathing. I ran to the nursing station. In a flash, five or six staff were at her bedside. She was transferred to the intensive care unit, where she could be watched continuously. She stayed there for a week or so. I think that she would have died had I not been there.

Just how remarkable a woman she was, was revealed during those final 10 years. She was in the hospital for about four months. On Christmas morning we visited with our two children and gave her a picture of the four of us. I remember her showing it to the nurse with great pride, saying that this was her son and daughter-in-law and children, yet in fact she was taking this on our word. She had no idea who we were. When we visited her, she would often tell us about a wonderful dinner party she had hosted the night before. It seemed to be set in the 1930s, in Halifax. But, wherever it was, it certainly had been a gala event, and she was able go on about it in great detail.

Gradually she regained her memory and strength and was able to return to the apartment she shared with a friend, Bun Agnew. Once I got a call at work from my sister, Maureen, who said, "Mom is having people over for lunch, and you won't believe what she is serving: peanut butter on toast, covered with tomatoes and mushroom soup!" I called Mom, chatted a bit, and then, when she informed me of her luncheon plans, I asked, "Mom, are you sure those ingredients go together?" "Well," she said, "I am certainly glad I did not invite you!" I never again interfered with her entertainment plans.

Bun died quite suddenly soon after Mom went home from the hospital, and Mom moved to the seniors' home at 185 Smith Street. Every time we visited, there was some little chore to be done. Somehow it took me back to my early childhood when I was always doing things for her. Only in later life can you realize just how hard it is to have to depend on others to do the things you always did for yourself, and how hard it is to ask for help. I have reached that stage in my own life. Without question, it is much easier to give than to receive.

Many times Mom told us that she would let us know when it was time for her to move to a nursing home. When that time did come for her, remembering only too well her struggles when her own mother and father lived with her, she understood that moving in with us would not be wise. The disabilities of our children were becoming more pronounced and difficult to deal with, and, as much as we would like to have had her with us, we had to make other arrangements. I remember the sadness and the guilt I felt the day I took her to Fred Douglas Lodge. Yet, the next day, when a friend of hers suggested that she should "get out of that place," Mom told me, "I said to her that I'm determined to be happy here." She lived at Fred Douglas for about three years. At first, she went to the dining room for her meals but gradually began having them brought to her. She was confined to bed for the final year of her life.

About nine months before Mom died, my sister, Maureen, was transferred by her religious community to Winnipeg, and, as luck would have it, the sisters had a house on Burrows Avenue, just a block away from the nursing home. This was a great treat for Mom, very important to Maureen, and extremely helpful to us. We all tried to visit as often as possible, but, as time went on, Mom remembered less and less. "I am so lonely," she said one day. "It seems ages since I've seen anyone." "Oh Mom," I said, "Esmé left just half an hour ago." "Oh, isn't that wonderful," she answered. Catherine, our daughter, loved to visit her, and Mom called her "my little nurse." About our son Vincent she said one day, "Now, don't be too hard on him," and it reminded me of how she "protected" us from our strict dad when we were children. We kept a little notebook in her room to record the comings and goings of visitors. It often helped us through conversations with her; we could remind her about who had been there. The notebook showed that she really had a large number of visitors.

Maureen often read to Mom and discussed things spiritual.

I remember asking Mom one day if she found prayer easy or hard and if she had a sense of being in the presence of God. She seemed to me such a holy woman, and I anxiously awaited her answer, expecting some special insight. But, instead, she was very matter of fact—no, she said, she did not have any sense of the presence of God. When Maureen spoke to her of heaven, she turned her head a little in bed, looked up, and said, "I'm not particularly anxious to go there yet. You won't be there." This was almost the same answer she'd given one Sunday two years earlier when Maureen had said, "It's the Feast of Christ the King today, Mom, do you feel ready to go to heaven?" She paused a moment and then replied, "I'm not in any hurry!"

Mom died on the 5th of April 1990. Her funeral was a fitting testimony to a faithful daughter of the Church. Almost every priest in the diocese was there, as well as Archbishop Adam Exner. John celebrated the Funeral Mass and also spoke about Mom. Maureen had reminded him of something Mom had said earlier in her life when someone had suggested how proud she must be of all the successes of her children. "I'm not proud," she had said, "but I am very grateful." At first, John's homily focussed on the passage from the gospel "Consider the lilies of the field." Then, he concluded his sermon with: "And so, if you ask me if I am proud of my mother? No, but I am deeply grateful."

In writing these reflections I did not have to embellish the positive or block out the negative. Whatever else I might have retrieved from memories of my family life would have had the same tenor to it. I simply had what I know was a privileged life—not from wealth and status but from the love and principles that were part of my home environment and continue to sustain and inspire me. For this, I too am "deeply grateful."

CHAPTER 3

My Early Years in the Franciscans (1953–1973)

Left to right: Robin, me, Maureen, and John, 1964

How did I get from my life as a Franciscan friar and priest to that of a married man with two children? As any social scientist might expect, it was not the result of a momentous decision following a conversion experience in the tradition of St. Paul.

Rather, it resulted from a series of small choices made over a period of about 10 years. That is also the best way to describe how I decided to enter the Franciscans in the first place.

As a preteen, when I helped Mom clean the parish church every week, I always took special delight in dusting the pulpit. For me, there was a certain sacredness that permeated that spot. It was imposing, and its dark wood added a sense of austerity. More than once, I told Mom that I dreamed of preaching there one day. Part of the appeal at that time was that I loved to imagine myself as an orator. I had already had some success in public speaking. In Grade 8, I won my school's oratorical contest and then competed against winners from other Catholic schools across the city. That same year, my school selected me as its representative in the Catholic Schools Junior Parliament. I was thrilled when, after I gave my address as a cabinet minister, the page boy brought me a note from the Speaker of the House. The Speaker thought my address was "one of the best of the session."

I had other teenage dreams too: to be a political commentator on radio or a lawyer defending individuals in the courtroom. The common thread among these career aspirations was their people-helping characteristic. In our home, we recognized our privilege and understood that we should spend our lives helping others. My uncle and aunt who were social workers in Minneapolis also had a significant effect on my life in this regard. And the lives of the saints were well known to us: Theresa of Lisieux, known as "the little flower" in Catholic circles for her sanctity achieved through a life of simplicity; Ignatius of Loyola, founder of the Jesuits; and the Canadian Jesuit martyrs are just a few whose lives were an inspiration. (It is interesting that the recent Pope John Paul II canonized more saints than any previous pope because he wanted to provide role models for the world.) Of course we had our favourite saints, and mine was St. Francis of Assisi. Not only was he the founder of the Franciscans, but also, his chosen life of poverty and simplicity, his love of nature and animals, and his desire to preach the gospel made him important to me and also one of the most beloved saints in the Catholic Church.

As well, the Franciscans whom we knew personally and invited to our home for dinners were loveable characters whose warmth and humour provided delight for the whole family and made a powerful impression on me. One evening over dinner, just before I left for St. Anthony's College in Edmonton for Grade 10, Father Godfrey McSweeney and Father John Forest listed all the reasons to support my *not* entering the Franciscans. They recounted some of their own less-than-pious experiences. For example, to have their sense of humility tested, as young friars they were sent to the local grocery store to buy both pork-and-beans and toilet paper. When a friar visited the guardian* of the friary, he was to get down on one knee and say "Bless me, Father" at the beginning of the conversation. Father Godfrey once taught a newly arrived friar from eastern Europe who did not speak English that the greeting was "Kiss my ass." The guardian knew immediately who the culprit was. This story-telling made for a memorable evening of laughter and likely helped me see the fun-loving, human side of these men, who were dedicated to a spiritual mission.

Following my graduation from high school in June of 1952, I did go back to St. Anthony's in the fall to study philosophy. But I was full of confusion and indecision about whether to enter the Franciscans and study for the priesthood. I left my studies and returned home to Winnipeg before Christmas. My confusion was compounded by my attraction to Noranne. However, two circumstances with my siblings also had their influences on me. A year earlier, my brother John went through a terrible crisis before he entered the seminary. He had completed his B.A. and was very much in love with one of his university classmates. I could see his suffering as he weighed his decision whether to pursue the relationship or go to the seminary. His decision to enter the seminary despite his feelings for his girlfriend was an example that must have had an effect on my own decision. Then, in May of 1953, I travelled with Mom and Dad to Albany, New York, to visit my sister, Maureen, who had entered the Convent of the Sacred Heart the previous year. She was obviously happy; in fact *radiant* would be a better descriptor. I wonder now how much her mood affected my decision to study for the priesthood; our visit occurred exactly when I was trying to make my decision. I entered the Franciscans in August, in Sherbrooke, Quebec. I don't remember a defining moment when I made the decision to enter in the same way that I remember my decision to leave 20 years later. I had certainly not forgotten Noranne, but, as John eventually did, I felt confident that I had made the right decision. It was the fulfillment of a long-held dream. I was rather immature at 19, but, nevertheless, I made the decision entirely on my own, without any pressure whatsoever from Mom or Dad. I certainly understood that in a Catholic family at that time, to dedicate one's life as a priest or religious was without question "the highest calling." The attitude prevails today that a person accepted into the priesthood or religious life has a "vocation"—that is, he or she is answering God's call. It is this attitude that undoubtedly influenced my decision to go into the ministry, and—as I discovered—it is also what made it so difficult to leave.

I do not look back with regret on my 20 years in the Franciscans or the 13 years ministering as a priest. As I recall those years now, I recognize again the incredible experience a life of religious service can provide a person, and I am thankful that I had the chance to discover it from the inside.

At the time I entered, the Franciscan authorities in Rome held the enlightened view that all Franciscans in Canada should be bilingual; therefore we Anglophones were sent to Quebec, where the Franciscans date back to the arrival of the Récollets priests in 1615. There was also a much larger contingent of Franciscans in Quebec than elsewhere in Canada; in Quebec there were over 500 members and only slightly over 100 friars in western Canada. The largest contingent in the West, the one in rural Saskatchewan near Regina, originally came from Germany. When I arrived in Quebec, I began seven years of speaking French almost all the time.

I undertook the customary training for the priesthood within the Franciscans. I lived for a year in the novitiate in Sherbrooke, learning about religious life and the Franciscan tradition in particular, then spent two years studying philosophy in Quebec City at the friary on rue l'Alverne. That was followed by four years studying theology in Montreal in the area of Rosemont.

My novitiate year as a Franciscan began in a beautiful four-storey building, set on the hill that separates Sherbrooke from Lennoxville. The walls, with their large, dark, rectangular stones and ivy growing up the sides, gave off a distinct centuries-old monastery aura. In fact, though, I was entering a friary, not a monastery. Monasteries are older in the Christian tradition and are characterized by their isolation from the world; anyone interested in meeting the monks have to go to the monastery. The Order of Friars Minor, or Franciscans, as the group is more commonly known, was founded in the early 1200s by Francis of Assisi. His vision created a type of community that was a radical departure from earlier forms of religious life. The friars are to go out among the people, two by two, to preach the gospel. Pope Innocent III accepted this vision of Francis, and later the Order of the Friars Minor became one of the four communities in the Roman Catholic Church upon which all other communities base their fundamental rules of procedure and conduct.

As friars in Quebec in the 1950s, we lived very much in the centuries-old traditions. Inside the locked door of our friary, the vestibule gave way to long, wide, but sparsely furnished corridors graced with simple arches. On the top floor, each of our small rooms had only a desk, a lamp, a bookshelf, and a single, wooden bed covered with a mattress of straw. Our appearance and attire, too, were spare. We wore the tonsure—that is, a band of hair around the head about two fingers wide just above the ears, all the hair above and below shaved off. We had no clothes other than two identical sets of the familiar brown habit with a cord and cowl, and underclothes. In winter we wrapped ourselves in large woollen capes. We wore these whether we were in the friary or walking from Montreal to Quebec City. And did we ever walk! A life of poverty was so central to the vision of St. Francis that we never even touched money.† If we needed to move from place to place in the city or between cities, we simply walked until someone picked us up. It was so common for people to offer rides to Franciscans that, if we went out for a walk and did not want a ride, we would walk on the side of the street facing the oncoming traffic; even then, people would stop. If we were offered money, we graciously refused it. In Sherbrooke, our community of about 75 had one Jeep. The brother in charge of begging would take the Jeep to the market and go about his errands, leaving the vehicle unlocked. When he returned to drive it home, it would be filled with bags of groceries left by people who shopped at the market. We received so much food that we not only fed all the friars but also gave away bags of groceries on a daily basis to any family that asked for help.

The generosity of the community toward us was humbling. I remember well that there was a large bakery in town that regularly donated two- or three-day-old pound cake with a cream or chocolate icing. If we did have dessert at our meals, it was almost always this pound cake, but we certainly didn't complain;

---

† *Diocesan priests, those who are responsible for most Roman Catholic parishes in Canada, do not take a vow of poverty. They receive a personal salary and can own property, unlike priests in a religious order such as the Franciscans.*

we felt lucky to have dessert at all. I remember little else about our meals, except that we fasted during the 40 days of Lent before Easter, and during Advent, the four weeks before Christmas. Fasting meant that we ate only one full meal a day, the other two consisting of half the normal portions.

The leader in the community was called the guardian. St. Francis did not want a hierarchy in the community, someone who was superior to the others. The guardian's term was limited, after which he was replaced and would return to the ranks. I was comfortable with this concept of leadership as a service and also found it appropriate in the university setting. I later served as guardian at the retreat house at Cochrane, Alberta (from 1965 to 1967).

I had to get used to limiting my conversations to set times during the day. We usually ate in silence, seated at two long tables, one on each side of the dining room. Perhaps two or three evenings a week, halfway through the meal, the guardian would announce *Benedicamus Domino* (Let us bless the Lord), to which we eagerly responded *Deo Gratias* (Thanks be to God) and then engaged in lively conversation. Because we did not have access to newspapers, radio, or television, the conversation certainly was not focussed on the news of the day. But we never were at a loss for topics. We also had about a half-hour following lunch for conversation, after which the friary bell would ring to signal a 30-minute quiet time. Following the evening meal, we had around an hour of free time for walking or playing hockey or baseball (all done, of course, in our robes). That period of activity was the hardest to leave, as we always had great fun playing sports, and it went by far too quickly.

At the beginning of the evening meal, or sometimes at lunch, there was an opportunity called the Chapter of Faults for one or two of us to kneel in the centre of the refectory and publicly state, or "confess," our violations of the rules of the friary. After the confession, the guardian would give a "penance," which usually involved saying some prayers in private later on but might include kissing the bare feet of one or another friar sitting at the meal. This was possible because we wore sandals with no socks.

I mention this practice because it helps describe the medieaval environment in which we lived. While it could inspire a sense of humiliation, I don't remember it that way. I don't remember anyone ever being obliged to make such a public confession, and any one individual seldom did it more than once every several months. It was useful as a form of social control in that it fostered the internalization of the rules of the friary; more important, it fostered in us a sense of humility, considered in all the writings of the saints throughout history to be the key virtue for those aspiring to holiness. Yet, to achieve humility is just as difficult in a religious order as it is in the secular world. Myriad types of social class and other rankings pervade our society. Academe, for example, is filled with competitiveness and rankings, from the quality of journals in which one is published to the very academic rank one has achieved. Why should we imagine a religious community to be any different? The only difference, I think, is in the criteria. Am I "holier" than others? Do I pray longer, fast more, violate the rule of silence less? The Chapter of Faults was probably begun to help individuals keep their own lives in perspective, to help them reflect on their own limitations.

Behind the Chapter of Faults was the same rationale as for the ritual in the Catholic Church on Ash Wednesday. At the beginning of Lent, Catholics are invited to have ashes placed on their foreheads in the form of a cross as the priest says, "Remember man that thou art dust and unto dust thou shalt return." Have we not all heard of the slave who ran before the Roman Emperor to remind him of his frailty? But not all of life in the friary was this dismal. On one occasion, three of us were trying to pull a heavy object with a rope when the rope broke. On a lark, we decided that at the next meal we would wrap the rope around our necks and publicly confess to breaking it. Thankfully, even the guardian saw the humour of our mock confession. On another occasion, when a friar was asked to kiss the feet of another as penance, he was appalled to discover that the feet smelled. Without the slightest hesitation he took the foot and sandal in his hand and rubbed the arch with the stubble of his beard!

Our prayer life was very much in the monastic tradition, the Divine Office* chanted at the appropriate times of the day: Matins and Lauds at midnight, Prime before Mass at 6:00 a.m., Tierce after Mass, Sext at 11:45 a.m., None at 2:00 p.m. after our naps, Vespers at 5:45 p.m., and Compline at 8:00 p.m. In fact, this set of daily prayers is required of all priests in the Roman Catholic Church. Therefore, if any of us missed the community prayers, we were expected to complete them on our own. Divine Office was composed mostly of the psalms and other texts from the Scriptures. It was chanted in Latin, and as the years went by I gradually understood more and more about what I was singing or reading. I had studied Latin in high school at St. Anthony's, but we did not have specific Latin classes during our studies as novices. This put those of us from western Canada at a distinct disadvantage; the young men who entered from Quebec had completed a classical high school education, including a great deal of study in Latin.

In addition to Mass each day, we had two one-hour periods of silent meditation—in the late morning and just before dinner. These were somewhat unpredictable hours for me. At times, no significant thoughts or prayers came to mind, and I would read spiritual books. And, like others, I occasionally dropped off to sleep. But I also had some powerful moments during these times when I felt an intimate connection with the Divine. The routine of daily prayer remained almost unchanged during the seven years of my training. It was the framework into which our other responsibilities fit. In the first year, we did a fair amount of manual labour and heard lectures on Franciscan spirituality, and later we took classes in philosophy or theology and had hours of study time. These were happy years for me. The sense of being part of a spiritual world provided great satisfaction.

In the summers, we had the opportunity of going to a lake in the Mont Tremblant area for almost two months. A number of the other English-speaking students headed off to the University of Ottawa for summer courses, but, frankly, I preferred the quiet of the lake. It turned out to be a very important spiritual time for me. One summer, I read the whole Bible and would often take a theme and try to follow it through. With my feet resting in the water at the shore one day, I followed the theme of *living water* from Jeremiah and Isaiah through to the Apocalypse. Another theme that particularly moved me, and one that I later used frequently when hearing confessions of individuals, was that of *forgiveness*, as is evident in the passage "The Lord, the Lord God, slow to anger, rich in kindness and fidelity, forgiving unto a thousand generations wickedness, crime and sin" (Exodus 34:6).

The spirituality we were steeped in provided a world view in which all events were easily interpreted within its framework. One experience that took on special spiritual meaning for me was sailing a 16-foot boat built by one of the brothers in the community. Our lake was nestled in the valley between two of the Laurentian Mountains, which acted as a wind tunnel. The arrival of the wind was like the arrival of a spirit moving across the water, providing invisible power to move me onward.

As friars and mendicants, not monks, we were not cloistered but went out to minister as requested. About half of the 60 who lived in this friary were students studying for the priesthood. About 10 others were brothers—that is, they chose to live in the community with the same vows of poverty, chastity, and obedience as the priests, but they carried out the maintenance tasks of the community, from cooking, to plumbing, to carpentry. Another two dozen were already ordained priests. They went about Quebec giving retreats or helping out in parishes. Others did research on a critical edition of the writings of the mediaeval theologian Duns Scotus (who was a Franciscan), while others were our professors. All our professors had doctorates in their areas of expertise from universities around the world. Most of the friars who were priests worked in poorer parishes, while a small proportion worked in universities, and an even smaller number in the higher echelons of Church administration.

As I reflect now upon those days in the friary, as well as on my later experiences living in the Bronx in New York, visiting the poverty-stricken areas in South America, and more recently travelling through South Africa, I would not say that we lived a life of poverty in the friary. It was, indeed, a simple and austere life, but it was also a life free of the insecurities associated with the real poverty in our world. Nor did we experience the disdain typically heaped upon the poor. On the contrary—we were held in high respect by others, which led to the offer of many benefits, and we had to decline things we did not need or should not have had. This is not the experience of the poor.

My ability to live within the vow of chastity was not difficult during my seven years in Quebec. It is perhaps hard for many to understand that it was possible, indeed natural, for me to live a life of chastity in the friary, but the expression of sexual desires was simply not an issue. My life was so filled with theological and spiritual interests and satisfying friendships with a number of friars that the vow of chastity was not problematic. I did not engage in, nor have any interest in, homosexual relations, nor did I know other friars who did. This was simply not a high-profile issue in those years. In the mid-1960s, however, when I was asked to lead the recruitment of candidates for the Franciscans in western Canada, I took the initiative to indicate openly to potential candidates that if they had homosexual tendancies they would likely find it particularly difficult to live in an all-male religious community. Of course the public climate toward homosexuality has changed dramatically since those years. The issue of religious leaders leading an active homosexual lifestyle is being fiercely debated in virtually all Christian religious organizations. Within the Roman Catholic Church, I believe that respect for individuals with a homosexual lifestyle has dramatically increased, although it is by no means universal. Nevetheless, I think it more than highly unlikely that the Catholic Church will ever legitimize an active homosexual lifestyle for priests. It should be obvious that, no matter which sexual orientation a Roman Catholic priest has, either heterosexual or homosexual, he is expected to live a life of continence, or abstinence from sexual activity.

The issue of priests being married is more complex. Currently there are close to 15 rites in the Catholic Church, of which the Roman rite is the largest. A rite sets out the manner in which the sacraments of the church are celebrated as well as many other practices, such as even the date that Christmas is celebrated. Celibacy for priests is currently the norm in the Roman Catholic Church but is not the norm in all other rites that are part of the Catholic Church, such as in the Ukrainian Catholic Church. Also, even within the Roman rite, there are priests who are married, such as Anglican priests who joined the Roman Catholic Church after their marriages and ordinations as Anglicans. Recent popes have all upheld the celibacy of priests in the Roman rite. Whether this will hold in the years to come is, in my view, unlikely. However, for members of religious communities, whether they are priests or brothers or sisters, the vow of chastity involves, by its very nature, celibacy and total continence.

It should be obvious that it is possible to live a life of celibacy and be happy in that state. There are many who do so, including many lay people who never enter a religious community. I was happy living a celibate life in the Quebec friary. But the demands of the vow of chastity were a more challenging issue for me after I left Quebec. This departure coincided with my ordination to the priesthood and the beginning of a phase of constant public ministry. I moved from the protected life in the large friaries in Sherbrooke, Quebec City, and Montreal, each including about 60 members, and back west into Franciscan communities that never numbered more than 15 or 20, and could number as few as five or six. Therefore, I was embarking on interaction with the public in ways from which I had been sheltered during the period of philosophical and theological training in Quebec. In particular, interaction with women became a part of my ministry, and I found many of them to be stunningly attractive. I was, at that point in my life, quite naïve about women. But once I returned to the West, the new and daily interaction with women awakened my somewhat dormant sexual feelings, and I had to come to terms with it. It was probably close to a year before I could comfortably accommodate my chosen way of life and ministry, which included a vow of chastity, with daily encounters with women.

A significant change, much greater than my personal adjustment, was occurring in Quebec just as I was leaving that province to return to the West. The Quiet Revolution in 1960 in Quebec, which began with the death of Maurice Duplessis in 1959, was associated with the declericalization of Quebec society. Cardinal Leger in Montreal had decided that no religious order of men should continue to wear their religious garb on the street. Franciscan priests, therefore, like members of all other religious orders, began wearing only the Roman collar common to all priests, even those who had not taken a vow of poverty. These changes came about just as I was leaving Quebec that year. It meant, of course, that we had to adjust our way of life significantly, as we were no longer recognizable in public as Franciscans. The most significant change was that we had to carry money and engage in daily commerce. In my mind, a kind of pact between the public and the Franciscans was forever shattered by Cardinal Leger's decision. Catholic clergy had not generally worn religious garments in North America for a long time, except in Quebec. This is one reason that Quebec has always had a special place in my heart. It is where I entered the Franciscans, and the wearing of the robes within a supportive social setting was one way that allowed us to live our Franciscan ideals.

When I entered the Franciscans, my immersion into Francophone life was immediate and complete. I was among five or six Anglophones from the West brought together with about 20 young men from Quebec, all of us entering into a community that already had at least 50 older French Canadian friars. I had studied only high school French, but within the second week after entering the friary I was taking my turn at meals reading publicly in French. (The consistency of the accent in French, always being on the last syllable, certainly gave us an advantage over those Francophones who were learning to speak English, in which the accent can be on any syllable. But they did not have to read in English in public!) In my first such experience, I began with great confidence reading a chapter (Chapître Quatorze) from a book about the life of Father Frédéric, a remarkable friar who lived in Trois Rivières some 50 years earlier. However, instead of pronouncing the title of the chapter correctly as "Coup sur Coup," meaning "Blow after Blow," I said "cue sur cue," or "ass over ass." Even in the strict environment of the friary, this caused a good laugh, for reasons I obviously did not understand at the time. I just had to keep on reading.

Nevertheless, learning French was relatively easy for me. I was extremely proud that by my third year I was commenting about the Mass on the daily program broadcast on a local radio station from the friary in Quebec City. By the time I returned to the West, I was thinking in French and had to pause to find the proper English word. We were committed to a truly classical education, including studies in Greek, Latin, and Hebrew as well as philosophy and theology. I had a much easier time with French than with the other languages, for some reason. Perhaps this was because we had a French-speaking maid, Bertha Beauchemin, in our home for over a year when I was four. My mother was ill, and, with four young children at home, Dad felt this was necessary. Bertha and I had a wonderful relationship, and I loved picking up French sentences from her, some of which I remember to this day. In the friary, all our courses were taught by French-speaking professors, of course, although some of our textbooks were in Latin, and one of our professors liked to lecture in Latin.

Not only did I learn French, but also I became somewhat immersed in Quebec society. I say "somewhat" because, especially during the first three years, we did not leave the friary often. Nor did we watch television, read the daily newspapers, or listen to the radio, all of which were considered to be worldly distractions. In my last four years there, however, during our theological training in Montreal, I travelled a bit throughout the province and began such forms of ministry as teaching catechism in Montreal schools.

By the time I left Quebec, I had become sympathetic to the frustration and sense of alienation from Canada felt by most of the Francophones whom I knew, including the friars. For example, I was embarrassed by the naming of the Queen Elizabeth Hotel in Montreal and by the fact that all cheques issued by the federal government were in English. I enjoyed the popular song "Le Manique," with its strong nationalistic overtones, as well as the folk songs of Félix Leclerc. Seven years after leaving Quebec in 1960, while I was in graduate school at Fordham University in New York studying sociology, I organized a seminar on bilingualism and biculturalism, inspired by the 1965 preliminary report of the Royal Commission on Bilingualism and Biculturalism. We attracted eight Canadian and American students as well as one professor. My own paper in that seminar dealt with language as power and traced the sense of identity of Quebec from its roots in faith as the "faithful daughter of the Church" to the then-recent statement of a prominent Quebec cleric who proclaimed, "Perdre la langue, c'est perdre la foi" (To lose your language is to lose your faith).

There has never been any doubt in my mind that Quebec society has a distinct culture and that we would be an impoverished nation without respecting and fostering it. Franciscans played a role in supporting the language and the life of the Francophones in western Canada. Almost all of us were bilingual, and some were asked to be pastors in French parishes in the dioceses of Winnipeg, Regina, Edmonton, Vancouver, and Victoria, and more than once I preached in French.

My knowledge of French has enhanced my work both in the ministry and in my academic career. I have been able to serve on several national committees in the social sciences, such as on the executive of the Canadian Sociology and Anthropology Association, the board of the Social Science Federation of Canada, and the Data Liberation Initiative,† and I currently chair the Research Data Centre National Coordinating Committee. As dean of the Faculty of Arts, my knowledge of French has facilitated communication with members of le Collège Universitaire de Saint Boniface and with many other French-speaking people.

Had I not gone to Quebec, I would no doubt have studied much more classical English literature, which I certainly would have enjoyed. However, living in French-speaking Quebec, I was reading authors such as Molière, Camus, Bernanos, and Sartre.

---

† *The Data Liberation Initiative is a very successful effort to make all the public-use data collected by Statistics Canada, such as the census, available to the academic community across the country by taxing the universities rather than individual academic users.*

What remained, though, was an intense interest in literature. On Charlene's initiative, during the last 10 years in particular, we have taken great delight in reading award-winning literature, such as Nobel-Prize, Governor-General, Booker, Pulitzer, Orange, and Trillium award winners. We have developed a special interest in Canadian literature, and we find it stimulating to discuss the books with each other. My love of literature as well as my knowledge of another language, which blossomed in my Quebec period, served me well as dean of a faculty that included both the humanities and the social sciences.

In 1998, Shirley Neuman, then dean of the Faculty of Arts at the University of British Columbia, and I jointly conducted an evaluation of the Faculty of Arts at Dalhousie University. A professor of English and a member of the Royal Society, she told me a story about the CEO of a large company who described to her the kind of employee he wanted. "I don't want an arts graduate," he said. "I want someone who can come into my company and understand the culture of my business, learn all the dimensions, interpret behaviour, and understand the motivations of my customers." "Ah," said Dr. Neuman. "What you need is someone who knows how to read a novel, someone who can enter an unfamiliar world, understand it, and critically analyze it. That is indeed an arts graduate."

My years in Quebec were stimulating and happy. I was pursuing the spiritual ideals of my youth, I was immersed in the extraordinary spirituality of Francis of Assisi, I entered an academic world of philosophy and theology at a time of enormous change in the Catholic Church, and the setting for all these discoveries was an entirely new culture for me, that of the French-speaking environment of Quebec society.

CHAPTER 4

My Studies in Philosophy and Theology (1954–1960)

In my Franciscan habit, Lennoxville, Quebec, 1954

At the end of my novitiate year in Sherbrooke in August of 1954, I moved to the friary on rue l'Alverne in Quebec City to finish my studies in philosophy, which I had begun in Edmonton two years earlier. The importance of ideas—indeed, their life and society-changing potential—became clear to me. One of the most influential teachers I had at that time was Professor Constantin Baillageron, one of the Franciscans who taught us modern philosophy. Starting with Descartes, we moved through other great thinkers such as Spinosa, Kant, Hegel, Feuerbach, Engels, Marx, Marcel, and Sartre. The course was an extraordinary lesson on the effect that ideas have on the transformation of human society, as well as the effect of society on ideas. This was heady stuff for a 21-year-old, and I found myself totally enthralled. I began to understand why we categorize whole periods of Western history by the predominant thinking of the time: the Dark Ages, the Renaissance, the Reformation, the Age of Reason, the Enlightenment, and Romanticism. Immanuel Kant (1724–1804), one of the leading figures of the Enlightenment, was among the thinkers I studied. He was interested in what we can know independently of experience and perception. And his conclusion was that we know very little. That turned out to be an explosive idea that still has relevance today. It defied much of the previous thought on human behaviour that stressed that religious belief, for example, should be based on tradition, the Scriptures, the authority of the Church, and apologetics (a defence of the faith against competing belief systems). Kant strongly influenced Schleiermacher, who became one of the forebears of the experiential basis for religious faith that has been prominent both in evangelical circles and in a number of new religious movements.

Karl Marx's argument was opposite to Kant's. Marx stated that "it is not the consciousness of men that determines their existence, but their social existence that determines their consciousness."[1] This powerful statement has for many years influenced the way I interpret much of human behaviour. By the middle of the 20th century, more than half of all people in the world were under the influence of various ideas articulated by Marx or espoused his ideas. This included the governments of more than 20 countries, such as most of eastern Europe (including the Soviet Union), much of Asia (including China, North Korea, and Vietnam), as well as people in many other countries without communist or socialist governments. In this context, I am surprised that so many people that I know dismiss the effects of the social setting in which they live on their ways of thinking and their interpretation of reality. Reflecting my personal bias, I believe that a sociological approach to reality is needed to complement our typical psychological or individualistic mindset.

I had occasion to visit the museum in Marx's honour at his birthplace in Trier, Germany, when I presented an academic paper at the University of Trier in 1990. Earlier, Charlene and I had seen his place of work in the British Museum, and we took the London tube up to see his burial site in Highgate Cemetery. That was in the mid-1970s, and we clearly had a sense that we were being watched by the groundskeeper; he appeared to be far more interested in us than in tending the gardens. Marx's tombstone had been bombed on several occasions and no doubt needed some security. It is ironic that the cemetery in which the best-known socialist thinker of all time is laid to rest is privately owned!

Later, with the advent of the women's movement in the 1960s, I realized that we had been studying only male philosophers. Of course, that in itself is a perfect illustration of the effect of society on ideas. Women had traditionally been deliberately marginalized within society, and it is not surprising that women thinkers were ignored. It will be interesting to follow the effect of women theologians in the Catholic Church as their roles become more recognized and more women are encouraged to join their ranks.

Will women ever be permitted to be ordained as priests in the Catholic Church? An interesting question. Between 1965 and 2005, there has been a 40-percent decline in the number of priests in the United States and a 65-percent increase in the number of Catholics. The decline of priests in Canada in the same period was over 50 percent. By 1995, 12 percent of parishes in the United States had no resident priest, and 81 percent of the administrators of those parishes were women. I doubt this demographic reality will have a bearing on the thinking in Rome. Personally, I expect that the ordination of married men will be permitted before women are allowed to be ordained. The long and extra-ordinary contribution of women as directors of hospitals and universities within the Church also has no effect on the current thinking of Rome on the issue of ordination. I don't think the issue will die. (There is a thoughtful, well-documented website advocating the ordination of women in the Catholic Church easily accessible through Google.)

Later in my work as a university professor and administrator, I obviously profited from the contribution of many women, including a very competent president, Emöke Szathmáry at the University of Manitoba. I want to highlight one example in the area of research. In the early 1980s, at a time when family violence was emerging as an important research area in Canada, I remember reading an article that reviewed 43 studies that dealt with psycho-social aspects of life in single-resource communities. The review indicated that 15 of the 18 studies conducted by males did not inquire about family violence, while 16 of the 17 studies conducted by females did. I have never forgotten these findings, and since the early 1990s I have supported the centre for research at the University of Manitoba on ending violence and abuse and have served for a decade on the board of Prairie*action* Foundation that supports these research efforts to end violence.

I was fortunate in the seminary to have studied philosophy, literature, art, music, and religion—the heart and soul of a liberal-arts education—and these areas have shaped my interests throughout my life. My studies in the seminary included a wonderful course on the history of art. It sowed the seed in me of an abiding passion for both the natural and the built environments around me. Cathedrals, sculptures, and paintings, both public and private, are all sources of life, and Charlene and I have filled our home with all the art we have been able to afford. My studies also included several summers at the Benedictine Monastery at St. Benôit du lac in the Eastern Townships of Quebec, where I learned Gregorian chant and earned a diploma *(quatrième étage)* that qualified me to direct Gregorian chant choirs.

The friary in Rosemont, a section of Montreal, was the largest in Quebec, and it served as my home between 1956 and 1960; it was where we studied theology. The Catholicism I encountered when I arrived in Quebec included a strong residue of 18th-century Jansenism among many of the laity. Jansenism† practised an austere form of piety, and promoted a strict, rigorous interpretation of morality. However, within the leadership of the Catholic Church, an extraordinary reform was under way. The cohort of theologians and bishops in Quebec, more so than those in English-speaking Canada or in the United States, became world leaders in the Vatican II Council called by Pope John XXIII in 1959 and convened in 1962. For example, I began my theological studies at a time of intense debate over such issues as the nature of the

† Jansenism was a powerful movement of religious reform, especially in France in the 17th and 18th centuries. "Jansenism emphasized original sin, human depravity, the necessity of divine grace, and predestination. According to Jansenist thought, human beings were born bad, and, without divine help, a human being could never become good. This meant that one had to be very careful about one's choices, exhibit a high level of piety and moral rectitude, and prepare carefully through prayer and confession before receiving Communion (which is why Jansenists favoured less frequent reception). The Jansenist idea of predestination, based on Augustine's writing and close to that of Calvinism, was that only a small number of human beings—that is, the "elect"—were destined to be saved." (This text is licensed under the <a href="http://www.gnu.org/copyleft/fdl.html">GNU Free Documentation License</a>. It uses material from "http://en.wikipedia.org/wiki/Jansenism_variable.)

incarnation of Christ—another example of the effect of ideas on human behaviour that deeply affected me. While the belief that Christ became man was fundamental to teachings of the Catholic faith, for me, the recognition that the resurrection of Christ really was the perfection of his incarnation led to a new appreciation of human life and nature. In my view, Catholicism never accepted the notion that human nature was corrupted by sin but, rather, that it was weakened. However, the influence of Saint Augustine, and the Jansenism inspired by Augustine, led to a distrust of the human and the idea that all creation was a source of evil and sin rather than a vessel through which the divine could be manifested. Even though Jansenism had been formally repudiated by Pope Pius X (1835–1912), it was the theological debates in the Church and the culmination of those debates in the writings of the Vatican II Council (1962–1965) that brought about this renewed understanding of the incarnation. Unlike in the 19th century, when it was more important for Catholics to go to church on Good Friday than on Easter Sunday, this new understanding led us to appreciate the Passover† as a single event with several stages, that is, a passage through death to the resurrection on Easter. It allowed us to celebrate the liturgy* with new appreciation and respect for the natural ingredients of water and wine, bread, candles, and incense, as well as the word of Scripture. All of these elements are to be understood as creations of God, good in themselves, capable of being blessed and becoming signs, sacraments, and vehicles of communication with the Divine. God became man, and in the resurrection we see the perfection of the incarnation of Christ and our hope for the future. F.X.

---

† *The Last Supper celebrated by Jesus was a Passover meal in the Jewish tradition—that is, a remembrance of the belief that God "passed over" the homes of the Jews in Egypt when he was slaying the first-born child of the Egyptians, thus allowing Moses to lead the people out of Egypt to the Promised Land. The Christian liturgy of Passover celebrates the passage of Christ from death on Good Friday to his resurrection on Easter Sunday.*

Durwell's *The Resurrection of Christ*[2] was the most influential writing on that theme that I remember. Without denying sin and evil, of which we are all well aware, Durwell's approach led me to a greater awareness of the goodness around me and a greater ease at celebrating life. It is a liberating theology. It replaces the notion of fear of the Divine and embodies hope. At the same time, it promotes a sense of awe of the intimate relationship between the human and the Divine. The Gospel became for me truly what the word means—"The Good News"—that which needs to be proclaimed. This was the rich context surrounding me as I prepared for the priesthood.

The other major shift occurring in the Church at the time of my theological studies was in the area of moral theology. The key insights for me came from German theologian Bernard Häring,[3] author of *Moral Theology: The Law of Christ.* This was the first of 45 books that he published. He died in 1998 as one of the most influential moral theologians in the Catholic Church in the 20th century. Häring refused to view morality as adherence to a series of rules and regulations. The text in moral theology that we were using in class before several of us discovered Häring's work was Herbert Jone and Urban Adelman's book entitled *Moral Theology,*[4] which was translated from German and published in 1953 in its 13th edition (a sign of its popularity). A humorous example of its obsessive attention to detail is the following, found in the section on fasting:

> Eating between meals is also forbidden but liquids, including milk and fruit juices, are allowed. The usual amount of cream in coffee or tea is permitted. Milk is understood as ordinary or homogenized, but does not include such combinations as malted milk or milk shakes. However, combinations based on skimmed milk and a coloring or special flavouring such as "chocolate milk" are rather a drink than a food and therefore, permissible. . . . To interrupt the

> principal meal for more than half an hour without reason would be a venial sin; should the interruption last more than an hour it would be seriously sinful. For a proportionately good reason (e.g., to assist the dying) one may interrupt his dinner for several hours.[5]

Häring stressed the inherent goodness of people and the presence of the spirit in them. The result was a greater focus on personal responsibility and the need to live by one's conscience. This approach led to fierce debate in our classes as well as in the larger Catholic community about the role of authority in the Church and the basis of that authority. I have always viewed the Church as a body of people searching for meaning in life and for behaviour that is consistent with that meaning. Within this framework, theologians, bishops, ecumenical councils, and the pope provide lampposts that guide us along, not one of them necessarily having all the answers, or even the right answers, at any particular moment in history. There are simply too many examples in history of the wisdom of the people, and of changing social and economic conditions also informing the authorities, for me to accept a single way of knowing, or arriving at, the truth.

Michael Novak used the term *non-historical orthodoxy* to describe the approach of those theologians who opposed the changes of Vatican II in the 1960s.[6] I think the term is highly perceptive. It describes a theology that is disembodied and unchanging, one that assumes that the discovery of truth about God has little or no relationship to the day-to-day struggles of people and that owes nothing to our human endeavours to know the universe and our place in it. It is almost a denial of the implications of the Christian doctrine of the incarnation—that is, that God became man in the person of Christ. The human and the Divine are forever linked. The nature of the relationship between them is the great mystery.

There are a number of issues that have been addressed by the

Church in a new manner because of changing social circumstances. They reflect newer understandings of both faith and moral behaviour. One example is of the Catholic Church's understanding of baptism. Baptism is a sacred ritual that creates a covenant, or bond, between the individual and Christ through the Christian community. However, the *absolute* requirement of physical baptism for salvation was abandoned during the period of the Renaissance. Faced with the experience of the discovery of new parts of the world, Renaissance theologians recognized that a large number of people in the world would never have an opportunity to hear the Christian gospel, much less make an informed choice about whether or not to accept it.

Before the Renaissance, before there was widespread knowledge of the size of the earth and its human population, Thomas Aquinas argued that, if some people did not know of Christ, God would send an angel to the sides of the uninitiated before death to give them the opportunity to come to a belief in Christ. The teaching about the existence of limbo reflected the dilemma of the need for baptism on the one hand and, on the other, the unlikelihood of millions of people ever hearing the Gospel. This new information on the size of the world and the sheer number of non-Christians in it challenged the belief that baptism was necessary for salvation. Far too many people would be permanently excluded. "Special intervention" by God or His angels, as Thomas Aquinas was suggesting, would need to be constant, and would defy the sense of the extraordinary, exceedingly rare occurrences that are a characteristic of miracles. Therefore, the Church gradually moved to recognize the importance of the individual living by his or her conscience as the most significant requirement for salvation. The formal expulsion from the Church of Father Francis Feeney in Boston in the 1940s by Cardinal Cushing (who was in effect backed up by Rome under Pope Pius XII) because he wished to continue the old interpretation, namely that the physical act of baptism plus membership in the Catholic Church was required for salvation, shows the extent to which the Church revised its position on the matter.

Another example of a shift in theological thinking over time has been in the area of economics. Interest rates for borrowing are monitored daily in every country throughout the world. In the Middle Ages, charging interest at any rate at all was considered not only illegal but also immoral. It was called *usury*. The condemnation of this practice was taken so seriously that the Third Lateran Council (1179) decreed, as punishment for practising it, both excommunication and the denial of a Christian burial. This thinking certainly has changed.

The concept of religious liberty has only a recent history of acceptance in the Church. The American experience of freedom of religion over the two centuries of its existence no doubt had a profound effect on John Courtney Murray, an American theologian. His book of essays entitled *We Hold these Truths: Catholic Reflections on the American Proposition* supports religious pluralism—that is, "the coexistence within one political community of groups who hold divergent and incompatible views with regard to religious questions."[7] Given the Roman Catholic view that it is the one true Church, this exploration of the separation of church and state and the genius of the American solution was difficult for Rome to accept. Although Murray initially suffered greatly for his views, his interpretation of religious liberty was ultimately accepted by Vatican II.† The new tolerance embodied in

---

† Just how much the thinking in the church has changed on this matter is reflected in the recent beatification of Pope Pius IX (1792–1878) in September 2000. Not only the Jewish communities throughout the world, but also many Christians, including Catholics, were appalled by this action because of the "kidnapping" and baptism of a young Jewish boy by Pius IX. The current pope took the unusual step of referring to the controversy during the ceremony of beatification and stated that this recognition of holiness of the pope should be acknowledged in spite of behaviour that simply reflected the beliefs and values of the time.

this acceptance opened the way for the Church to appreciate individuals committed to other religious traditions and to respect the existence of other beliefs, even in a traditionally Catholic society.

The theological changes that emerged from Vatican II led as well to a greater appreciation of the laity* as the people of God. The long history of the emergence of democracy in Western cultures is a significant factor in the evolution of this more accepting way of thinking. The priesthood remains a distinct office in the Church, but the sense of the "holy" priest and the "sinful" people that had previously prevailed is replaced by a sense of the presence of the spirit in all people. This understanding—that is, a sense of the presence of the spirit in all people—does not in any way deny the presence of sin and evil, either in the clergy or the laity.

It is a vivid and contemporary understanding of Paul's Epistle to the Romans (8:1–17), in which Paul marvels at the power and glory of God manifested in the weakness of humankind.

These are just a few examples of the shift in theological thinking associated with the changing social circumstances that were important to me. The pace of change in the Catholic Church may be much slower than I would wish, but a long view of the Church suggests to me that it has shown itself more open to change than many people realize.

I want to mention one other result of the new approaches to theology, one that has affected me directly: a new spirit of ecumenism.* The term *ecumenism* I understand to mean the effort to find and appreciate manifestations of the Divine in all forms of religious expression, especially those previously considered simply erroneous. Protestants, for example, were no longer "heretics" but rather "separated brethren." In 1966, I spent a month in Dubuque, Iowa, at the Aquinas Institute of Philosophy and Theology studying various aspects of theology among 40 clergy, which included an equal representation of Roman Catholics, Lutherans, and Reformed churches.

This month of study was extremely important in my life. I was just 32, one of the youngest at the workshop, and I interacted with men who had consecrated their whole lives to pursuing the truth of the Gospel. They were honest, searching, humble men, who taught me to respect others with different beliefs. Ecumenism should not be confused with relativism (which teaches that it doesn't matter what you believe as long as you believe something), but it certainly cannot exist in a climate of ideological intransigence. The Vatican II document on this topic states that ecumenism requires respect for others, dialogue, cooperation wherever possible, and a good deal of self-examination. (Recently—on the 10th of July 2007—Pope Benedict XVI issued this statement: "The Catholic Church is the only true church of Jesus Christ." It certainly reflects what the Catholic Church has always taught. But it appears to be a kind of bragging about the sense of superiority of the Catholic Church, and, occurring just decades after an acknowledgement in the Vatican II Council of the spiritual treasures of other religious bodies, it seems inappropriate.)

In addition to attending the theological discourse in Dubuque, Iowa, I had several other opportunities for involvement in the ecumenical movement. I was invited to give lectures to Anglican clergy, to preach in several United Churches, and to conduct research for the United Church and the Mennonite Central Committee. One of my most memorable events occurred near the end of the Vatican II Council in 1965. Doug Roche, then editor of the Western Catholic Reporter and later a Conservative member of Parliament in Ottawa and a senator, organized a six-part series of lectures in Edmonton entitled "Vatican II and You." I was invited to give the lecture on ecumenism to a packed basilica.

I think the appreciation of the beliefs, attitudes, and values of others that I learned while studying theology with the Franciscans served me well when I became a sociologist and during my whole academic life. My own department of sociology has been reasonably tolerant of various theoretical perspectives. However, when visiting other departments across the country, several times as an outside assessor, I saw examples of units torn asunder by an ideological intransigence of colleagues toward one another. I am uncomfortable with "true believers," be they proponents of political, social, or religious ideologies. Eric Hoffer[8] described a "true believer" as one who can tolerate no differentiation in his or her disbelief system. For example, a true believer in capitalism can see no good whatsoever in socialism; and neither could a true believer in socialism see any good in capitalism. The same intransigence of course has existed among religious bodies and has led to wars and other forms of serious conflict. In 1992, I had a wonderful opportunity to co-edit a book entitled *Fragile Truths: Twenty-Five Years of Sociology and Anthropology in Canada.*[9] In the introduction, we wrote, "The 'truths' that inform the work we do (as sociologists and anthropologists) are truly fragile ones that cannot be easily separated from the various (and usually hierarchical) social structures in which they are embedded."[10]

~

Moral theology is a particular branch of theological training. In our times, the most obvious and controversial areas of morality (if not for the Church hierarchy,* then certainly for the laity) has been related to sexuality. The advances in reproductive technology have had a profound effect on what is considered to be ethical sexual behaviour. My first real experience with the dilemmas faced by individuals and couples came in the confessional. Of all the experiences in the priesthood, without question, "hearing confession" (or, more accurately, granting forgiveness for sins to those confessing their guilt in the ritual act of confession) was for me the most moving and profoundly spiritual event. The humility of the people who came to ask for pardon from God for their actions was remarkable. I felt empowered by the office of the priesthood to assure them of the forgiveness of God. The peace they experienced after confession was often palpable, a reaction that was inspirational to me, in the true sense of the word. The words of Scripture would come back to me: "The Lord, the Lord God, slow to anger, rich in kindness and fidelity, forgiving unto a thousand generations, wickedness, crime and sin" (Exodus 34:6).

However, individuals in a marriage wishing to live by the teachings of the Church on sexual matters often came to confession with dilemmas. They were not sure if their behaviour was sinful, and they were looking for guidance. What were they to do if the circumstances, for various reasons, dictated that they should not have another child? And in that situation, what if their experience around the rhythm method of contraception simply did not work? It is in this area that the writings of Häring were most helpful to me. He taught that one must live by one's conscience, especially when it is informed and inspired by one's faith, even if it is at odds with what appears to be the explicit teaching of Church authorities. I remember well talking with a couple in a counselling session who expressed, reluctantly, that they would have to find another church because they simply could not live by rules they felt the Catholic Church was asking of them.

This kind of crisis, which a priest experienced daily in the confessional, not to mention the crisis as it was experienced far more directly by couples themselves, came to a head in 1968 when Pope Paul VI issued the encyclical *Humane Vitae: Encyclical on the Regulation of Birth,* in which he reaffirmed the position "that each and every marriage act must remain open to the transmission of life" (25 July 1968). I was at Fordham University in New York City in graduate school at the time, still in the priesthood. The response of the bishops in the northeastern part of the United States was one of unmitigated solidarity behind the pope's statement. At

Fordham, a liberal-thinking Catholic university, the reaction to the encyclical was anger and outrage, and it was publicly expressed immediately. At the same time, a prominent Canadian theologian, Gregory Baum, apparently wrote a note to one of the key bishops begging him and his colleagues not to release a commentary on the document until they had a chance to hear from and consult with the theologians. (Baum had already published a chapter in the book *Contraception and Holiness*, calling for a change in Catholic teaching. He wrote, "There are areas of teaching where assistance of the spirit enables the Church to teach with authority, without however, claiming to speak infallibly."[11] The bishops apparently agreed to consult the teologians, and, at a meeting in Winnipeg of the Conference of Canadian Catholic Bishops, attended by 75 bishops, they issued a statement indicating that, while upholding the thrust of the encyclical, they left room for the individual to live by his or her own conscience. What amazed me was that priests in the Diocese of Washington, D.C., were being suspended from their priestly duties by their bishops for issuing statements that were almost identical to the one issued by the Canadian bishops in Winnipeg. Recently, when I was recounting my memory of this incident to Don McCarthy, a philosopher and avid historian of modern Catholicism at the University of Manitoba, Don immediately pulled from his files the document issued by the Canadian bishops. The pertinent section is worth quoting:

> 26. Counsellors may meet others who, accepting the teaching of the Holy Father, find that because of particular circumstances they are involved in what seems to them a clear conflict of duties, e.g. the reconciling of conjugal love and responsible parenthood with the education of children already born or with the health of the mother. In accord with the accepted principles of moral theology, if these persons have tried sincerely but without success

> to pursue a line of conduct in keeping with the given directives, they may be safely assured that whoever honestly chooses that course which seems right to him does so in good conscience.[12]

The last sentence of the section is extremely powerful. To those not familiar with the Catholic Church, the whole statement might sound confusing. A year later, in the face of a great deal of criticism within the world-wide Church, the Canadian bishops felt the need to reiterate that they stood by their statement, which was probably the most contentious reaction to the *Encyclical* in the whole Catholic Church. But there is a saying, well known in some Catholic circles, that "laws are made in Rome, read in France, and obeyed in the United States." Of course, this last statement might seem inconceivable to individuals who think that the Catholic Church is much more monolithic than it really is. It might also seem quite flippant to those caught in the agony of making a personal decision in the face of a decree from Rome that seems impossible to live by. As a priest at the time, I was being asked by Catholics what they should do. Personally, I was completely in support of the statement by the Canadian bishops. In the face of a moral code that I could not in good conscience embrace unequivocally, I found their statement an example of "liberating uncertainties." In my view, there is no inconsistency between a search for truth and the sense that the goal is ever elusive.†

The moral codes within the Catholic Church prior to Vatican II were considered by most Catholics as unequivocal and absolute. In one of his early works in the sociology of religion, Andrew Greeley presented three types of Catholics: those who went to Mass and received communion; those who went to Mass but abstained from communion because they were practising birth control or were

---

† *My friend Herb Weil told me that the term* liberating uncertainties *was one originally used by author John Updike. I was immediately attracted to the power of the concept.*

not fasting; and the many who stopped going to Mass because they could not abide by the Church's teaching on birth control but did not want to be identified by remaining seated while others went up to communion. Many of us knew individuals in this last group. Either they failed to trust their own judgement or felt that they did not have the right to a personal judgement on the matter. Some started attending church again after their childbearing days were over, but far more did not. Since Vatican II, many members of the laity no longer consider practising birth control to be sinful and continue to go to Mass and receive communion. Birth control was an issue for me only in the sense that I was asked for advice by Catholics.

I want to return to the role of bishops in this historical period. Canadian bishops and archbishops operated differently from the way their American counterparts in the 1950s and 1960s did. In the United States, cardinals Spellman in New York, Cushing in Boston, and McIntyre in Los Angeles were without question the leaders of the American Catholic Church. When bishops convened, the senior cardinal chaired the session. In Canada, Cardinal MacGuigan of Toronto was the senior prelate in the country and should have chaired the sessions. I understand that he was not particularly keen to do this, and so Canadian bishops began a system of rotating chairs. This initiated a much more collegial and less hierarchical approach than that which prevailed in the United States, and it allowed for much more open discussion of issues. It served them well when Vatican II introduced national councils of bishops.

Having grown up theologically in Quebec, I was not surprised by the differences of opinion among bishops, both within and among countries. Two incidents touched me personally. Shortly after I had resigned from the ministry in 1973 and was teaching at the University of Manitoba, I was asked to give some lectures on the sociology of religion to priests and deacons in Winnipeg. About a month before the lecture dates, a controversy arose involving Rome and the Faculty of Theology at the University of Montreal. The Faculty had been strengthened several years earlier when a number of theological seminaries run by religious orders in Quebec were closed and the best of these theologians were hired by the University. All the seminarians* were now to attend the University for their theological studies. Over the years, however, several of the priests on staff decided to resign from the ministry. They were tenured academics by this time, and the University saw no reason to dismiss them for personal decisions that, in the judgement of the University, did not affect their teaching and research. On behalf of a papal committee that he chaired, Cardinal Garrone in France threatened that, if these individuals were allowed to continue on staff, the University would no longer be recognized by Rome as a centre for theological studies leading to the priesthood. The matter was eventually resolved, but I was infuriated by Cardinal Garrone's reasoning that these former priests could not teach seminarians because, in his own words, these priests were "morally flawed." When I heard about the threat, I immediately dashed off a letter to Cardinal Flahiff in Winnipeg, indicating that I certainly should not give the planned lectures, because his clergy might be influenced and thus contaminated by a morally flawed individual. True to his pastoral style, he wrote back within days, calmly assuring me that he did not share Cardinal Garrone's view of the situation and gently requesting that I carry on with the lectures. I did.

The second incident involving the actions of a bishop was related to my by my close friend Leo Klug, who preached at our wedding. When he himself later resigned and wished to marry, he approached Archbishop O'Neil in Edmonton about having his wedding at Newman College, the seminary in Edmonton where he had taught for years. Archbishop O'Neil wrote back, telling Leo that he (Leo) had served the Archdiocese of Edmonton so well over the years that he, the bishop, would be most pleased to grant this permission. His action in this matter was extremely touching to me and was another sign of the diversity and tolerance found within the Church.

Two other moral issues of the time that deeply troubled me were the Church's attitude toward war and toward abortion, which I saw as linked. In 1967 and 1968, while I was studying in New York, I had been involved with other students in demonstrations and walks against the war in Vietnam. At the time, I was living with two other priests in an apartment close to the University, where we were all students. One of the priests had been a fighter pilot in the Canadian air force before he entered the priesthood and felt that the Americans should "bomb the bastards." The other was a priest from Belfast, Northern Ireland, who was sick and tired of the fighting going on in his city. We argued over these issues regularly. It was at this same time that Cardinal Spellman of New York, who was named by the pope as the apostolic vicar to the armed forces, was widely quoted as having repeated the old saying "My country right or wrong, my country."[13] To this day, I do not understand how Church officials can have such an unequivocal opposition to abortion under any circumstances, yet can speak about a just war "under the principle of a twofold effect." (Jone and Adelman's book, *Moral Theology,* which I quoted earlier, concludes its section on atomic warfare as follows: "Therefore, while the use of atomic weapons must be greatly restricted to the destruction of military objectives, nevertheless, it may be justified without doing violence to the principle of a twofold effect."[14])

This is certainly not an apologia for abortion. In the 1980s, I found myself in a position that had a modest effect on the implications of the Church's approach toward abortion. At that time, I had begun to serve on the board of directors of Villa Rosa, a home for single expectant women in Winnipeg. It was opened in 1899 by the Sisters of the Misericorde. By 1987, I was chair of the board. Our board was successful in initiating a second residence on the same grounds for young, single moms who had just given birth. Because most of these young women were planning to parent their children, we felt that we should help them learn how to parent. We began this initiative above all because of the needs of the young women, but we also reasoned that, since the Church was opposed to abortion, it had all the more reason to care for these young moms, both prior to their babies' births and afterward. Not all our board members were Catholics. But we all respected Villa Rosa and its mission, and we were unanimous about the need to continue supporting these young moms.

When the new facility opened in 1985, I began a research project that included interviews with the young women for over 10 years. Each woman was interviewed when she entered Villa Rosa, when she left, and then a year after that.[15] We evaluated the services of Villa Rosa and identified the most pressing needs of the young women living there. Villa Rosa could now focus its energies on addressing these needs—for example, raising their levels of self-esteem, widening their social-support networks, and helping them come to terms with any abuse that they might have experienced. It was rewarding to see the seriousness with which Villa Rosa's staff took our research.

Before leaving these reflections on my theological studies in Montreal, I would like to make several final comments. Studying theology was not just a disembodied adventure, nor was it four years of simply memorizing a catechism. On the contrary. We had fierce debates within the friary about various theological perspectives. In fact, our small community was almost a microcosm of the larger church with its ongoing debates. Our classes were often hotbeds of discussion, professors and students alike arguing about the theological approaches of Vatican II. In retrospect, I don't think we were as open-minded about one anothers' views as we might have been. However, I do feel indebted to one of our professors, Father Cantius Matura, who was clearly the most influential theologian in the community and who was an advisor to one of the bishops in Quebec during the Vatican II Council. He would come to my room and give me the latest book on theology, for example. Within a couple of days he would be back to pick it up and give it to another student. When he picked it up, he expected me to have read it and be ready to discuss it. These discussions covered such topics as how to live a life of real poverty and how to make the liturgy of the Mass more meaningful. We also discussed extensively the scandal of the division of Christian denominations. Most people take for granted the presence of so many Christian denominations in the world. Yet, it is considered by Christians in a large number of denominations to be a real scandal in the sense that all Christians should be outraged that we present such divisive views of Christianity to the world. Scandals of all types weaken the moral fibre of a society. When so many Christian bodies each claim to have the truth, the credibility of each one is weakened. Why should any be believed? A week of prayer for Christian unity (January 18–25) has been observed around the world since 1908. French citizen Paul Irénée Couturier, one of the originators of this movement, wrote in the late 1800s: "The quest of Christian unity can no longer be thought of as a reversion to the past, but rather as an integration, to be attained in the future, of all Christian values."[16]

These divisions are especially noticeable in Jerusalem and other sites in The Holy Land, and they lead to disputes among the various Christian groups even at these sacred sites. In our Franciscan communities, this has been a particularly vexing issue. In 1309, a document was signed by the Moslem supreme authorities in favour of the Franciscans as "guardians of the Christian holy places." This role has continued almost uninterrupted since then. Our discussions in the community over the divisions of Christians and efforts toward Christian unity were based on our historical role.

The debates in our seminary went beyond the classroom. I remember one incident in particular. As chair of the liturgical committee in the friary, I was involved in some changes in the celebration of the Mass. In preparation for a visit from Cardinal Emile Léger to the parish attached to our friary in Montreal, I had written a commentary on the liturgy of the Mass that included some use of the vernacular, in this case French. The guardian of the friary felt that this was a violation of the existing rules for the celebration of the Eucharist, which required the use of Latin, and that we were initiating changes before Rome had approved them. We had a strong disagreement over this issue. Finally, the guardian told me that, if I wanted to proceed, I should find out from the cardinal ahead of time if he would permit what I proposed. I think he expected me to drop the matter at that point. However, I knew that the cardinal supported the proposed liturgical changes, so I called his office and explained the situation to his secretary, who told me to wait on the line. Several minutes later the secretary returned and stated, "The Cardinal does not wish to be asked the question." Obviously, I understood the implication of the answer and proceeded as we had planned with the reluctant permission of the guardian.

Theology is a living science. Theologians can and do engage in the same kinds of disagreements and discussions that we take for granted among economists, philosophers, and sociologists. In the Catholic Church, however, there is a body of wisdom and knowledge, articulated primarily through a set of ecumenical councils held over the centuries, that does not so much set boundaries as it inspires theologians to apply their best thinking to the relationship between the human and the Divine. When Pope John XXIII called together the bishops of the world to discuss doctrine and practice for the Vatican II Council in the 1960s, many bishops brought along as advisors those whom they considered their best theologians. Some of these theologians had an enormous effect on the documents that came out of the Council. Some of them have also been critical of aspects of the Council and of the direction of the Church since the Vatican II Council. The Church is most alive when all its members engage in healthy, respectful, open discussion of every aspect of the human condition. This is the theology that I learned and the one that still inspires me.

Chapter 5

My Early Years in the Ministry (1960–1967)

Blessing a member of the congregation following my first mass, Winnipeg, 1960

I finished my theological studies in 1960 and was ordained a priest on the 5th of June of that year in St. Mary's Cathedral in Winnipeg by Archbishop Philip Pocock. For me, the most memorable part of the ceremony occurred after Mass when the whole congregation was invited to come forward, receive a blessing, and kiss the consecrated hands of the newly ordained priest. The faith of the people was a profoundly moving experience for me.

That was during the time when Mom was looking after the house of Archbishop Pocock on the banks of the Assiniboine River in Charleswood, so I stayed with her in her separate quarters. Of course the location brought back memories of my childhood when we lived on the Assiniboine less than a mile away but on the other side of the river. Mom and I had a wonderful three weeks together, including a trip to Flin Flon to see my cousin Bill and his wife, Chieko. Bill's experience with a particular priest in Alberta when he was preparing to marry Chieko, who was not a Catholic, was an unpleasant one, and I found myself in a pastoral role very quickly, even in the family. A clear message of disrespect, such as that given by this priest, is hardly a message that comes from the Gospel. And this is what I conveyed to Bill and Chieko. One may not agree with marriage between a Catholic and a non-Catholic but should respect any couple who wishes to do so.

After my holiday with Mom, I headed to Regina, where I spent a year studying at the Franciscan Institute for Pastoral Theology. This extra year of theology, which was to focus on the pastoral dimensions of the priesthood, was instituted directly as another result of the Vatican II Council. It was to be an internship year, during which young priests could continue their studies and practise carrying out ministry. I attended classes during the week and every weekend went to the Church of Our Lady, a parish on the south side of Moose Jaw, to serve as an assistant. I had plenty of opportunity to preach, hear confessions, visit the sick, and prepare couples for marriage; I carried out most of the responsibilities of the average parish priest.

In the fall of 1961, I was hoping to get permission to go to graduate school in liturgical studies. I had spent the summer at the University of Notre Dame in Indiana studying liturgy with

Josef Goldbrunner. The more I progressed in my philosophical and theological studies, the more I developed a passion for learning. My earlier doubts about my academic abilities seemed to melt away as my interest in the specific topics I was pursuing took hold. However, much to my disappointment, I was assigned to the friary in Edmonton to become the first directorof vocations* for the Franciscans for western Canada, a position I held for the next four years. I did not brood even for a day, however, as I was faced with enormous challenges. Having lived in large friaries in three cities in Quebec and then in Regina, I now found myself practically on my own, designing a job that had not previously existed. My new position also required a great deal of travel. From 1961 to 1965 I travelled at least 30,000 miles a year by car, from Winnipeg to Victoria with stops at almost every town in between, in both the northern and southern areas of the four provinces. I travelled alone, often driving 400 miles a day, and I tried to make the trips themselves interesting. I read every historical sign I came across (something Charlene and I did later while travelling with our children). I remember marking up a map of western Canada near the end of this period and finding few roads I had not been on.

There were three things that I kept close to me in the bright red station wagon furnished by the community: my breviary to pray the Divine Office at the appropriate times of the day; a book on theology or a novel; and my bathing suit in case I should come across a lake or some other place to swim.

I learned to love the West—its topography, its rural and urban strengths and differences, and its history. I also came to appreciate the differences in the economies among the provinces. Much later, when I studied sociology, these experiences served as a useful background when I taught courses in urban sociology.

Western Canada is vast as well as diverse. I found that my lifelong interest in art enlightened these travels. Recently, while visiting museums in Santiago, Chile, I was struck by how few paintings there were of the majestic Andes Mountains. The art seemed to reflect a continuation of European impressionism, still life, and portraiture. I thought of the Group of Seven in Canada and their contribution to our appreciation of the landscape of our land. I thought as well about how such Canadian artists as Emily Carr, and more recently Clarence Tellenius, Robert Bateman, and Ivan Eyre, interpreted our wildlife and our landscapes. Our artists have helped me enormously to appreciate the beauty of even the most common features of our surroundings.

During my travels in the western provinces, my audiences were made up mainly of high school students. I was given a specific goal of recruiting students to St. Anthony's College in Edmonton and to identify the students who were thinking of entering the priesthood. I felt much more comfortable, however, helping all the students think about their goals in life. I talked with both girls and boys. I was only 27, and my own high school days, filled with a sense of confusion about what I wanted to do in life, as well as my sexual awakening, did not seem long past. I soon came to the conclusion that the rigid Catholic moral code that these teens had to follow was destructive. The insights I had gained from the moral theology of Bernard Häring now came to life. I was most anxious to dispel the view that one spends one's youth going up and down like a yo-yo between a state of mortal sin* and a state of grace (two commonly known theological concepts). Rather, even if the choices one makes on a day-to-day basis are indeed important, the more essential issue is the basic direction of one's life. Rather than instill a fear of God into teens for things they might do wrong (an inevitable occurrence, since we are indeed all sinners), I wanted to help them experience and believe in the love of God as the dominant message of the Gospel: "The Lord, the Lord God, slow to anger, rich in kindness and fidelity, forgiving unto a thousand generations, wickedness, crime and sin" (Exodus

34:6). I wanted them to go forward with confidence, believing that "nothing can separate us from the love of God" (Romans 8:35). I preached this basic message at two-day high school retreats in over 30 cities and towns in all parts of the four western provinces during the years I spent travelling the West. I felt that this was an extremely useful ministry, and I received a great deal of satisfaction from listening to the young people who attended and observing the sense of peace, hope, and confidence they gained at the retreats.

I have never lost my interest in young adults. I did my doctoral dissertation on the religious and social beliefs, attitudes, values, and behaviour within a city-wide sample of 750 young adults between the ages of 15 and 24 in Calgary. As well, I conducted research at Villa Rosa, a home for young, single moms in Winnipeg. And, of course, I had a long and satisfying academic career at the University of Manitoba, where much of my focus was on young adults. At the splendid reception given for me when I retired as dean of the Faculty of Arts, I was particularly touched by the gift from the Arts Student Body Council. It was a small clock with the inscription "Arts: Education for Life," a theme I had often referred to during those years.

As I travelled the western provinces, I usually preached in a different parish every Sunday. In small towns, when a parish priest knew I was coming, he would often take advantage of my presence to get away for a few days. But many others stayed to visit with me. I often heard their confessions and talked with them by the hour over meals in their rectories. Because these years were right in the middle of the Vatican II Council, and I was still deeply immersed in readings on the Council, I often found myself trying to explain the theology behind the enormous changes being advocated by the Council to clergy who had read nothing about the issues. I would often provide information about the best books to read on the topic. A few of these clergy, however, felt that this young whipper-snapper (me) had nothing to say to them. But, however I was received, the importance of the role of the priest in the parish soon became clear to me.

From a theological point of view, the Church is above all else the people of God. However, the hierarchical structure of the Church means that the leadership of the priest, or the lack thereof, has a disproportionately large effect on the theological, spiritual, and moral life of the parish. All the priests whom I encountered in my travels were good men who were dedicated to their vocation. However, in my view, their roles and responsibilities were not well-articulated. My observation was later reinforced when Charlene and I headed off for our six-week honeymoon trip to Latin America, which included time in Panama, Colombia, Peru, and Ecuador. Other than our visit to the extraordinary sites of Cusco and Machu Pichu, we combined our holiday with interviews with various priests and bishops, anthropologists, sociologists, and economists, including a number of religious women. These interviews were part of a research project that I was conducting on the role of the clergy in social change in Latin America. Most of the time we stayed in the poorest areas of the regions, guests of priests or sisters. When we arrived at Iquitos, in the Peruvian Amazon, the Canadian Franciscan who was bishop of the area came to the government hotel where we were booked, took us to the front counter, and simply informed the attendant we would be checking out. "You will learn nothing staying here," he said. He insisted that we stay each night in a different mission station along the river. Each day at 4:00 p.m. for a week, the village priests would communicate by wireless radio to arrange our accommodations when we arrived at the next village. We travelled the half-mile-wide Amazon in boats that ranged from 40-foot hewn-out logs to vessels large enough to hold an entire village of 50 people as well as their chickens and pigs.

The simplicity of the life and the ingenuity of the villagers to cope with the jungle was best illustrated to us one day when we were taken to see a little hut, about double the size of an outhouse, where the village's electricity generator was situated. For reasons of economy, the villagers had decided that the electricity should be turned off at 10:00 p.m. But, because there were snakes in the area, and by 10:00 it was absolutely dark, no one wanted to take the narrow sidewalk to the generator to shut it off. When we were shown the little hut, we saw how the villagers had solved the problem: They had nailed a clock to a table top and attached a short string to the dial at the back of the clock that was used to wind up the alarm. The string led to a large coffee tin, which was filled with little rocks and situated precariously on the edge of another table. A second string went up from the coffee tin to the on/off lever on the generator. At 10:00 p.m., the alarm went off, turning the dial at the back of the clock and thus shortening the length of the string. This pulled the coffee tin off the edge of the table, and as it dropped, full of stones, the string attached to the generator lever pulled the lever down, turning off the power. This is an example of the social context in which ministry was carried out in the Puruvian jungle.

The contrasts among the ministries of the priests in these villages were stark. We were struck by the power and authority that the clergy in some villages held. Here we met the most conservative, hierarchically oriented individuals whom we have ever encountered. They ruled the villages with an autocratic colonialism and knew nothing about the Vatican II Council, which was held some 10 years before. "I am building this new sidewalk all through the village," one priest proudly told us as he stood in his white, short-sleeved shirt, while three natives were bent over, sweating in the oppressive heat, cutting away the high bushes.

But we also met priests who were totally committed to the economic and spiritual development of all the women and men of the village and who worked according to the teachings of the recent Vatican council. These priests effectively used the resources of the United Nations, especially in support of education, and by doing so were true leaders, both spiritual and otherwise, in their communities. My point is that the perception that an individual priest has of his role (whether controlling and authoritarian or democratic and at the service of the people) has an enormous effect on the life of the people in isolated villages like the ones we visited in Peru, where the separation of church and state is not as clearly defined as it is in North America.

The deliberations and documents from the Vatican II Council have had other positive effects: For one, they have empowered the laity to take leadership in areas where they are obviously more competent and urged the clergy to recognize and nourish this leadership. The matter is not simple, however. Two examples come to mind: Soon after I began working at the University of Manitoba in 1972, I was asked by the Archdiocese of Winnipeg to serve on a committee that would implement the findings of a sociological study called *Priests in Canada.*[1] One of the authors was Bob Gaudet, a classmate of mine at Fordham University. One of the most important observations in the report was of the extraordinary discrepancy between what priests reported about their ministries (what they were doing) and what they thought they should be doing. The priests themselves recognized that the specifically spiritual leadership that had attracted them to the priesthood in the first place was often lost in the morass of administrative and other responsibilities that they had assumed.

This discrepancy was brought home to me in June of 2000, when my sister, Maureen, shared with me the evaluations of her work with a program in the Catholic Church to train laity in spiritual leadership. When she was required to relinquish her role in the training of these lay people because of her ill health, her evaluators repeated over and over that she was most valued for the manner in which she had taught them to truly pray.

These were very moving testimonials. "Teach us to pray" was one of the requests of the apostles to Jesus. To be able to pray is obviously a deep thirst of many people, but to teach them is not an easy task. And it is a task often neglected by the clergy.

Another example of how priests have found it difficult to empower the laity as precribed in Vatican II is within Catholic education. In the early 1990s, when I was asked to study the feasibility of setting up an integrated Catholic school system linking the three archdioceses in Winnipeg† (the Archdiocese of St. Boniface, the Archdiocese of Winnipeg, the Ukrainian Catholic Archeparchy of Winnipeg), I recruited Lance Roberts, a colleague at the University of Manitoba, as my co-researcher. Together we conducted interviews with individual clergy, parents, principals, trustees, and teachers, and then we presented a report to the archbishops in the three archdioceses. We found that many parish priests exercised power and authority over the running of the Catholic schools in Winnipeg far beyond their expertise in education. We also found that many parish priests found it difficult to trust in the laity, including those trained specifically in education. Far too many clergy were engaged in tasks outside their expertise and consequently tended to neglect the very spiritual leadership that was required of them.

† *It is interesting to note that there are three archbishops in Winnipeg, but there is no bishop. This is the only place in the world where this occurs other than in Jerusalem. Normally, if there are several bishops in an area, such as a province in Canada, one bishop is appointed as archbishop. The reason for the situation in Winnipeg is that, when the Vatican decided to separate St. Boniface and create a diocese in Winnipeg in 1916, conscious of English-French relations in Canada, it did not want to create an inferior situation for either the French or the new English-speaking Bishop, so both were made archbishops. The Ukrainian Catholic archbishop was then created for the same reason. The effort to create a common school division among the three archdioceses was one of the rare inter-diocesan initiatives.*

In 1965, after four years as vocation director at the friary in Edmonton, I was appointed guardian of the friary in Cochrane, Alberta. Set in the foothills of Alberta, just west of Calgary on the old No. 1 Highway, with land both above and below the plateau where the main buildings were, the friary complex included a 35-room, Spanish ranch-style retreat house, a pig barn, a small herd of cattle, and hay fields. It later became the training centre for the six new candidates to the brotherhood* —that came in every year. These were men who were attracted to the Franciscans for its religious life rather than for the priesthood. The brothers would all become skilled in a trade of interest to them, such as mechanics, farming, accountancy, or even sculpture or painting. The staff included a retreat director and a farm director, and I was responsible for the overall operation of the complex as well as for the training program of the brothers. I was, as well, to be part of the retreat team for preaching and counselling. I thoroughly enjoyed my two years at the Cochrane friary. The setting was extraordinary, the quietness soothing, the ministry highly worthwhile, and my responsibilities satisfyingly diverse. We renovated parts of the retreat house. We found ourselves one night near midnight having to fight a major fire that destroyed the whole barn and threatened the retreat house before we brought it under control with the help of the local volunteer fire department. I even took part in the annual branding of the cattle. I often drove through the foothills and the mountains and remember vividly walking a trapline out of Canmore one winter. I climbed the mountains in the Valley of the Ten Peaks and frequently hiked in the Kananaskis. What I enjoyed most of all at the Cochrane friary was the opportunity to read extensively, to write, and to lecture. I was happy to give up the long hours I had been spending on the highways.

Franciscans throughout the world are divided into 41 geographic areas called *provinces*, of which there are two in Canada. The leader of a province is called the *provincial*. Every four years, the Franciscans hold a *chapter*, when the state of the province is assessed by two friars who come from another Franciscan province. They visit each friary and each friar individually and make recommendations that usually lead to a number of changes in the responsibilities of individual friars. It is very much like the academic review of departments in universities, except that the outcomes for individuals can lead to a move to another job and even to another city. During the 1967 chapter, one of the recommendations was that I be permitted to go on to graduate studies. I was 33 at the time, and I think both my provincial and I felt that it was "now or never." I had requested such an opportunity in 1961, and the request was denied, so the permission now came as somewhat of a surprise, since there clearly were not enough personnel across the West to fulfill all the requests for ministry that our community received. Nevertheless, I was thrilled.

The opportunity to go into graduate studies was a significant turning point in my life. I was intensely interested in the relationship between social structures and ideas and had already resolved to study sociology. This resolve was nourished by my early training in philosophy as well as by the Vatican II Council documents, one in particular entitled "The Church in the Modern World." My first task was to seek out the appropriate university. I visited the University of Toronto, where I was told that, because I did not have an undergraduate degree, I would have to start in first year. I was simply stunned. I had studied philosophy for two years in Quebec City and had taken courses in sociology, trigonometry, chemistry, physics, Greek, and Hebrew —all in French. I then studied theology for four years in Montreal and possessed a document indicating that my course of studies was recognized by the University of Montreal as equivalent to a Licence ès sciences religieuses. I had a diploma in Gregorian chant. I also had studied pastoral theology for a year in Regina, then put in a summer of liturgical studies at the graduate level at the University of Notre Dame in South Bend, Indiana. In 1966, I spent a summer at the Aquinas Institute of Philosophy and Theology in Dubuque, Iowa. The demand by the University of Toronto that I begin in first year simply confirmed my already strong sense of the arrogance of those who saw Toronto as the centre of the universe. I left the city as quickly as I could.

I then went to New York and visited Fordham University in the Bronx. Father Joseph Fitzpatrick, later honoured by the American Sociological Association for his research and work with Puerto Ricans, was head of the Department of Sociology. Recognizing that I had a great deal of background in philosophy and theology, as well as some sociology, he suggested that I take two undergraduate courses in sociology (theory and methodology), and then, if I did well in those courses, I could enter graduate studies. I did well in my two courses and was admitted to the graduate program in the fall.

Fordham University is situated in the North Bronx, and the street life in the Bronx was an education in itself. The University was in the middle of Irish, Italian, and Jewish enclaves, and tensions among the various ethnic and racial groups were extremely high. Over the years when I was there, I lived in three different apartments, the longest period on Belmont Avenue, one of the settings for the film *The Godfather.* One of Sidney Poitier's early movies *Blackboard Jungle* was filmed at Theodore Roosevelt High School which was just around the corner. Mount Carmel Elementary School was just three blocks away. In the mornings, Mount Carmel mothers on our street would walk their children to school and wait across the street at noon and after school to walk them home again. This area had been predominantly Italian, but African Americans were starting to move in from the

South Bronx, and Puerto Ricans were coming in from the South Bronx or directly from Puerto Rico. A spray-painted message right in the centre of the street in front of our apartment described their reception: "Spics and Jiggs get out!" (*Spics* was a derogatory name for Puerto Ricans, and *Jiggs*, equally offensive, was assigned to African Americans, I was told, because they could dance so well.) I was well aware of the social context in which I was living and studying.

While I was taking those two courses in sociology in the summer of 1967, there were riots and burnings of buildings in New York in protest against the Vietnam War. That was the welcome I received when I arrived in the city.

Chapter 6

My Graduate Studies in New York (1967–1972)

Dealey Hall, Fordham University
(photo courtesy Nicholas D. Lombardi, S.J.)

Two significant changes in my life occurred the moment I arrived in New York. The first was that I was full-time student again. The second was that I requested and obtained permission from my religious community to rent an apartment in the Bronx, close to Fordham University, where I was studying, rather than live at the Franciscan friary about 30 minutes away. My reason was straightforward, but I admit that I did not feel the need to share it with my community. When I arrived in New York, I felt that I needed time alone, away from the large religious community. I had visited several Franciscan communities in the New York area previously, and I perceived a spirit there that was different from that in our friaries in western Canada that made me uncomfortable. I thought it too "worldly," an ironic conclusion in the context of my later choice to leave the Franciscans and the priesthood. The term *worldly* is clearly pejorative in religious circles, connoting as it does a world view that is not sufficiently focussed on the spiritual dimensions of life.

My arrival in New York occurred early in the period when priests were beginning to shed the Roman collar in public, and I was among those. I didn't like the trappings that came with my public identification as a priest. I realize now that this attitude was inconsistent with my earlier disappointment that the Franciscans in Quebec (as well as members of all male religious orders) were directed by Cardinal Leger not to wear their religious garments in public. At that time I disagreed with Cardinal Leger's directive. I reasoned that our Franciscan habit was a symbol of a simple way of life, but the Roman collar had become more a symbol of prestige. So when I arrived in New York, I did not want to wear it. But I made one exception. On Sunday mornings, out of respect for the conservative pastor in the parish where I assisted every week for most of my five years in New York, I did wear my Roman collar when I went over to the parish. But when I got on the bus and the driver would place his hand over the ticket box and would not let me pay, I felt embarrassed.

In wanting to live on my own, I was not trying to distance myself from the priesthood. I sought out and found two other priests, who were also graduate students, to share my apartment. My identity as a priest was well-known to the other graduate students. I frequently celebrated Mass in the chapel in Dealey Hall on campus, and I was often asked to celebrate a Mass in one of the other Catholic students' homes. Though I did not wear the collar and lived in an apartment, not in a friary, I certainly lived as a priest. I prepared my homilies very conscientiously, but, looking back now, I think my immersion in academic studies led me to neglect far too frequently my daily recitation of the Divine Office.

I was also experiencing a number of troubling doubts about my faith. It was during my two years at Cochrane, prior to going to New York, when these doubts first surfaced. I never did, and still do not, feel an ounce of bitterness, disdain, or indifference toward the priesthood or the Franciscans. But I wasn't clear about my doubts. What did I doubt? I think now that they can most simply be described as doubts about the very existence of God, the possibility of revelation, and, if it were to occur, how it might happen.

The content of my homilies changed while I was in New York. Before I began doubting the existence of God, my typical homily proclaimed the Gospel with great assurance to those who did not know the "good news." But I became a "struggling wayfarer," and, just as I was doing in my own life, I started urging my congregations to try to discover how the Gospel was relevant in their lives. More and more, I saw the Church as a lamppost that could be helpful on the path yet often seemed a hindrance to truthful living rather than as an institution with all the answers. I felt that the Church should not only teach its members but also learn from the rest of society.

This was the state of my thinking, then, when, in the spring of 1968, I was privileged to attend a series of lectures entitled "Truthfulness in the Church" given by Hans Küng, the noted German Catholic theologian, at Riverside Church, a beautiful Baptist church located on Manhattan's Upper West Side near Columbia University.[1] Küng's appeal to the Church to be truthful to itself and its relationships to those outside it was a compelling message for me:

> Truthfulness is more than honesty and straightforwardness. Honesty and straightforwardness concern man's outward behaviour in regard to the other person, straightforwardness emphasizing more than honesty the disposition behind this behaviour. Truthfulness, however, concerns first and last the attitude of man to himself. A person is truthful, therefore not simply outwardly —in relation to his fellow-men—but inwardly—in relation to himself.... Truthfulness is a recent, a present-day, concern. As long as in former times there was not the modern tension between individual consciousness and community, but harmony with society was self-evident, truthfulness could not yet acquire importance as a virtue. In this sense, truthfulness is a modern virtue, possible only from that time onwards when a self-conscious subjectivity began to develop.[2]

I have always been very much in tune with Trappist monk Thomas Merton, who wrote that all serious Christians at times experience doubts about their faith. This view was reinforced dramatically for me in the summer of 2007, when newspapers reported that the writings of Mother Teresa reveal that she had years of doubts about the very existence of God and experienced no sense of His presence. One of the most powerful dimensions for me of Graham Greene's novel *The End of the Affair*[3] is the heroine's visit to an atheist whom she'd heard preaching in Hyde Park. She had made a promise to God not to see her lover again because she felt that God had answered her prayers and saved her lover's life during a bomb blast. Yet she desperately wanted to see her lover again. She began to doubt the existence of God. If this preacher could convince her that God did not exist, she reasoned, then she would be freed of her promise.

Later in my life, in my sociological research, I had several opportunities to study and test the coexistence of doubts about faith, religious belonging, and religious commitment. I found that the way various people deal with their doubts depends on the denomination in which they were raised. In my study of youth in my doctoral dissertation, the Catholic youth often reported that they were still Catholic even when their commitment was extremely low or nil. Those who were brought up in the United Church tended to report that when they lost their commitment they also gave up belonging to any denomination. Evangelical youths who lost their commitment tended to leave their denomination and seek another. Reginald Bibby and Merlin Brinkerhoff call this phenomenom "the circulation of the saints."[4] These youth were the least likely to view doubts about faith as a normal part of Christian life. There is an abundance of literature about the rise of conservative churches that suggests that one of their attractions is precisely the certainty with which the Gospel is presented.

I am struck by the work in the American Academy of Higher Education by Ernest Boyer ("Ways of Knowing"[5]) and by Eugene Rice ("Making a Place for the New American Scholar"[6]). Rice suggests that there are two key challenges that we must face in our times. The first is a tension between the various approaches to knowing and one's own development as a scholar. It deals with how knowledge is perceived, either from an abstract, analytical approach or, on the other hand, from an experience-based approach, which values contexts and relationships. This requires some clarification, and radio talk shows offer an interesting example. If a guest with expertise based on years of study offers a general statement on a public issue, such as crime, for example, people calling in to the show will often respond with personal stories. If the general statement given by the guest does not match the individual experience of the caller, or even contradicts it, the caller treats the expert's statement with a great deal of suspicion. To just dismiss the reactions of such callers can miss some key insights into issues. In our search for knowledge, then, how do we know what the best balance might be between an experience-based approach and the more abstract, analytic approach? The experience-based approach is receiving a great deal of attention today in both religious and academic circles. Theologically, it can be explained as follows: If the spirit does indeed reside in the people, then the personal experiences of the people must be taken seriously as a source of understanding of faith. But the Catholic Church has not followed this approach to knowledge as much as I would like.

The second dimension that Rice describes has to do with how knowledge is processed. The tension, or strain, is between *intellectual reflection* and *active practice.* In other words, one way we can learn is by doing and by watching what others are doing. The Catholic Church holds to the Latin statement *Lex orandi, lex credendi.* A simple translation is: "If you want to know what the Church believes, watch the way it prays."

When I was granted permission by the Franciscans to go to graduate school in 1967, I chose sociology as an area of study because I was interested in the effect of society on theological thought. For some time I had been thinking about writing my doctoral dissertation on the relationship between Divine revelation and sociological thought. Assuming that the phenomenon of revelation were to occur (obviously one that is beyond direct sociological verification), God would have to communicate with us humans in a way that we could understand, in a way that would match our human experiences. Rice was not talking about theology here, but his discussion of the tension in "ways of knowing"—that is, between abstract reasoning and experience-based learning—is relevant. It is important to note that Rice's approach also questions the exclusivity of any one approach at uncovering truth.

As I embarked upon my graduate studies, I found a great affinity between doubts about faith and the search for "truth" in the academic enterprise. In discussing reasons for studying the humanities, Walter Kauffman states, "We do not teach so that our students know all the answers, but rather to lead them to examine their own faith, morals, assumptions, as well as the consensuses by which they are surrounded."[7]

A critical difference, of course, between faith and knowledge is that faith cannot be found by testing and retesting hypotheses. I now recognize that, as I pursued these serious questions, I did not nourish my faith as I might have. I neglected time in prayer and meditation. Jesuit priest Father Daniel Berrigan, strongly identified with anti-war and social-justice issues, came to the University of Manitoba to lecture for a term in the academic year 1972–1973, shortly after I had returned to Manitoba. Because of a strike by support staff on campus, I invited him to stay off campus, at the friary where I was living at the time; I was therefore able to spend some time with him that I otherwise might not have. He attracted an enormous amount of attention from the media, students, and the general public. I was deeply impressed by his priority of finding at least an hour every day to go off for quiet meditation and prayer, even one day when a *New York Times* correspondent came to the door waiting for an interview. "I came all the way from New York to interview you," pleaded the reporter. "I did not tell you to come," replied Father Berrigan. "I can see you in a little over an hour," he added, as he headed out for a quiet walk.

I read about God in the Scriptures and other books. I study religion. I listen to what the liturgy says, and I am moved by its internal consistency, by the world view upon which it is based. But I don't seem to have a sense of a personal relationship with the Divine. I live my life the way I do because I think it is the right way to live. But I think, having grown up as a Catholic, that

I expected to have God as a companion on my journey through life, a spiritual presence that would help me to know that I was on the right track and to encourage me. This was a naïve expectation. Nevertheless, there is no doubt in my mind that I am a Roman Catholic "jusqu'au bout des ongles" (to the tips of one's fingernails), as the French would say. I am, at the very least, a seeker of truth, and of that relationship with the Divine. I am not sure how common my situation is in this regard.

I believe that my decision to live in an apartment in New York just off campus influenced the manner in which I carried out my studies. My reference group became other graduate students and not the Franciscans. Most of these students were part of the approximately 75 who were in the sociology graduate program; the majority were Americans but there were also Canadians, Europeans, and South Americans.

I lived a disciplined life. Most days I arrived at my study carrel in the library at 8:00 a.m. and stayed until it closed at 10:40 p.m. I left only for meals and for classes, which tended to start around 4:00 p.m. For most of the first year, I ate my meals with several other students on campus in order to save the time it would have taken to go home and because I enjoyed the other students' company. On Saturdays, I would leave the library early in the afternoon to run errands and take a breather. Sunday mornings, I went to my parish in the Bronx to celebrate Mass and then came home to spend a couple of hours reading the New York Times. It used to publish one article a day about Canada; in those days it kept a correspondent in Canada, a practice that I gather is no longer the case. Because I kept well informed about Canada in other ways as well, I used to assess the coverage of *The Times* on Canada to judge whether I could trust its coverage of other countries. Most of the time, I gave *The Times* more than just a passing grade. I enjoyed its attention to issues around the world and also its coverage of the arts, literature, and theatre.

After my first year of graduate school, I was funded by a Canada Council doctoral fellowship. The result of this was that I completed my master's program in one year and my doctorate in fewer than four years. Even more important, later I felt relieved that I had not burdened the Franciscans with the cost when I decided to leave it just one year after completing my studies.

Charlene lived about five blocks away from me, just outside the Italian area, on a street with predominantly African Americans and Puerto Ricans. She was in the religious order of the Sisters of Charity of Nazareth, Kentucky, and had moved from her home in Louisville to New York to undertake graduate studies in sociology at Fordham. I met her about six months after I arrived in New York in a seminar on urban community. I was impressed by some particularly astute comments she'd made in class one day, and we continued a discussion after class. We found that we shared a common interest in many of the issues of urban life, including migration, immigration, ethnic relations, and integration. We became friends very quickly.

She, along with Barbara Doherty and Joan Range—two women from two different religious communities enrolled in the theology faculty at Fordham—applied to live in a high-rise located several blocks from where I lived. The superintendent of the 15-storey complex was delighted, as this was a building designated for integration and he was having trouble attracting white tenants. A later superintendent of the building, Mr. Kola, was an immigrant from Albania and was highly active in the Albanian ethnic community. He was surprised that these religious women wore regular street clothes; they were not devout enough for him. "Nuns used to want to get T.B. and die," he lamented. Charlene found herself helping him write letters to President Nixon asking to have another Albanian, whom he felt was wrongly held, released from jail, and she once acted as an advocate when a delegation of Albanians approached Mayor John Lindsay for funding for the community. "Don't worry," Mr. Kola said, pointing to the gun in his suit-coat pocket as they headed to the subway, "I'll protect you."

As most of the other graduate students in the program had, Charlene experienced a New York mugging. It happened one day when she was walking to her apartment from the subway with her grandmother, who was visiting from Kentucky. Afterward, the police drove them to a station in the South Bronx and urged them both to identify as the mugger a young African American male who had just been arrested. "If he didn't do this, he did something else," they stated. When Charlene and her grandmother refused to comply because they were not sure, they had to argue to get a ride home from the police, who seemed about to leave them stranded in the South Bronx to find their own way back.

I was never mugged, but the front windows in our apartment were broken one day. I was told by an eyewitness that a man who lived in an apartment across the street thought that our landlord was renting to African Americans. The police told us, "Try to get the eyewitness to come to court and spend a day or two waiting to testify, then press charges; otherwise, don't bother." We didn't bother. On another occasion, we found that a number of the cars parked on our street overnight had been put up on blocks, all their tires missing. On still another occasion, several car hoods were up in the morning, the car batteries gone. Hermann Strausser, a graduate-student friend from Germany, did not get off so lightly. He returned to his apartment one day to find it completely empty. Thieves had brought a truck and emptied the entire contents; the neighbours simply watched, thinking that he and his wife had decided to move.

One day shortly after Martin Luther King was assassinated in 1968, it happened that we were to have a Holy Thursday liturgy at the apartment of one of the graduate students, Louise Weston. Part of the ritual for Holy Thursday Mass is the washing of the feet of some of the congregation, commemorating the action of Christ just before his crucifixion. While the priest performs the ritual, members of the congregation either read or sing the text from the Gospel of St. John, in which Christ exhorts the disciples to love one another. Given the death of Dr. King, however, which was a source of profound grief for all of us, I suggested that I might substitute the washing ritual by polishing the shoes of a number of the students; polishing shoes was a menial task associated with many poor African Americans. The liturgy was powerfully moving according to the 15 or so people who attended. It certainly was for me. The following year, we repeated the event, but somehow it had lost its power. From this experience I came to understand even more clearly the importance of maintaining liturgical symbols, like the washing of the feet, that are universal and timeless.

The forming of intense relationships among graduate students is a common phenomenon. Even given this, I believe our cohort of students was unusually close. We were not a single group of students but rather a set of over-lapping groups. Because Fordham University is a Catholic institution,† it attracted a large number of priests and sisters as well as lay students, particularly to its programs in philosophy, theology, religious education, and

† *This matter caused Fordham a significant financial crisis at the time. Marshall McLuhan had been invited by Fordham to be visiting chair of the Communications Department. The State of New York was at the time offering universities $100,000 each to host such distinguished scholars. Shortly after Fordham was awarded this position and McLuhan had accepted, a complaint was lodged with the government that, according to the notion of the separation of church and state, Fordham, as a Catholic university, should not have been offered the award. The funding was withdrawn, but Fordham decided to honour the commitment to McLuhan anyway. Almost immediately after he arrived, McLuhan suffered a stroke from which he never recovered. So, from both a financial and an academic point of view, the event was a great disappointment.*

sociology; one of the key reasons was the intellectual and spiritual renewal of the Vatican II Council.* The intellectual life at Fordham was incredibly stimulating. I think we formed a new student culture in sociology there. We discussed our classes, theories, and other ideas among ourselves, we studied for comprehensive exams together in small groups, and several of us presented our proposals to our small group for feedback before having the formal presentation in the Department.

Our student life was also our social life. Those of us who were religious, however—quite naïvely, I believe, and without explicitly discussing it—espoused the view that there was a "third way," a common notion in those days, in which we priests could be close friends with women as well as with men, both lay and religious, without romantic involvement. Thus, many of us got together socially with other graduate students; we often went to dinner, the theatre, or bars such as The Jug of Punch on Jerome Avenue. And, in spite of the dangers of being mugged or otherwise injured, we loved living in New York. We learned how to take precautions, and nothing deterred us from a thorough enjoyment of that great city.

Life as a student was far more exciting than I could ever have imagined. The city of New York itself became a laboratory for research. The course I took in urban politics is a good example. In it, we undertook a daily analysis of political events in the city, to be understood within the context of various theories of political science at the time. It was the period when John Lindsay was mayor and Albert Shanker was head of the union that carried out the first teachers' strike in the United States. Using as a counterpoint the city of Chicago and the power of Mayor Richard Daly to effect change there through his control of the Democratic political machine, our professor highlighted the powerful bureaucratic constraints on Mayor Lindsay in New York as he pursued social change. It was an insightful exposure to the various political models and their effects on the workings of a city.

One rather humorous incident occurred relating to the course in urban politics. Our professor was hired by CBS Television to help the network be first to predict the results of the 1968 presidential elections in New York State. He was to do this based on results from a small sample of polling stations that he judged were good predictors of the total State vote. In more recent years, we have all become accustomed to the prediction of election results within a few minutes after the close of polls. But it was rather a new idea then. Those students who wanted to take part in the project were given a tour of the CBS studio from where Walter Cronkite would be reporting. We were each assigned a polling station from which we would report back to CBS headquarters, and, to prevent other networks from calling in bogus results, each of us was given a secret code when we phoned in the results.

Early in the evening of election day, I made my way to my assigned polling station in the Bronx, where I obtained permission from the polling officer to remain in the station after the close of the polls as an official reporter for CBS. I then headed out to find the closest pay phone so that I could report to CBS that I was in place. When I returned to the polling station, news had spread that CBS was going to report from that poll, and, with my CBS identification badge in place, I suddenly found myself surrounded by polling workers wanting to appear on television. As I was trying to explain the process, from the back of the small group I heard a voice address me: "Hi, Father, what are you doing here!" One of the parishioners from the congregation where I ministered on Sundays was working there, and my very modest role was quickly revealed. The small crowd dispersed, and my moment of fame dissipated. I might add, however, that the results from the sample of polls provided an accurate prediction of the State-wide results. I learned a great deal about sampling in the process.

One very special New York experience for me occurred on New Year's Eve, as 1970 approached. An older graduate student, Clarence Dye, had a beautiful apartment in Manhattan, about a 10-minute walk from Times Square. He invited six of us in for some frozen daiquiris, after which we would head out to the Square for midnight. I estimated that there were about half a million people approaching the Square from all directions. The Vietnam War was winding down, and some troops were being withdrawn, but, even though there were still major demonstrations in the United States, the mood of the country was improving—it being the beginning of a new decade—and there was extra excitement in the air. As midnight approached, the crowd became more and more excited, and people pressed together as if we were all trying to get on a subway at rush hour. The expectation of the arrival of the precise moment of midnight was palpable. When the ball dropped, the crowd could no longer contain its excitement. Everyone turned to greet those beside them with a warmth, a sincerity, and a sheer sense of joy and celebration that defies description. Suddenly, we realized that we were surrounded by various races, languages, and nationalities. We were a microcosm of the world, and it was wonderful, an amazing, magical, long minute. I say *minute* with good reason. Part of what made it so powerful was the fact that, as we began to make our way out of the Square just after midnight, we all went back to the standard, essential precautions of life in New York City, and we instinctively protected our wallets and purses. We were again surrounded by strangers. But, for a moment, that special minute surrounding the transition to the new year, we were simply humankind sharing the planet Earth.

I was part of two other enormous crowds during my years in New York: the tickertape parade when Neil Armstrong and his fellow astronauts returned from the moon and the throng present when President Lyndon Johnson and Vice-President Hubert

Humphrey arrived at St. Patrick's Cathedral for the funeral of Cardinal Spellman. Neither of these events, however, came close to providing the emotional high that I experienced when I celebrated the advent of the new decade at Times Square with people from around the world.

My major interest in graduate school was the sociology of religion. Three courses in particular were relevant to the relationship between ideas and social structures. One was a fine course on the theology of revelation given by Gabriel Moran at Manhattan College. How could Divine revelation occur to humans in ways that humans could receive such revelations?—that was my interest in the course. Another was the sociology of religion and the sociology of knowledge given by Werner Stark, who had just published his fourth book on the relationship between these two areas. The third was on early socialization, taught by Eva Sandis in my first semester at graduate school. Eva Sandis soon became solicitous of my academic progress. Even though I was still struggling in my own mind with the theories and methodologies of sociology, she urged me make a trip to Harvard to see if I could transfer there after finishing my master's degree. I did, and I had an interesting meeting with Harvey Cox, author of *The Secular City*—a popular bestseller for a decade—but my visit occurred well past the deadline for applications for the following year, and so I decided to stay at Fordham.

With that settled, Eva helped me articulate what I might do for my doctoral dissertation. The master's was to be simply the stepping stone, and it was on her advice that I took a comprehensive exam for the master's instead of writing a thesis. This was a common pattern in many graduate programs when individuals were certain that they wished to proceed to a PhD program. She advised me to organize all my courses around my proposed doctoral topic, which I did. For example, in my master's methodology class, I wrote the required paper as a proposal for my doctorate dissertation. It was on the relationship between religious and social values among a sample of 750 young adults, between the ages of 15 and 24, in Calgary. Because of the contacts I had made in Calgary while living in Cochrane, which was only 20 miles away from Calgary, I raised $17,000 from various religious denominations there to carry out my proposed doctoral study.

Even though they were not central to my doctoral project, there were two sets of questions on the survey that are pertinent to this discussion of Divine revelation and the sociology of religion. One focussed on the relationship between the search for meaning and religious commitment. I found that, indeed, the two approaches to religion were different and independent among young adults. Not all those who scored high on religious commitment revealed a high level of searching for meaning, and the reverse was also true. I presented a paper about my findings at the Scientific Study of Religion conference in San Francisco in 1972, but I did not submit it for publication, as I kept feeling that the issue was much more complex than I had shown it to be. Over the years, I have modified the paper a number of times, and I still hope that one day it will be ready to submit for publication.

The second relevant theme in my doctoral project, about which I did publish a paper, was the experiential dimension of religiosity. Following earlier research by Charles Glock and Rodney Stark,[8] the two pioneers of quantitative research in the sociology of religion, I confirmed that the religious experiences of youth tended to follow the same gradual progression toward intimacy as do relationships between people. In other words, while many respondents in my study reported having had a sense of the presence of God, far fewer reported a more intimate experience, such as being asked by God to do something or having a sense of unity with God. In fact, the ordering of the five experiences formed what is called a "Guttman Scale." That is, the ordering was so consistent for the respondents that a researcher could know exactly *which* experiences had been reported by knowing *how many* were reported.

I also attempted to test another idea—that the most intimate experiences are the most important experiences. This hypothesis was eventually not supported, but, nevertheless, it brought to light a different, but clear, pattern. I found that the more experiences individuals reported, the more important was each of the reported experiences. In other words, what emerged was an experiential approach to religiosity that seemed to be the very basis of a religious faith. The message seemed to be: I can believe only what I have personally experienced. The teachings of the Scriptures, of dogma, of apologetics, and of tradition paled in comparison to personal experience as a basis of faith. There is much to commend this approach, but, after reflecting on it for some time, I wrote another paper on the subject, this one focussing on the limitations of what I consider to be a reductionistic approach to religious commitment. I think that religious commitment must be based upon more than just having a good feeling about one's relationship with the Divine.

The City of New York was a wonderful lab in which to study the sociology of religion. During one discussion of religion and ethnicity, Father Ed Lamano, a graduate student from Brooklyn, offered to take several of us to visit two churches in his borough, one Puerto Rican and the other Italian. The two churches couldn't have been more different. The Puerto Rican church was small, intimate, and decorated with folk art, and the Italian one was like a traditional baroque cathedral. When we entered the Italian one, we were met by a large statue of an angel holding a huge spear that was inserted in a statue of a prostrated Satan, who just happened to be portrayed as an African American! The two donation boxes at the back of the church each had razor-sharp edges that pointed downward so that anyone thinking of putting a hand in to steal the money would be quickly deterred. The ceiling featured a large fresco of the Blessed Virgin in an apparition to the children of Lourdes or Fatima. I have never forgotten that the painting of the apparition included likenesses of several local members of the congregation who were said to be part of the mafia. The statue of Mary at the front of the church had jewels around the neck, arms, and even the toes. We were told that, following a recent theft of the jewels (which the thieves were quickly convinced to return, by the way), an alarm system was installed between the sanctuary and the pews, and two guard dogs were brought in to patrol the church at night. After our visit, Ed was planning to take us to a restaurant thought to be a favourite of the mafia, but it was fully booked, and we ended up in a diner across the street from it. We were convinced of Ed's claims, however, when we observed a number of limousines glide up to the door of the restaurant and discharge several muscular individuals who could easily have been bodyguards.

Another anecdote about the ethnic climate of New York, and particularly of the Bronx, deserves to be recorded. On the recommendation of her dissertation director, Mary Powers, Charlene became the survey research director for Dr. Albert Scheflan at the Bronx State Hospital. One dimension of the project was to find a location for a mental health facility that was situated so that individuals from the various ethnic and racial groups in the area would not have to cross one another's boundaries to get there. The vast data she gathered became the basis of her doctoral dissertation. She hired me as one of her 20 interviewers. I, too, was becoming interested in survey research methodology, and we had discussed this before she asked me to be one of her interviewers. As she sat in her locked car on Webster Avenue handing out interview forms with specific addresses to her team, Barbara Doherty and I would head to one of the five- or six-storey apartment blocks lined up along the street. I would go to a door with

Barbara and, once she was satisfied the residence was safe for her to enter and she was admitted, I would then go off to conduct my own interview nearby and return to pick her up. Once I arrived at a building where a burnt, overturned car sat in front. I entered the building and headed up to the second floor on stairs that were themselves partially burned out and supported by only a couple of new pieces of unpainted two-by-fours. I was admitted to one of the apartments by a polite, six-foot-five African American man. To my questions about fear of living in that neighbourhood, he replied as he continued polishing his shoes, "Why should I be afraid? I'm a policeman, so I always have my gun. And there are two officers who do nothing but patrol this street. Besides, this is a fourth platoon area. Because we've found that most crime takes place after 8:00 p.m., in addition to the three eight-hour shifts for police, we added a fourth, creating a double night shift, in high crime areas." I left after the interview not at all comforted by all the firepower around me.

The cultural life of New York was a treasure that Charlene and I began to share more and more. We reserved Saturday evenings to go to plays, concerts, or other such events. As a foreign student, I paid eight dollars a year for a pass that entitled me to attend up to 100 events in the city each year. These could be concerts at Carnegie Hall, rehearsal nights for new plays on Broadway, and many off-Broadway productions. We would also attend opera productions at the botanical gardens that were next to the Fordham campus and Shakespeare productions in Central Park, where we saw some memorable plays directed by Joseph Papp. I also found the museums of New York, the New York Public Library, and Columbia University Library extraordinarily nourishing. As often as not, we went to these places as part of a group.

As I approached the end of my first year in graduate school, Fred Williams, another Franciscan from western Canada who was studying at Fordham, came to stay with me for a week and did my cooking and laundry, and made trips to the library for books while I wrote my master's comprehensive exam. I had recently moved and was living alone at the time. I was given 10 days to write my answer to the exam question; it was in the form of a major paper. I still remember the question: "Scientific innovation, economic growth, and secularization are said to be three interrelated processes over time. What was their early historical relationship, and, since World War II, what has been their relationship?" It was a daunting task, but it was made so much easier by Fred's assistance.

In late 1969, Charlene asked me to participate in a discussion group on secularization that Barbara Doherty was organizing. This was a very hot topic at the time, as church attendance was declining across North America. An abundance of sociological literature was emerging. Since my comprehensive paper was on the topic, I was delighted to join the discussion. We continued the group for over a year. Later, at the University of Manitoba, I offered a seminar on the same topic.

I finished my classes in May of 1969, wrote my doctoral comprehensive exams in October, and then flew to Edmonton with Charlene to the Population Research Laboratory at the University of Alberta to draw the complex sample for my proposed study. In the spring I asked Charlene to accompany me to Calgary to conduct the study. She stayed with Dave and Adele Pogue and their three children, whom I had known when I'd previously lived in Calgary, while I lived at the friary.

Near the end of the period when we collected the data, I made visits to a number of universities in Alberta and Manitoba to explore the possibilities of academic positions once I completed my doctorate. Several expressed some interest, and so I returned to New York determined to wrap up the dissertation as soon as possible. During the analysis phase of my study, the sheer size of the sample required a large number of computer runs, and

Fortran, the computer language of the day, was far from user-friendly. Missing a simple comma in a two-page program written to create a scale of items, for example, would cause the computer run to abort. It might take half a day to find a single error in logic, syntax, or simple punctuation. Nevertheless, with great confidence that I would finish by Christmas of 1971, I accepted a position at the University of Manitoba. I specifically requested a January 1972 start date so that I could finish my dissertation before starting. I experienced enough aborted computer runs to cause significant delays in my project, and it was with great embarrassment that I arrived at the University of Manitoba without having finished. So, as soon as classes were over in May, I returned to New York and completed the dissertation before the fall term began.

Leaving New York and returning to the Prairies to start my academic life at the University of Manitoba meant that I was leaving Charlene, which was not easy. In The Jug of Punch bar one evening, a group of us were listening to a live-band rendition of John Denver's song "West Virginia." As the words "take me home" were sung, Charlene and I both happened to look out the window at the same time and see a moving van go by. The enormity of our impending separation struck us, neither of us having said a word. The memory is vivid. She had won a tenure-track position at the University of Kentucky in Lexington. The separation was expected, known far in advance, and made only a bit easier because we were both embarking on new academic careers. Yet, we had shared so much in New York; without question, these had been the most exciting times of our lives. We both were embracing sociology, a new discipline for each of us (Charlene had majored in history in college). The intellectual discussions that the two of us shared on all sorts of topics were at the heart of my graduate school training. New friendships with very bright and interesting people from all over the world had begun and promised to last a lifetime. The treasures of New

York provided through academic lectures and extraordinary cultural events that attracted the very best performers in the world were at our fingertips. Yet, simply living the daily life in a city that was tense with racial strife and suffering from the trauma of the Vietnam War required energy, openness, and a good deal of risk-taking. We had few personal responsibilities other than to be studious, which made the situation even more enjoyable.

When Charlene and I married in 1975, it did not come as much of a surprise to those who had known us in graduate school—at least, so they told us years later! Yet, when I left New York to begin teaching at the University of Manitoba in January of 1972, I still had no intention of resigning from the priesthood and no intention of marrying, even though I harboured considerable doubts about my faith.

However, eventually I did leave.

For a priest or religious to resign is a hugely traumatic event. In accepting ordination to the priesthood in the Franciscans, I had taken vows of poverty, chastity, and obedience, and the notion of leaving religious life was daunting. We know how unacceptable divorce has been in the Catholic Church at certain periods in history; I would say that leaving the priesthood was considered even more unacceptable. At the same time, I now realize how naïve I was in allowing myself to become so close to Charlene while still in the priesthood; without understanding what I was doing, I was creating grounds for a major life shift. I understood that I was very fond of Charlene, but I did not realize until I had left New York just how much I loved her.

While some other priests and women in religious life who were part of our student network did remain in their vocations, certainly a large number resigned. In a sense, our experience was symbolic of the life of the Catholic Church in North America at that time. It was the period of the largest number of resignations from the priesthood in the 20th century. Since the 1980s, a request to Rome for a dispensation to resign from the priesthood but at the same time remain a Catholic has been much harder to obtain. I simply don't know what I would have done or how I would have coped had the Vatican refused my request for laicization. Since I've been married I have often said to others that I am not only committed to our marriage, but I am committed to the commitment. In practice what that has meant, among other things, is that at any conference or academic setting where I might interact with women academics I make a point of speaking of Charlene early in a conversation in such a way that there is no ambiguity about my allegiance. Yet the same approach that led me to be so open about my priestly activities while at Fordham obviously did not protect that allegiance.

When I returned to Manitoba in December of 1971 to take up my position at the University of Manitoba at the beginning of the new year, it was the first time I had lived in the Province of Manitoba for any length of time since I had left for high school in Edmonton in 1948. Mom was in Winnipeg, of course, as were my brother John, who was also a priest, and my brother Robin and his wife, Irene, and their three children. I settled in at the friary that had just been built on Edmonton Street, around the corner from St. Mary's Cathedral. There were about eight of us living in the friary at the time. From its central location in the city, the friars offered a noon-day Mass and had a priest available almost all day and early in the evening for confessions. I helped out on weekends at the friary, but my first responsibility was the preparation of classes and my research at the University. On campus I was assigned an office at St. Paul's College. There were about 30 faculty members whose offices were in the College, usually one or two from each of various departments in the humanities and social sciences, and several from science. It was an interesting interdisciplinary academic environment.

I didn't really become well-integrated into the life of the College. In 1974, I asked to be moved to the Department of Sociology, which was located across campus in the Isbister Building. I was concerned about the tenure process. I felt that being located in the Department itself rather than in the College would help me become better socialized to the norms and expectations of the Department. But this was not the whole story.

Now that I think back, I realize that I wanted to establish myself as a sociologist, not as a *Catholic* sociologist. I cannot recall making this choice consciously. I do know that I was embarrassed by some positions held by the Church, particularly on issues of sexuality and about women. Perhaps my embarrassment had simply to do with the process of secularization occurring in my own life. For the most part, I avoided doing research on Catholicism, which was clearly a poor decision, given my extensive theological knowledge and understanding of the organization of the Church. I did help the Archdiocese on several projects, but I viewed that more as community service than as research.

My first few years at the University of Manitoba was a period of turmoil for me regarding my future as a priest and Franciscan, and my move from the College was perhaps prescient of my later decision to leave the ministry. In October of 1972, I flew to San Francisco to give a paper at the meeting of the Society for the Scientific Study of Religion. On the way back to Winnipeg, I spent a Saturday night in Vancouver with my cousin Kathie and her family. I was so depressed that, for the only time in my life, I did not care if the plane had crashed. Kathie had arranged for me to say Mass at her parish on the Sunday morning, and when I arrived at the church I found that the pastor had also expected me to preach; he was nowhere to be found. I hated preaching without adequate preparation. However, the Scriptural readings dwelt on doubts about faith, and it was an issue I was personally experiencing at that moment in my life. I simply spoke from the heart, and after Mass I was extremely touched when a middle-aged man stopped me at the back of the church to say how much the homily had helped him.

Shortly after I returned to Winnipeg, I attended the regular monthly meeting in the friary. I remember making recommendations for six rather minor changes. Every one of them was dismissed as impossible, unnecessary, or unwise. I was devastated and depressed, not so much by the rejection of my suggestions but more by the realization that I shared almost no interests with the people in the community. I put on my hat and coat and went out through the back door of the friary as fast as I could. As I walked past Eaton's, I remember concluding, "I am like an alcoholic in that I can't solve this depression alone." Making this decision gave me a great sense of peace, and the next day I went to the Psychological Service Centre at the University. Terry Hogan, the director, agreed to see me, and it turned out that he could not have been more helpful.

I was not sure at the time why I was so unhappy. Over several months, as the issues became clearer, Terry advised me to try to separate the two issues that were concerning me: the priesthood and my relationship with Charlene. "If she were to die tomorrow, what decision would you make regarding the priesthood?" he asked. I was thunderstruck by the question and went on to wrestle my way to an answer. By February, I felt I had the answer. I requested a leave of absence from the Franciscans. This is not intended to diminish the importance of Charlene in my decision. Very recently I learned that, when Charles Davis, the most prominent Roman Catholic theologian in England, not only resigned from the priesthood but also left the Church in 1968, he stated that it was only a woman's love that gave him the strength to leave the Church. In spite of the perceptive question that Terry Hogan had posed to me, and in spite of the fact that a year later I formally proposed to Charlene (that is to say, I did not take for granted that we would marry), it is important to acknowledge that it may indeed have been her love that gave me the strength to do what I needed to do about my commitment to the priesthood.

When I left the friary in February of 1973, I went to live with my brother John at his parish rectory, which was attached to St. Vital Parish on Pembina Highway. I had been turning my salary over to the community every month, so I had no personal resources. I would simply have to start from scratch. The friary helped out by giving me the old car that I had been using to get back and forth to the University. In April, I submitted a carefully worded six-page letter to the provincial of the Franciscans describing my life in the ministry and how I had come to the point of seeking laicization. The provincial sent the letter, with his own recommendation (which I never saw) to the headquarters of the Franciscans in Rome. Headquarters then wrote to the appropriate secretariat of the Vatican. About six months later, I received word from the Franciscan Provincial that the laicization had been granted. There was nothing more to be done.

I look back with no regret at all on the years I spent in the Franciscans. Nor do I regret my decision to resign. My resignation took place at a time in the Church when such action was not unheard of. But my decision provoked a great deal of surprise, disappointment, and, indeed for some, a sense of betrayal. Some people have said to me that it does not seem fair that a priest can receive a decree of laicization and later marry in the Church while a married person cannot remarry in the Church after a divorce. Since both ordination and marriage are sacraments, it is indeed hard to understand. However, all I can say is that I have always been at peace with the decision I made.

No other part of my life has been as difficult to write about as this. Does Pascal not say it best? "Le coeur a ses raisons que la raison ne connait point? (The heart has its reasons of which reason know nothing.)[9] My goals in trying to articulate it were not rationalization or justification, as some people might judge. My doubts about my faith were real and difficult to deal with; at the same time, I was starting to understand how limited a priest's life really can be in terms of family, friends, and the other acquaintances who comprise our social network.

A marriage is a union of families. This is illustrated beautifully in the Jewish marriage ritual, which calls for parents and future in-laws to crowd up under the *chupah* (or marriage canopy) during the exchange of vows. Aboriginal customs that stress the importance of an extended family, whether or not they might all be blood relatives, reflect the same reality.

In our culture, marriage is the culmination of, or better yet, the lifelong commitment to, one particular friendship, probably the most intense friendship that any of us ever experience. Of course, other friendships can coexist, can arise later, can come and go. Some friendships are so strong that, even after a long separation, a reunion can seem almost a continuation of the previous week's interaction. Other friendships remain only as memories. Still others—for example those that arise in the workplace—are time-bound; when the work situation changes, the interaction ceases, but the friendships were nevertheless meaningful.

Relationships among people in religious life include all these kinds of friendships. Some are deep, wonderful relationships. However, in my case, after ordination I found that usually I was not living with any of my close friends in the community. We all put our preferred ministries, our work, before every other consideration, and my friends were dispersed across the West. I found myself living with individuals with whom I shared a common spiritual goal but very little personal bond. Without meaning any disrespect, in other circumstances, I probably would not have asked any one of them to share a meal even once a year. Furthermore, our theological understandings were so diverse (a conflict between pre- and post-Vatican II theology) that there was little common ground even spiritually. In very small children we observe "parallel play." Daily life in the friary was reduced to "parallel prayer." It was not enough for me.

After leaving New York and starting to work at the University of Manitoba, I often found myself enjoying the company of women. I certainly was not looking for dates, and I still had no intention of leaving the priesthood. But the interaction with women in a wider social context than the Church and graduate studies at a Catholic university made me dwell upon my relationship with Charlene. I determined very quickly that I would not seek out, initiate, or even allow a relationship with another woman to develop.

In my letter requesting laicization, I discussed all the overlapping factors that led me to the decision to leave the priesthood, including my relationship with Charlene. I do not presume to describe Charlene's arrival at her decision; that is another story, and one for her alone to tell if she so desires. But one related incident deserves mention. After seeking counselling from Terry Hogan during a visit to Winnipeg, Charlene shared part of her conversation with Terry to her dad. "How much did you have to pay him to tell you that?" he responded, "I could have told you that for nothing!"

I have not regretted my decision to resign from the ministry, and certainly a prominent reason has been my enjoyment of our marriage. We have been through a great deal together, and all our experiences have done nothing but strengthen our bonds. Charlene has supported me in every initiative that I have ever wanted to pursue. She has rejoiced in all my successes and has understood my frustrations. We share an interest in ideas, in academic life, in theatre, art, music, and novels—I read aloud to her almost every evening since retirement—and we travel together to experience other cultures; we feel extremely privileged and grateful to have so much in common. And, without question, our common religious background has nourished our relationship and kept us close. We have shared extraordinary relationships with both our families, and we have also been privileged to have a good number of precious friends who have often been a great support to us. Our week in the Amazon, travelling the wide, powerful river in a hewn-out log boat with no life jackets and only a 12-year-old boy at the front watching for "deadheads," has become a symbol for us of the adventure in our lives and our ability to face unpredictable adversity.

Following our honeymoon in South America, we arrived in Winnipeg on the 1st of July and took up residence in an apartment on Pembina Highway. Several months later, we purchased our home at 1060 Grosvenor Avenue, at the edge of Crescentwood, a neighbourhood lined with Dutch elms that form a beautiful canopy over the streets. I think the most important financial decision we made since our marriage was buying a home that we could afford on one salary. We reasoned that, if one of us became ill, we would not want a burdensome mortgage. This decision not only permitted us to pay off our home relatively quickly but also allowed us to travel regularly. As our friend Jane Ursel put it, we lived in "faded elegance." In 1994 we moved to our new condominium on Victor Lewis Drive. We traded the majestic Dutch elms with their shade for a home with a southern exposure that basks us in sunlight almost all day long. And today, as I write these memoirs, we are still living there.

Chapter 7

Our Marriage and the Beginning of my Academic Career (1972–1990)

Our wedding day, the 24th of May 1975, Louisville, Kentucky

By the time Charlene and I were married, I had already spent over two years at the University of Manitoba. After spending 20 years in the Franciscans (1953–1973), I was now about to embark on what turned out to be 28 years at the University of Manitoba (1972–2000) with only one year of overlap.

As we were planning our wedding, with Charlene at the University of Kentucky in Lexington and me at the University of Manitoba, we quickly decided that we would seek job openings for both of us close to at least one of our two families. While there was nothing open in my areas either at the University of Kentucky or the University of Louisville, Charlene was offered a one-year term position at both universities in Winnipeg. She chose the University of Winnipeg because, during the interview at the University of Manitoba, she was asked constantly if my presence in the same department would cause a problem. "Because they asked me about it so frequently, it obviously does matter to them," she told me, so she decided upon the University of Winnipeg. Anyone in academic life will know what a tremendous sacrifice that was for her to make; she gave up a tenure-track* position in Kentucky for a one-year position in Winnipeg. The following year, a very unusual opportunity arose when a faculty member decided to move. Charlene won the competition for the position and was able to spend the rest of her academic career at the University of Winnipeg.

Charlene's move to Canada was a signficant career interruption for her. She lost a very strong infrastructure of support when she left the University of Kentucky. More challenging was the steep learning curve she faced in order to become knowedgeable about Canadian society so that she could teach introductory sociology at the University of Winnipeg. When she asked me to explain the role of our governor general, I knew she had a lot to learn! But she was diligent; she spent long hours of study in the evenings and on weekends and came through with flying colours.

I don't recall any difficulties making the switch from being a priest to being an academic. While I found myself facing some professional circumstances that I had not experienced before, there was also some "home ground" for me in my new role at the University, which is not so surprising when one considers that many early universities began from religious communities. Indeed, periods of monastic silence and isolation from others in the pursuit of knowledge are not unknown to university professors. These conditions of work are essential to both the priesthood and academic life, but the core commonality is the search for a balance among knowledge, truth, and wisdom. What was new for me was the manner in which I found myself undertaking the search. One enormous difference concerned the relative importance of the roles of teaching and research.

One the one hand, within the Church, there is a real distinction between the roles of parish priests (the teachers) and theologians (the researchers). On the other hand, academics in universities are normally expected to be both teachers and researchers. In the ministry, I was always involved in preaching and pastoral counselling, but, other than taking a few graduate courses in liturgy at the University of Notre Dame and in ecumenism at Dubuque Theological Seminary, I had no graduate training in theology and didn't claim to be a theologian. When my preaching and pastoral work allowed, however, I did as much reading about theology as I could, because I was interested. I certainly prepared my homilies carefully, indeed as carefully as I later did my classes at university, and I gave a number of public presentations while I was in the priesthood, but I didn't have many opportunities to write with the precision necessary for the preparation of academic conference papers or articles for publication. Nor were there any formal peer reviews of the theological writings I did put out. The teaching dimension of my ministry was, for the most part, a bit like offering an introductory course in theology, a different topic covered each Sunday.

I came to the conclusion that the close link between teaching and research at universities is healthier than the distinction between the two that was expected in the priesthood. It is easier to be intellectually lazy in the ministry than it is in academe. The constant evaluation that goes on in universities is a clear deterrent to coasting. Every course I ever taught at the university level was evaluated by students, and the evaluation was then reviewed by the head of the department. In a way, it was stressful, but I welcomed this feedback as a chance to constantly improve my teaching. In my research, the publications I valued most were those that were reviewed by peers. In the ministry, my sermons were evaluated only occasionally, and that was in the first year after my ordination, during my year of pastoral theology.

Another way that the ministry and academic life are different is that a university pays attention to and rewards the high quality of an individual's performance. Over the course of my academic career, my curriculum vitae grew to over 35 pages, including a list of the degrees I've earned and honours I've received; my areas of expertise, courses taught, research grants received; committees I've served on; the books, chapters, articles, and conference presentations I've published; graduate students I've supervised; programs I've evaluated at other universities; and editorial responsibilities I've undertaken. These activities constitute the life of the academic. This long list was accumulated quite easily, actually, because of the annual evaluation reports I had to turn in for a tenure hearing, for merit pay consideration, and for promotion to associate professor* and later to full professor*, as well as the annual activity reports to the vice-president while I was dean of the Faculty of Arts. One criterion in the evaluation process was quality of teaching. Another was the extent to which one's research was contributing to new knowledge.

Such evaluation was never a part of the ministry. Now, having witnessed the benefits of continuous tracking of professional growth in the academic world, I believe it would be beneficial if bishops and other religious leaders asked clergy for an annual report of their activities, perhaps a prime benefit being the opportunity for bishops to acknowledge the high level of commitment that priests bring to their ministries. I know of nothing more satisfying to individuals than recognition of their achievements.

My key observation here is that one spends one's academic life "proving" to others that one is competent to do one's job. This is decidedly different from the role of the individual in the ministry. Max Weber, the famous German sociologist, has provided the best explanation of the differences. An academic position in a university is what he would call an "achieved role," where the individual not only works hard to get the appropriate education but also must constantly prove himself or herself worthy of keeping the position. Having said this, I probably need not add that universities have not always been successful in addressing incompetence. (Later, as head of the Department of Sociology and then dean of the Faculty of Arts, I found that this particular responsibility took up a great deal of my time.) Max Weber would call the priesthood an "ascribed" role—that is, a position acquired simply by birth, by lineage, or by rituals such as marriage or, in this case, ordination. While priests also undertake long years of study prior to being ordained, after ordination, the priest's position is considered ascribed. This can have two negative consequences. The first is that, because the priesthood is viewed by the Church as a sacred calling that imparts an indelible mark on the individual ("Once a priest, always a priest"), it is viewed as a scandal when a priest leaves the ministry. The second is that bishops in many dioceses within the Church and leaders within the religious communities are extremely reluctant to take appropriate action when individuals have been incompetent or have brought the ministry, by association, into disrepute. I personally felt that there were far more institutional guidelines to monitor my performance as an academic than there were to monitor my priestly activities.† Having said this, I must also say that, in my judgement, there is not a single profession in our society that has not had difficulties in addressing the failings of some of its practitioners.

I certainly worked as hard and as conscientiously when I was a priest as I did as a professor. However, the life of the priest is not expected to be focussed upon his own achievements. In Christian theology, ultimately the truth is embodied in a person: Jesus Christ. "I am the way, the truth and the life" (John 14:6). He proclaimed. John the Baptist articulated a sharper contrast on the issue when, speaking of Jesus, he said, "He must grow greater, I must grow smaller" (John 3:30). When I was first a priest, I thought that the truth we were seeking was somewhere "out there." I wanted to help others achieve knowledge of, and intimacy with, a being who transcends us, yet with whom we can communicate, indeed, in whom we can find salvation from the obvious limitations of our existence. But, over time, I came to realize just how much change is occurring in the development of the knowledge of God, as well as in other aspects of theology. These changes often are a result of changes in society. The theology that I now value is very much a live, ever-changing discipline, much like all other academic disciplines. It innovates as well as it preserves. And therefore "truth" is not just a given but needs to be sought after. Theology informs and nourishes faith.

In academe, when we discover new knowledge, there are two outcomes. First, the new knowledge itself often improves our society. Finding a cure for a form of cancer, improving treatments for strokes and heart attacks, building safer bridges, or creating music, sculptures, or a play that makes the human spirit soar—

† *For example, to my regret, I am not aware of a single bishop in the world who has been removed from office for allowing priests who were pedophiles to move to other parishes, where, unfortunately, many continued their criminal behaviour.*

these are the kinds of improvements I mean. The university is one of the foundations of civilization, one of the great civilizing forces. Second is the acknowledgement of the researcher for the achievement. We have elaborate rules dealing with plagiarism and with "intellectual property," the ownership of, and the right of the individual to benefit from, anything that he or she has created.

The various rituals that take place in the two institutions reflect the differences between them. The liturgy of the Church is primarily a "communion" service, an individual's communion with Christ and with other individuals. The rituals of a convocation in a university celebrate the achievements of individuals; each graduating student receives his or her diploma and individuals receive honorary doctorates for "distinguished achievement in scholarship, the arts, or public service."

But there are commonalities, too, between the two institutions. One of the most significant is that both are committed to creating a better human community. If "love one another" is the common linguistic framework used in the ministry, "respect for human rights" and "community development" are the common terms used in the university setting, particularly the social sciences. In both, there is always intense debate about the meaning of such terms and about how to achieve the goals identified by them. I feel privileged to have served people through my membership in both these institutions.

In the same way that I studied theology at a time of enormous change, I entered into academic life in the social sciences in the Canadian university system at a time of great change. Sociology was coming of age, and I was excited to be part of it. When I was hired in 1972, there were almost no textbooks that analyzed

Canadian society from a sociological perspective, an appalling situation. The introduction-to-sociology textbook that I had to adopt was published in the United States and contained not a word about Canada. G.N. Ramu, who was hired at the University of Manitoba the same year as I, edited a pioneer introductory text with Stuart Johnson that became one of several to be adopted across Canada. I contributed an article, on the sociology of religion in Canada, to the first edited book in that field.[1] Scholars in such sub-disciplines as social class, health, ageing, ethnicity, demography, and criminology began writing monographs and publishing specialized journals.

These publications were at the heart of what became known as the "Canadianization issue," which was characterized by serious divisions in sociology departments across the country and intense, acrimonious debates at the annual meetings of the Canadian Sociology and Anthropology Association. There were few doctoral programs in Canada in the social sciences at the time, and most members of sociology departments, as well as of other social-science disciplines, were Americans. Was it appropriate to be teaching about and researching social issues in other countries (read, the United States) to the point of neglect and even ignorance of our own society?

We know that the very issues chosen by researchers often reflect their particular biases and of course their backgrounds and values. For example, because the academic positions in medical schools have more frequently been held by men, more research has been conducted on illnesses more common to men than to women. If one wishes to see differences between the United States and Canada, then teaching an introductory course in sociology is one of the best ways to discover the differences. Whether one is comparing the political systems, the justice systems, the health systems, the role of Aboriginals, the origins of the countries, or the approaches to multiculturalism, the differences are more than superficial. In the early 1970s, we desperately needed to understand our own unique social realities. The decisions to begin a plethora of Canadian doctoral programs in the social sciences and to develop and hire more Canadians to teach and conduct research in them was an important advance in our national consciousness.

The debate about hiring, however, was framed in other terms: should we be hiring the very "best" academics we could attract, or should we be hiring Canadians? (The inference was that the "best" could not be found among Canadians and we could save a lot of bother if we didn't have to look at Canadian candidates!) The debate raged on about whether the two ("Canadian" and "best") were mutually exclusive. It's amusing that at a time when there was almost no social-science research on Canadian society, some scholars were already arguing that we would end up in a situation of parochialism if we were to concentrate on Canada. What we needed was new hiring policies that would search for experts who would not only research Canadian social life but also engage in international comparisons. The Canadianization issue was eventually resolved by legislation from the federal government that encouraged us to hire "the best" but required that we look first at the pool of Canadian applicants, a policy I thought eminently fair and sensible. Identical concerns arose in the mid-1980s but focussed on hiring women, Aboriginals, visible minorities, and people with disabilities. Certainly, the debates within universities about these issues were pivotal in helping the federal government arrive at fairly comprehensive policies, even if the implementation has been excessively slow.

While this was the political climate when I began my academic career, my early years were filled with course preparations and efforts to publish. I taught undergraduate courses in the sociology of religion, social problems, and urban sociology, and a graduate course on survey research methodology. Conducting and interpreting research based on surveys has been the methodology of choice during my entire career. It began in graduate school in New York. Although I had interviewed young African American students in a head-start program in Manhattan, my first major experience was serving as an interviewer for Charlene's research at the Bronx State Hospital. That project was supervised by Mary Powers, our doctoral dissertation director, who also taught us survey research methodology. In her course, I proposed a sampling of 750 young adults in Calgary for my doctoral project. The technical term for the method I chose is a *four-stage, stratified random sample.*† Such a study was rather unusual in 1970 in Canada, and, as a consequence, it was easy to get publicity about the project and therefore to achieve a high response rate. Over the years, I have conducted or advised others on hundreds of such sampling frameworks for survey research projects, but my own thesis sample remains for me the most satisfying.

The ethical guidelines at universities for any research that involves human subjects have become more and more strict over the years. A university committee must review every request to do a survey and examine the protection of privacy of individuals as well as the appropriate disclosure to the respondents of the aims of the research. It is this sense of responsibility to respondents that led me, in addition to publishing in academic journals, always to report the general findings to participants. In 1973, I gave 19 lectures, mostly in Alberta, on the results of the study that I had conducted for my doctorate. After I conducted a nation-wide study of 1,600 Mennonites from six different conferences on attitudes toward, and their use of, alcohol, I visited Mennonite communities across Canada to report the results, which highlighted the

† *According to the four-stage, stratified random sample, at the first stage in the Calgary study we took a random sample of enumeration areas in the city. At the second we took a random sample of city blocks within those enumeration areas, then took a random sample of houses on the selected blocks, and finally a random sample of youth in the selected households that had more than one youth between the ages of 15 and 24 living in that household.*

wide interpretation of norms that coexisted in Mennonite conferences and even within Mennonite congregations. When I began the annual Winnipeg Area Study in 1981, we established a tradition of always sending a summary of the results to the homes of those selected in the sample.

Of course many people are annoyed when an interviewer comes to the door or, more frequently, calls on the telephone to conduct a survey, especially if it is a market survey. And especially if the call is around the dinner hour! Researchers from universities are now experiencing similar resistance. The inconvenience from the sheer number of surveys to which one is subjected, the fear of losing one's privacy, and the fear that findings may be selectively reported and manipulated are some of the reasons for resistance. Perhaps another is the question of how a sample of a little over a thousand people in Canada can tell us anything accurate about the views of a population of 33 million? Many people do not trust the fact that, properly selected, such a sample can be amazingly accurate.

In some sociological research, we are trying to find out what people think and/or how they behave. Some surveys can dispel the "shared ignorance" that exists in a community. Some can address the implications of existing attitudes and values and even the laws governing our behaviour. I was particularly pleased to have played a significant role in a survey of Winnipeggers on mental health issues. We tackled such questions as: Are people with mental disabilities dangerous to others? What happens if people are afraid that they are? What is the origin of this fear? How will this fear affect the treatment of these people? Will we face objections if we place mental health facilities in particular neighbourhoods? Because our own daughter suffers from autism, I was personally gratified by the positive attitudes of the majority of Winnipeggers on these issues. The NIMBY (not in my back yard) phenomenon was prevalent in many cities at this time, and so it was reassuring to know that this was not the majority view in our city.[2]

In 1981, the year after my experience with the mental health study, with the assistance of my wife, Charlene, and my sociology colleague Leo Driedger, I designed the Winnipeg Area Study. It was designed to be an annual study, and my goal was to provide academics with a high-quality, annual city-wide sample of 750 households† for their own research and to provide graduate students with training in survey research in a course connected to the survey. Some 70 academics have used the study since 1981. Some have used the data gathered by others to analyze an issue of interest to them. Most, however, have developed their own questions for the survey, confident that the staff of the Area Survey would gather the information according to professional survey research standards.

I believe that my key contributions to research have been in providing academics and students with advice on methodology. Each year, we included several experiments on the Winnipeg Area Study to test the validity of our procedures with the goal of advancing the discipline of survey research. Furthermore, because the University of Alberta had developed a similar survey (indeed, it was the first such survey developed in Canada, and its director, Les Kennedy, was of great assistance to me), together we were able to support researchers at the two universities to exchange questions that compared our cities on 11 different projects without ever exchanging money. Over the years, I have been invited to give lectures on the Winnipeg Area Study at half a dozen universities. It was exciting to launch the Study and guide it through its growing pains.

The Winnipeg Area Study led to a number of academic

---

† *My frequent use of 750 households stems from the statistical fact that a sample of that size in a city of over 500,000 is accurate 95 percent of the time, plus or minus 5 percent.*

opportunities for me that I had not anticipated. One that I was particularly proud of came in 1997, when I was asked by Statistics Canada to serve on the External Advisory Committee of the Data Liberation Initiative (DLI) that Wendy Watkins, Chuck Humphrey, and Ernie Boyko had established the previous year, an outstanding initiative. Until the DLI was established, the hundreds of surveys taken by Statistics Canada, including the census data gathered since the late 1800s, usually sat in the archives in Ottawa with very little call upon them, largely because of the high fees imposed for access. Statistics Canada was obliged by government to charge any researcher a high fee to use the data for analysis; it might cost $50,000 or more.† The job of the DLI, then, was to facilitate less-expensive access to the data, so that they could be used more effectively for the benefit of Canadians.

In my judgement, the DLI project is one of the most significant innovations that has ever been developed in the social sciences in Canada. Survey research is only one methodological approach in the social sciences. Nevertheless, the vast data base in Statistics Canada provides essential information for historians, economists, geographers, community health researchers, anthropologists, sociologists, and researchers in many other disciplines. Within the five years of the establishment of the DLI, its work has exceeded everyone's expectations, with almost every university in Canada participating. I have a sense of satisfaction about having had this small part in a very important historical development of the social sciences.

In the seventh year of their academic appointments, academics normally are given the privilege of a leave from teaching to concentrate full time on their research. When mine came up, I was successful in obtaining a Social Sciences and Humanities

† *The total cost of adding one single question on the Canadian census is in excess of one million dollars.*

Research Council (SSHRC*) research/study leave grant, and Charlene and I, with our two children, headed off to Berkeley, California, for the 1978–1979 academic year. It was an unusually successful year for me. Because I was not sure that I was a good enough sociologist to be at Berkeley, even as a visitor, I went with a great deal of trepidation. I had not forgotten a particular traumatic incident in New York during my graduate program. In 1970, I had received a call asking me to present a paper at the mid-winter meetings of the Religious Research Association in Manhattan. I told the organizers that I was not far enough along in my dissertation research to do it, but about two weeks later, when the program came out, I saw that they hadn't removed my name. After some thought, I began to feel that I could learn from the experience, and so I decided to go through with the presentation. At the time, I was funded by a Canada Council doctoral fellowship and was working on the theoretical perspective that eventually led to my city-wide study of the religious attitudes and values held by Calgary youth.

I was not far into my presentation when an individual near the back started to flip through the pages of my paper with quite a disdainful look on his face. I was upset for the rest of my presentation, and, when I concluded, he was the first to speak. "I certainly don't see how you got a grant to carry out that study," he began. I don't remember the rest of the comments, from him or from any of the others, but I certainly remember that I felt like the wounded wolf being attacked by the pack. The reception after the academic sessions was agony. When I left the meeting, I walked up and down the streets of Manhattan, and I like to exaggerate that I had a drink in every bar. It took me six months to recover from the humiliation and to find the confidence to go on with my work. Later that year, I went to a conference at Harvard and heard an eminent sociologist, author of some 10 books, attacked in an extremely personal manner by another eminent scholar. I realized that it was not my student status alone that provoked the attack on me.

Academic bullying is far too common "a game." Verbal aggression seems to be the weapon of choice for those who, were they not academics, might resort to using a knife or a gun to settle disputes. I swore that I would never humiliate a student or a colleague in that way, nor in any way, for that matter. I became passionate about creating a respectful environment wherever I worked. In fact, in my retirement, I now conduct workshops on academic leadership for department heads at universities across the country, and I always stress that the creation and maintenance of a healthy, respectful work environment is one of the major responsibilities of a department head.

There were 43 sociologists from around the world on research/ study leave at Berkeley the year that I was there. I was sponsored by Charles Glock, the pioneer in using survey research as a methodology to study the sociology of religion. While at Berkeley, I attended a large number of meetings about such new religious movements as the Summit Lighthouse, founded by Elizabeth Claire Prophet, Siddha Yoga and its spiritual head Swami Muktananda, and Erhart Sensitivity Training (EST). I was also invited to take part in the major discussion group of scholars in the Bay area interested in the sociology of religion, and I gave a presentation at one of the meetings. I remember clearly that Charles Glock disagreed with one of my premises, but his manner was so supportive that I welcomed the criticism. It was a clear contrast to my experience in New York. I had now experienced both the competitive, arrogant side of academic life as well as the collegial, supportive environment. Experiencing both served me well when later I became head of the Department of Sociology at the University of Manitoba.

One day at lunchtime in late January when I was at Berkeley, as part of my interest in new religious movements, I had my tarot cards read on the street close to the Survey Research Building, where I had an office. I was informed that soon I would be offered a promotion. I was fascinated by the prediction, as that very week I had received a letter from the dean of the Faculty of Arts at the University of Manitoba advising me that I had been nominated as a candidate for the headship of the Department of Sociology and asking that I let him know if I was willing to let my name stand. The request was indeed a surprise. I certainly was old enough at 45 to take on the headship, and I had been superior of the retreat house, the Franciscan formation centre, and at the pig and cattle farm at Cochrane, Alberta, but I was a relatively young academic (that is, I hadn't spent that many years in academe). More important, I was still an assistant professor, and I feared that people would not respect me as an academic. Nevertheless, I decided to let my name stand and then accepted the offer to be head when it was made.

At the same time, I decided to submit my request for a promotion to the rank of associate professor. During my year at Berkeley, I had completed six papers, all of which were later published. But they had not been accepted for publication at the time I submitted my application for promotion, and I was informed by the departmental committee that my application was premature and was turned down. I was annoyed for a day or two but quickly realized that their judgement was correct, and the next year my application was approved. A number of years later, when I was dean of the Faculty of Arts, I always counselled candidates applying for promotion not to tie up their whole identities with the decision of the committee. These are often very tense times in the life of an academic. When individuals were turned down by their departments and I supported that committee decision, it was helpful to be able to tell them about my own experience. I would then offer advice on how they might overcome the deficiencies the committee or I had noted.

When I assumed the headship in the Department in 1974, I knew that I was facing a climate that was characterized by serious divisions between faculty members. My concern about personal respect because of my inexperience in academe was quickly replaced by my efforts to encourage the 25 academics within the Department to respect one another. My first initiative was to meet individually with those faculty members with whom I had the least contact. My style was neither to impose my views nor follow those of others but rather, whenever appropriate, to raise important issues and guide discussions toward useful, achieveable consensus. Equally important, I refused to listen to anything that smacked of gossip. I believed (and still do) that it is acceptable, indeed to be expected, to raise serious academic concerns about a colleague in tenure or promotion committees. But gossip, rumour, innuendo, bullying, and isolation of colleagues can destroy the fabric of a department. I worked hard to eliminate any hint of these in my department. Soon I felt satisfied that people were back in their offices doing research and preparing their classes instead of plotting the obstruction or demise of their colleagues.

There is no question that my major source of satisfaction came from the successes of colleagues in the Department. It was easy to acknowledge their achievements. Who does not want to be recognized for having done a good job? Perhaps my mother's recognition of my little achievements when I was a child had influenced me. I also never missed an opportunity to inform the dean at the time, Fred Stambrook, when someone in the Department had achieved some success. This was important for morale in a dispirited department. I wanted to be a facilitator in the Department. But I also wanted to initiate a number of projects, the Winnipeg Area Study being one. As well, I managed to find monies through internal and external grant programs to have a visiting scholar in the Department every year.

I was particularly satisfied in being able to support a young scholar in our department, Neena Chappell, who had become an expert in the sociology of aging, a relatively new area of research in the 1980s. Neena believed that, if I could find a position for her, she would be successful in attracting a $500,000 national research grant from SSHRC to begin a centre on aging. President Arnold Naimark approved the position, and Neena won the SSHRC award.

The Centre on Aging has become one of the most successful research centres at the University, and it has achieved an international reputation. Its academic members have published successfully and are in demand for supervising theses and dissertations of students in other departments, and there is now an undergraduate teaching concentration on aging. It hosts an annual research day, which attracts several hundred local policy experts and service providers who learn about the latest research on aging. Members of the Centre have been consultants on policy issues relating to aging at all levels of government in Canada and abroad. Several years after the Centre was inaugurated, I was made an honorary lifetime member.

The five years when I was head of the Department of Sociology were among my happiest, both professionally and personally. As my term ended in 1984, our children had just begun school. Except for Catherine's excessive shyness, few of the problems that they experienced in later years had emerged, and I look back on this time with a great deal of satisfaction and gratitude.

I made it clear to the Department that I did not intend to seek a reappointment. I felt that I was leaving it in a healthier state than when I'd taken on the headship, and I knew that there were several very competent individuals who could take on the responsibility. I also felt that a new head would bring new ideas and approaches that would be good for the Department. While my publishing pace had certainly slowed during my headship, I still had managed to publish something every year, so I did not expect it would be difficult to leave administration and return to full-time teaching and research.

In fact, my involvement in administrative matters did not end. In 1985, I was elected to the national executive of the Canadian Sociology and Anthropology Association and given the specific responsibility of coordinating the annual national meetings. One of the most satisfying dimensions of this work was reading the several hundred abstracts of papers that were being considered for presentation each year. It gave me a strong sense of the theoretical, methodological, and substantive directions of the discipline. It also gave me the opportunity to meet some of the finest sociologists in Canada. I developed a network of friends across the country.

The growing maturity of the discipline in Canada led me to organize, on behalf of the Association, a display of Canadian books and periodicals at the American Sociological Association's annual meeting in Atlanta in 1988. I felt that the time had come for American sociologists to learn more about the work of Canadian scholars and come to a better understanding of the differences between our societies.

As part of my responsibilities at the national level, in 1987 I had the privilege of organizing the meetings in Victoria on the occasion of the 25th anniversary of the founding of the CSAA. A year before the event was to occur, I put together a committee that invited a number of scholars to prepare retrospective papers, which four of us later edited into a book entitled *Fragile Truths: Twenty-Five Years of Sociology and Anthropology in Canada.*[3] In preparation for those same meetings, I also had a hand in the Outstanding Contribution Award, which was instituted that year. I remember well the packed auditorium as colleagues from across the country waited to hear who the 14 pioneers of sociology and anthropology were to be so honoured. The awards are given to this day, usually to one or two scholars each year. Very much to my surprise, I was given the award in 1994.

CHAPTER 8

Suffering with our Children

Family photo, 1985

A dramatic change occurred in our home life on the 15th of April 1977, when we adopted Vincent, a little less than 10 months after his birth. It was not a difficult decision to adopt; we did not agonize over it. We'd both come from homes that were happy when we were growing up, and we felt we had much to offer as parents. At the same time, at the ages of 42 and 36, we felt that we didn't have a great deal of time to deliberate. Once the doctor informed us of our infertility problems and that we would likely not be able to conceive, we quickly began the process. My brother and his wife had already adopted three children, my cousin two, and my dad's mother had taken in a young man two generations earlier. My own parents had taken in our cousins when their mother died. This family history made the whole process of having children through adoption seem normal. Our children have always known they were adopted, and it was always presented in a positive context.

We had told our social worker that, while race, religion, or ethnicity did not matter, we didn't think we would be very good at parenting a child with mental disabilities. We now know how naïve a statement that was. We knew nothing about people with mental disabilities. We just knew that we were very busy professionals and could not imagine providing the extra time that a child with mental disabilities would require. Ironically, both our children turned out to have mental disabilities. The reality is different, however. Once you hold your baby in your arms, even in that first moment, such an indelible bond forms that your life is forever changed, and you just do what is required.

We visited the foster home in Transcona several times before bringing Vincent home so that he would be comfortable with us. As we entered the living room of the foster family the first time, Vincent was playing on the floor on his hands and knees with his back to us. He turned slightly to look at us, and I could see what a beautiful little boy he was, with a dark complexion and rich black hair set off by his little red outfit. We knew he was Aboriginal. Indeed, years later we found out that he was a First Nations Treaty member from the Peguis Reserve. During the adoption process we had asked the agency if an Aboriginal home were available where he could stay within his culture. They assured us there was not. In any case, the thinking of the time was that, as long as a child was placed in a middle-class home and given lots of love, all would work out. I'm quite sure that we bought into that myth ourselves. The politics of child placement are quite different now.

In the summer of 1978, a little over a year later, we went to a different foster home in Transcona to pick up the little four-month-old girl who was to be our daughter, Catherine. When we arrived, she was on the porch, on a small swing, rocking back and forth, an activity she chose for years to come, any time she was upset, and which came to symbolize for me her tremendous social isolation. Within a week of Catherine's arrival in our family, we packed up and headed out of the country for a year. Expecting the arrival of Catherine, we had planned that I would take a research/study leave from the University of Manitoba and Charlene would take a year's leave of absence without pay from the University of Winnipeg to be with the children. I was appointed a visiting research associate in the Sociology Department at the University of California, Berkeley, under the sponsorship of a marvellous human being and scholar, Charlie Glock.

Charlene was given a leave without pay from her university job, but not without difficulties. At first the leave was denied. It coincided with her application for tenure, and the administration did not want to give tenure and then a leave without pay to someone whom they thought might not want to return to work full-time after the arrival of a second child. This was only one of the problems that women in academic life faced in those days. The head of her department, Bill Greenaway, went to bat for her and got the decision reversed.

Our year in Berkeley was one of our happiest ever. I worked every day, but not in the evenings or on weekends. In fact, almost every weekend we packed up the children and headed out to discover California with Dan Cawthon and Penny Washbourn, who had also come from Winnipeg on research/study leaves with their two children, who were about the same ages as ours. One of Charlene's classmates in Kentuky, Rachel Thompson, and her husband, Bill Bates, lived in Berkeley and arranged for the home we rented, which was high up in the Berkeley hills and had a view of the Golden Gate Bridge. Charlene stayed home with Catherine all day, and we enrolled Vincent in a preschool class for half days. One of the delights for me that year was to come home on the bus to our children and to a new meal almost every day. Charlene was thoroughly enjoying herself, trying out recipes in all the cookbooks in the house, keeping a record of the recipes we liked for later use, back home. We had many, many visitors during the year, including Mom. She would play endless games of train with Vincent, lining up all the suitcases, straddling them with him, and leading him on a magical journey. And we had great fun with Kitty and Mose, Charlene's parents, including a wonderful trip through Marin County and its beautiful forests.

We returned to Winnipeg one month earlier than planned because I was asked to take up the headship of the Department of Sociology on the 1st of June 1979. We settled back into the wonderful home on Grosvenor Avenue that we had purchased in 1975. Andrea, my niece, who had also spent two months with us in Berkeley, agreed to come and live on the top floor of the house and serve as nanny for Catherine for a year. We registered Vincent at the University of Winnipeg daycare centre, and he went back and forth on the bus with Charlene.

My new position was a challenge. I took it for granted that I would continue my research in spite of the new administrative responsibilities, which meant that I rarely got home much before 6:00 p.m. I often worked after our children went to bed, as did Charlene. Still, we had wonderful times with the children. Catherine was excessively shy, although at that time we did not know that the reason was her autism. When we had guests over, even close family members whom she knew, she would hold on to Charlene's skirt for dear life. She would only whisper and then only to Charlene, and so quietly that even Charlene could not hear what she was saying most of the time. Because of Catherine's insecurities and her strong dependence on Charlene, we fell into a pattern in which Charlene would put Catherine to bed while I tended to Vincent. When I was a child, there was a program on CBC radio on Sunday mornings hosted by a woman who would tell stories to children linking three unlikely objects. I had always enjoyed her stories, and I developed a habit of creating such stories with Vincent as we lay down on his bed at night, me with my arm outstretched so that he could rest his head close to my shoulder. I would then weave my story of, say, a rabbit, a light bulb, and a chair, or a toothpick, a little boy, and a picture. These were unrehearsed stories, although I often found myself thinking about possibilities while driving home from work or giving Vincent his bath before bed. Occasionally, once I lay down on his bed with him, I would be so tired that I would fall asleep in the middle of the story. He would suddenly burst out laughing at me, and I would sheepishly try to remember where I was in the story so that I could continue.

We were determined that the children would not start off life with a television for a babysitter, so on alternate Saturday mornings either Charlene or I would get up when the children did and play with them while the other rested. After several years of this Saturday morning routine, we developed a new one that lasted until Charlene had a stroke in 1996. I would get up first and get coffee ready, and then we would sit up in bed together for at least an hour. The children came to know that this was our special time together and they had to give us at least an hour without disturbance. (Charlene always said that a woman who had her coffee prepared for her in the mornings would do well in life.) These Saturday mornings have been among the most precious times in our lives together. As the childrens' problems became more severe, these were our moments of sanity, of recovery from a week of stress. I once heard an expert state that 70 percent of couples with children who had autism ended up divorcing. I think our Saturday mornings with coffee and quiet time were our salvation; it was when we took the time to discuss our differences about how to deal with the issues and tried to work out new solutions, even though, in the early days, we didn't know the real nature of the problems.

One Saturday, I came home from the recreational vehicle show at the convention centre and convinced Charlene to go back with me. That afternoon we purchased a pop-up camping trailer. We sold the small Maverick car we'd been driving and began our search for one that could haul a trailer. A Ford salesman convinced us to buy a used taxi. We fitted it with a trailer hitch and were ready for camping. Our first trip was to St. Ambroise in the Interlake early in spring. The bird sanctuary on one side of the campsite and Lake Manitoba on the other were amenities from heaven.

After exploring Manitoba, we became much more adventuresome and travelled to Kentucky and back many times over the years and stayed every night at campsites along the way. During the day, we would pull in to rest stops every two hours. It was at these oases that Vincent learned to throw a ball straight, and, later, when he was about nine years old, he became an excellent pitcher on the Crescentwood community baseball team. I took great pride that I could set up the trailer and have dinner ready within an hour of arriving at a campsite. Over at the playground, under Charlene's supervision, Catherine would share a swing with Baby Beans and several of her other dolls, totally immersed in her own world. As we travelled, Charlene kept a diary of the events, including the expenses, but most of all to keep track of what the children said. As we headed back to Kentucky the year after Charlene started her diary, the first thing the children wanted to hear were the funny things they had said the previous year.

On many trips we included Charlene's parents, Kitty (Catherine) and Mose (Charles) Thacker. We took trips to Mammoth Cave, Kentucky Lake, and the Horse Museum in Lexington. We went to Hazard in Appalachia because Vincent was keen on the Dukes of Hazard, a television program. We ventured across the mountains to Vancouver and Victoria, all six of us crowded into the little trailer at night. Kitty would never let us get away with a nickel's expenditure that she would not share. Mose became resigned to the fact that we stopped at every historical site on the way. The two of them could drive the 1,300 miles to Winnipeg from Kentucky in one night and two days, while it took us, with the kids, at least three nights and four days.

Camping trips were not our only excursions together with Kitty and Mose. We drove to Florida with the children several times, visiting Disney World, Cape Canaveral, Busch Gardens, and St. Petersburg. In 1985, the six of us headed to Portugal, Spain, and Morocco for three weeks. By the time Catherine was seven, her autism was growing more noticeable. Unless we made a point of taking her out, her world was limited to the van that we rented, and she rarely even looked out the window. Vincent loved the sea and would simply throw himself into the waves with abandon whenever we found a beach. He would try every new fish that was served. Both children loved the camel rides and the belly dancer in Morocco who lifted her skirt up to polish Mose's glasses. I think it was our children who saved a lot of people from being seasick as we crossed the Straits of Gibraltar in a hydrofoil in very choppy seas. Oblivious to the danger, the children thought that the water splashing into the boat was a great joke, and their excitement kept most of the passengers distracted.

As our children began school, we were able to create an ideal after-school situation for them at home. We had met Mary Vollrath when one of her two teenage daughters, Charlene, was babysitting for us. Charlene hinted that her mother might be willing to help us in our search for some after-school help. For approximately eight years, Mary came to our home every day before the children got home from school and stayed until one of us arrived at 5:15 p.m. After Mary had been with us for several years, we found out that she had at first been reluctant to come to our home, as she feared being diminished by two "uppity" professors, an experience she had already endured elsewhere. She need not have worried. John Thacker, my wife's brother, said to her one day: "Charlene, you would never know you had a PhD!" Is that what is called a back-handed compliment? At any rate, we established a wonderful relationship with Mary. She was as sweet and loving as could be and extremely understanding of the disabilities of both the children. She had excellent judgement on when to deal with situations herself and when it was necessary to call us. She was frank about when she was unsure, and we had many conversations with her about the best strategies for dealing with problems. To this day, Catherine drops in to see her from time to time.

Ann Juskow was already an anchor in our home. When Charlene and I married, Ann was cleaning my brother John's home on a bi-weekly basis. We asked her if she would like to come to our home as well. She did, and for 25 years gave us order and a sense of control in our home. She and Mary together formed our invaluable family-support team.

By the time each of the children began going to school, their disabilities had already begun to manifest themselves. "I could weep forever as I think of how much our children have had to bear," Charlene laments. "However, they had a wonderful childhood," she adds, "and we should never forget that." This was confirmed to me recently when I spent two weekends with Catherine putting together an album of photographs, all records of happy times at our cottage. One does not take photographs of children in their moments of anxiety or hyperactivity, of course, nor of parents dealing with crises, but the album contains photographic records of so many happy memories that we can almost forget the difficult times.

Catherine: A Story of Love, Anxiety, and Promise

Although Catherine is the younger of our two children, her disabilities began to manifest themselves first. Vincent's came afterward. The range of disabilities was wide, stemming as they did from Asperger's syndrome (a form of autism) in Catherine's case, and both attention-deficit hyperactive disorder (ADHD) and foetal alcohol spectrum disorder (FASD) in Vincent's. Soon they became so pervasive that they overtook our family life. And they required different responses from Charlene than from me. Not by choice, but rather in response to crises, Charlene began to deal more with Catherine, and I managed the care that Vincent needed.

Around the age of four, Catherine began to experience "night terrors," which occurred almost every night for two years. We can trace their beginnings to just after she had had surgery to correct a wandering eye. Just when Charlene and I were ready for bed, Catherine would get out of her own bed and run around the house screaming in terror for up to an hour. We tried putting warm wash cloths on her face, we tried waking her, and at other times we decided to just let her sleep-walk her way through it while we simply followed her. Nothing worked. It was as if the cycle just had to play itself out.

We enrolled both children in French immersion kindergarten at La Verandrye School. At the time, we didn't realize Catherine had autism (we thought she was just shy), but we soon realized that it had been a mistake to put her into what turned out to be a stressful environment. After a year we moved her to Grosvenor School, where she repeated Grade 1. We had been attending teacher-parent meetings throughout the year and were astounded to hear from her teacher at the spring meeting, "Oh, I gave up on Catherine before Christmas. I could never get her to say a word." If this teacher had not been planning to retire at the end of the school year, we would seriously have considered calling for her resignation.

For grades 2 and 3, we arranged to have Catherine bussed to a special-needs program at Sir John Franklin School about two kilometres away. The parent-teacher meetings were never encouraging. Catherine would not interact with her teacher or the other children. She was not just shy; indeed, she did not respond in any way to the initiatives that the teachers suggested. She was totally silent. She went back to Grosvenor for Grade 4. By this time, we had engaged a social worker, who had organized a weekly group session with three or four other little girls for the sole purpose of encouraging Catherine to interact. This turned out to be of little avail. She hated school and constantly complained that other children were laughing at her. We enrolled her in various groups, including Brownies, but it did not take long for us to see that each and every placement was in her mind simply another competitive situation in which she failed. Halloween, birthdays, Christmas, and Easter were all disastrous times for her, because it meant interaction with others, and all she wanted was to be with Charlene.

Recently, when we were going out to the cottage, Catherine recalled some of these times. She remembers vividly events I have completely forgotten about. In fact, her memory is remarkable; for example, she can remember the names of all her babysitters and of all the children in every family she has ever met. She has a keen sense of humour and remembers some funny things that happened to her, but mostly the negative events. One of these is of a birthday party to which I insisted she go because she had promised the child who had invited her. "You should have known, Dad," she said to me, "I could not face these kids who did not like me anyway. You should have known!" In a completely other context, recently she told us, "You know, there are a lot worse parents than you out there. Some of them hit their children." Charlene and I looked at each other and smiled. The first part of her comment seem like a rather back-handed compliment. But, in fact, it is probably a very accurate description of our parenting skills. We made a lot of mistakes (including my insistence that she go to the birthday party) because, at that time, we did not know the full nature of our daughter's illness.

My own interaction with Catherine was initially limited. She did not want to be touched by anyone other than her mother, and even then would hug Charlene only on her own terms. I would never hug her without permission, and I did not get that permission until she was close to 19, an incredibly difficult burden for me to bear. Once I understood that she had many characteristics of children with autism and understood a little better how she perceived events, her inability to hug me was much easier to bear. She might have benefitted from using a hugging machine, a device that Temple Grandin, a marvellous woman with autism had built for herself because she also does not like to be touched or hugged. Temple Grandin, who has a PhD and works at the University of Southern Colorado, visited Winnipeg several times to lecture on living with autism and once described this machine and how it helped her. She would get into the machine, turn on the electricity, and relax as the soft sides came up and surrounded her. Oliver Sacks[1] has written an insightful article about her, and her own article in his book gave rise to its title: *An Anthropolgist on Mars: Paradoxical Tales.* Grandin has written other important books of her own, including *Thinking in Pictures: Autism and Visual Thought.*[2]

When Catherine was about eight or nine, we took her to play-therapy sessions at the Psychological Service Centre at the University of Manitoba. After about 10 weeks of providing therapy, however, the psychologist wrote a report basically repeating all the difficulties that we had submitted in writing when we registered her at the beginning. This was yet another disappointment in our search for help.

In retrospect, we are amazed that we did not identify her disability earlier. But we knew nothing about autism, or Asperger syndrome. The disability is receiving far more public attention today than it did in the early 1980s; were we to be raising a child with autism these days, we would certainly have related her symptoms to autism. Catherine had an extraordinary vocabulary, and she could interact well with others one-on-one, both of which masked the seriousness of her disability. Tobiah Goldstein, a little neighbour, was her closest preschool pal, and they could play together for hours. But Catherine could never have a good time if more than one child were around. She was possessive of her time with the one, just as she was with Charlene. She always wanted private conversations with Charlene, and so they would either leave the room or I would.

Few children could get beyond the barriers that she constructed and interact with her in any meaningful way. Paige Wilson was an exception, however; she was the one grade-school child with whom Catherine was comfortable. They went to Mini University summer sports camp together at the University of Manitoba, and without Paige I think Catherine would have been unable to stay in the program. Paige's support, combined with Catherine's very strong athletic abilities, allowed her to do very well in the program. By the time she was in Grade 4, Catherine had already passed most of her Red Cross swimming levels at the Boni Vital pool. But in every new social situation that we exposed Catherine to, I would always take the leaders aside and explain that Catherine was extraordinarily shy and could not be pushed, and that we would be there in the background to help as needed.

In 1996, when Vincent was 10 and Catherine 8, we decided to purchase my brother's cottage, and it was indeed an inspired decision. Little did we know how much Catherine would thrive there. The cottage is on Pelican Bay, just south of Petersfield on Netley Creek. It is a protected little community of about about 150 cottages and homes situated on Grand Circle. Here we could let Catherine roam out of our sight for short periods of time. She played and swam in the water by the hour, she rode her bike around Grand Circle, she loved sitting in the front of the boat as we went fishing or took Vincent water-skiing. She loved raking, and did so with such fervour that there was little grass left, and certainly not a leaf. On weekends we usually took along one of Vincent's many friends or, very occasionally, one of Catherine's.

The cottage is in an unassuming area, quintessentially Manitoba. Heading north on Highway 9, most people would never realize that Netley Creek is just a stone's throw off to the left, as it surrounded by fields of wheat, canola, hay, and what may appear to the uneducated eye as simply wild grasses. That is an observation many of our guests have made to us. The narrowest parts of the creek are hardly wider than the Assiniboine River in the centre of Winnipeg, yet there are several parts that look like a small lake. The creek is fed by a large number of springs, which shoot off one from one another to form a labyrinth of narrow passages, some only wide enough for two or three boats, and which are separated from one another by tall reeds. One of these passages leads into the Red River, which allows a boater to head either north to Lake Winnipeg or south to the City of Winnipeg.

Weekends at the cottage have been, and still are, without question, the most enjoyable times in Catherine's life. And it has been my salvation. Without the cottage, I don't believe I could have withstood the pressures of being dean and taking care of our responsibilities at home. The cottage is only a 55-minute drive from our home in Winnipeg, which makes getting there almost effortless.

During Catherine's year in Grade 6, Charlene and I spent hours visiting schools and talking to professionals, trying to plan the best junior high school for her. It was clear that she could not cope with regular classes in most subjects. While her vocabulary and drawing skills were excellent, she was not able to master even elementary mathematics at that time. We had taken her to the Sylvan Learning Centre twice a week for two years to try to improve her math skills, but, when we withdrew her from the program, she was still unable to tell time. We had seen doctors galore, had had her hearing tested at the Child Guidance Clinic, had arranged for testing at school, and had taken her to a psychologist weekly. After a meeting that we attended at Grosvenor School one day, Dr. McFee, the psychiatrist representing the school, said in passing as he was about to leave, "She may just have Asperger syndrome, you know."

Charlene has a strong grasp of medical terminology and did not forget that offhand comment. A couple of days later, I joined Charlene for the weekly meeting with the psychologist, Lynne Ryan, where Charlene repeated what she had been told. "That is beyond my competency," the psychologist answered immediately. "I think I should refer you to a psychiatrist, Dr. Choptiany." She left the room, and we heard her talking on the phone about "the interesting case" she wanted to refer. She also informed us that the Autism Society was having its annual educational forum in a couple of weeks at the Health Sciences Centre and suggested we go.

There were about 200 people at the forum, and each of us was handed a pamphlet that listed 14 characteristics of autism. Charlene and I were were stunned when we read it and immediately associated nine of them with Catherine. It was as though a thunderbolt had struck us. All I remember about that day was the incredibly dark cloud that had come over our lives.

In the sociological literature on criminology and social problems, the theory of *labelling* suggests that the act of labelling, such as we encountered at the Autism Society meeting, often damages the individuals associated with labels. Since there is no balancing "de-labelling" process, a criminal, for example, can never seem to shake the label attached to his or her previous criminal behaviour. Furthermore, it is usually the person, not the set of characteristics, who is labelled. Catherine is not disabled; she has a disability. She also has many outstanding abilities. It is much more appropriate to speak about a person's disabilities than to say she or he "is disabled." It is not just a matter of semantics; it is an important distinction.

For us, however, finally having a label attached to Catherine's disability soon opened all kinds of doors for her and for us. We found literature to read, we could now gain access to specialists, and, although it took three years, we finally were able to have her placed in a special-education program for children with autism. While we still do not understand the root causes of much of her behaviour any better, at least we now know that such behaviour is characteristic of people suffering from Asperger syndrome. It no longer strikes us as strange that she wants to smell absolutely everything: dinner plates, newspapers, bus tickets—everything. We know that the noise of the singing at Mass will lead her immediately to cover her ears; to her it is simply cacophony. The noise and commotion of a crowd in a mall will cause her tremendous anxiety. Charlene has helped her to articulate her anxiety in such situations. We now know that we need to leave a mall, or a movie, or any other anxiety-provoking situation immediately, and she can count on us to do that. We stopped taking her to Mass, which meant that we, too, stopped going on a regular basis for some time. We began going to drive-in restaurants. If we go to a "real" restaurant, we always ask for a booth, or we don't stay. We now know that she needs to talk to only one person at a time. We might see the lawn, but her focus is more likely to be a blade of grass. We learned that she can be so totally absorbed by her current thought that any interruption is greeted by what appears to others to be rudeness, but it really represents a distraction to her from her totally insulated, all-consuming world. Recently, I came into a room where she was vacuuming and called her name to get her attention. She responded with anger simply for being disturbed. She needs to finish what she is doing, without interruption. If she were filling ice-cube trays and the phone rang for her, for example, she would need to finish that task before she could pick up the phone, even if it took several minutes. Our expectation that she come to the table when she is called for a meal is still a struggle.

We now know that she will perseverate (that is, repeat over and over the same immediate concern that she has) literally by the hour. Perseveration is probably the most striking and enduring characteristic of her disability. It is also the characteristic that requires the most patience of us, her parents. Most often, it represents an anxiety that needs to be alleviated. But it could also be something she wants us to do or not do. It might look like an extreme case of "nagging," but it is not that at all.

We also know not be offended when, from time to time, she might simply say what is on her mind; she lacks the filter that keeps "normal" people from making socially unacceptable comments. For example, she might say, "Dad, did you fart?" "Dad, did you brush your teeth? You've got bad breath." "Dad, you're not listening to me." And one knows very quickly whether or not she appreciates a gift. We have come to understand that another key characteristics of those with autism is their inability—no, rather, the extreme challenge—to place him- or herself in the mind of "the other." "I am who I think you think I am" is a description of Charles Horton Cooley's "looking-glass self."[3] There are four components to Cooley's famous sentence ("I am—who I think—you think—I am."), and each one is essential to the definition of the "looking-glass self." Cooley explains that we come to know ourselves in the process of perceiving how others perceive us. People with autism find it difficult to understand how others perceive them and often assume inaccurate perceptions, with devastating consequences for their own self-image. Catherine as a child and a teen was always plagued with a feeling that others were laughing at her. She would verbally assail other children in malls, on the street, on the bus, or elsewhere for laughing at her even when, in fact, there was no provocation whatsoever. We now understand that the very term that identifies the disability—*autism*—highlights a self-centred focus.

Human emotions and behaviour can be understood as occurring on a continuum. Most people function in the middle of the continuum and therefore can easily adjust their behaviour to various social situations, but a person with autism functions at one end or the other and does not readily make adjustments. We constantly try to teach Catherine socially acceptable behaviour when she violates the rules, but there is a limit to how often one can correct another's behaviour without endangering that person's self-esteem. We have come to believe that it is far better to overlook some behaviours and stress the essentials, to help improve her self-esteem. Just as Catherine must, so too must we live with her disability.

There is another characteristic of Catherine's autism that requires constant adjustment on our part. She assumes that we know everything. Some of her favourite shows are *Cold Case Files* and *Unsolved Mysteries*. If we are watching one together, often, very early in an episode, she will ask us about the outcome, which, of course, we don't know. This trait affects an enormous number of everyday interactions among us, and it must be extremely frustrating for Catherine to hear us say over and over that we don't know what other people are going to do, for example, what other people are thinking, or what's going to happen.

Catherine constantly "puts away" things in the house, and it requires all of our imagination to figure out where they might be. This includes everything from the measuring cups in the kitchen to cleaning supplies, soap, and even some of Charlene's toiletries. What is even more frustrating is that it is highly unlikely she will put things in the same place twice.

Charlene has done a much better job than I have at truly hearing Catherine's needs and responding to them. I have not easily adjusted my priorities to what is within Catherine's capabilities. She cannot stand certain kinds of messiness. Messiness at the cottage includes fallen leaves in the dense bush surrounding the cottage. Before raking the front lawn at the cottage, with its wide-open spaces strewn with leaves from about 200 trees, Catherine will invariably head for the dense bushes to rake up those dead leaves. I would like the leaves in the bushes to rot and provide nourishment for the living trees. "It is not that important," says Charlene. I would like the small, growing trees that are brittle in the fall not to be stepped upon. I want these trees to grow and increase our privacy from neighbours. "Who cares?" repeats Charlene. I care—and I care too much! Surely, after four years of explaining and seeing no change of behaviour, I should be able to understand the frustration that the messy, fallen leaves present to Catherine in her need for orderliness. I surrender!

We learned the true nature of Catherine's disability shortly before she moved from Grosvenor Elementary School at the end of Grade 6 to River Heights Junior High. The principal almost begged us to send Catherine to River Heights, as the philosophy in the schools at that time was (and still is) to integrate children with disabilities, and he definitely wanted Catherine in his school. He promised special aides and attention. But the reality was quite different. It took us some time to understand why Catherine would usually come home from school angry. The immediate cause turned out to be that all the teachers and aides took their breaks at lunchtime, precisely when Catherine most needed support. She would go back into the classroom in the afternoon with a clear sense that she was the laughingstock of the school. And, of course, the very fact that she did show her anger (for reasons that the other children could not always understand), they saw her as "different."

The school situation was beyond redemption. In Grade 7, when she was 14, Catherine reached a crisis in her ability to cope. One day in the middle of the winter, we had to take her to the Health Sciences Centre emergency ward because we were so worried about her safety. Her constant anger was becoming uncontrollable for her and for us. "Do you want to die young," she taunted Charlene one day, brandishing a large knife. "It is a little late for that," Charlene responded quietly, and cautiously took away the weapon. I was awestruck at Charlene's ability to diffuse the danger so skillfully.

Catherine was admitted to the psychiatric ward of the hospital when we took her to the emergency ward, and the medical staff tried to find appropriate medicines to reduce her extremely high levels of anxiety and her inappropriate behaviour. She returned home after a month, but her stay was short-lived. When we went back to see Dr. Choptiany about the situation at home, it became clear to us that Catherine would have to return to the hospital. When he told us that, I got such a pain across my chest that I thought I was having a heart attack. Charlene drove home to get Catherine for readmission to the hospital, while Dr. Choptiany got a wheelchair and took me over to the emergency ward. The examination was thorough and the diagnosis quick. I had no heart problem but did have a very high level of tension and anxiety. Catherine stayed in the hospital until about mid-summer. Charlene and Kitty came in from the cottage almost every day to visit. At the end of Catherine's hospital stay, it became clear to us that she would have to go to a residential facility.

After agonizing over a choice of a very few facilities, we settled on Hydra House, specifically their residential home near

McPhillips and Jefferson. There were usually five or six children in residence there, all under 18 and all less-functioning than Catherine. She came home every Friday and stayed until Sunday evening, a pattern that has continued to this day. She was smart enough to know that she had autism and that she could not overcome her disability. Perhaps this understanding came a year or two after she went to Hydra House. And she simply hated her situation. "I can't believe I am not living with you," she said several times, a statement very hard for us to have to hear. She did not like the staff, but, rather than communicate directly with them, she would tell us everything that was wrong. We did not know whether or not to believe her. Furthermore, we could not ignore the many stories in the papers about people in care who were not properly treated. This was during the time when stories of the tragedies and injustices of residential schools were beginning to emerge. We felt obliged to check out every story, and we made many calls every week to her residence. Indeed, we did find out that one of the staff members had a problem with alcohol, and Catherine perceived that this person did not like her. Catherine spent hour after hour telling us about her. In fact, for a full three years after Catherine left the facility, whenever anything came up that upset her, she switched the conversation to talk about how "that woman" had treated her.

We were careful not to accuse the staff when we called. Rather, we pointed out what Catherine perceived and tried to help the staff understand her thinking. Unfortunately, our interventions had an unintended negative effect. Often, when an uncomfortable situation arose, Catherine's response was to inform her caregivers or her teachers, "My dad will take care of this." At times, this hampered the ability of caregivers and teachers to deal effectively with a problem and Catherine's own ability to face problems and find solutions. We tried to make sure that problems at Hydra House were dealt with at Hydra House, problems at school were dealt with at school, and problems at home were dealt with by Charlene and me. This plan was not always possible at first, but, as Catherine's living situations changed over the years, and we became more confident and comfortable with the arrangements we had made, we were eventually able to follow this approach consistently. It was particularly the case at Grant Park High School, where there were two extraordinary teachers in the autism program: Ruth Lee Tesky and Bruce Barkwell. Catherine didn't always comply with the plan, however. When to intervene and when to hold back have been among the most difficult judgement calls for us to make over the years. I don't pretend that we always made the right decision.

The staff at Hydra House tried behaviour modification as a treatment, but it simply caused Catherine further anxiety. To this day, if we tell her (or another caregiver does) that she will have a privilege removed if she does or does not do something, her perseveration on the forthcoming penalty will last for days at a time and the intended modification will simply be lost.

Returning Catherine to Hydra House on Sunday evenings was always a nightmare. We had to drag her into the car, and because she tried it several times, we had to be careful that she did not jump out of the car as we were driving. When we arrived at Hydra House, she would often refuse to go into the house. And if she did, she would often hold fast to my leg and not let me leave. Or, she would run out of the house after me and try to hold on to the car. When we were finally able to drive away, more often than not we would be in tears or simply in shock, and certainly always exhausted.

Shortly after Catherine went to live at Hydra House, I asked her if she would be interested in becoming part of the Special Olympics, for which she was eligible because of her mental disability. She had always been interested in exercise. I'd taken her to swimming lessons, taught her skating and cross-country skiing, and often taken her to the Y to run around the track. She could not function in groups, so we restricted her athletic activities to individual ones.

Catherine knew nothing about the Special Olympics but agreed to give it a try. It took the volunteer coaches only a couple of weeks to realize that Catherine was a wonderful runner. Soon they were suggesting that she take part in Special Olympic track meets. We were concerned that she could never cope with such public events. The first such event, held indoors at the University of Manitoba, with hundreds of people in attendance, was indeed traumatic for her, as it was for us. Her coach, bless her, had to run after her four times to get her to the starting line. Thank God, the starting line was on the far side of the track, away from the stands; otherwise I don't think she would ever have competed. She did run that day, however, and, much to her surprise, she won easily. Once the race began, it was as if her ability to be completely focussed on one thing took over, and she was oblivious to the crowd. After the race, she would not go near the podium to receive her medal. At the next meet, several months later, the same scenario occurred: she ran away, I stood outside the women's washroom and begged her to come out and get to the starting line, she ran a wonderful race and had another victory. Again, she would not approach the podium, so the wise and caring officials came over to where the athletes were gathered and gave the medals there. It was several more meets before she could approach the podium, but finally she did, at first with her coach and then, at the summer games, by herself in the University stadium. I was simply ecstatic that day, and as Charlene and I were driving her for a treat at the local Dairy Queen, I remember how surprised Catherine was that we were so excited for her. There was a visiting running coach from the University of Minnesota who saw Catherine at that meet and was reported to have remarked that Catherine had one of the best running styles she had ever seen.

In the fall, Catherine was invited to train four times a week as part of the Medallion program, which was designed for selected athletes to prepare for the national games in Halifax in the summer of 1994. This program was a Manitoba Special Olympics initiative that was originally not taken seriously by the rest of the country. Some of the leaders in the national Special Olympic movement felt that Special Olympic athletes were competing just for fun and therefore would not train seriously over a long period of time and become outstanding athletes. How wrong this view was! An interesting feature of autism is that it sometimes enhances one's ability to focus. Manitoba athletes began to succeed disproportionately at the games, and other provinces have now adopted the Medallion program.

During 1994, the staff at Hydra House drove Catherine all the way from the far north end of the city to the University of Manitoba for her practices two or three times a week. And she trained with me once or twice every week-end when I did my regular workouts. These training sessions were without question the highlights of her week. Charlene and I accompanied her to Halifax with trepidation, worried that Catherine might not be able to cope with the crowds, the noise, the excitement, and the fear of racing against athletes she did not know. We talked to her about winning and losing and doing her best, and about the Special Olympics pledge: "Let me win, but if I cannot win, let me be brave in the attempt." When a young woman from B.C. told her the night before the races, "I'm very good, you know, I've won lots of gold medals," Catherine was distraught. The next morning, the first race was 3,000 metres. Catherine won easily. It was her first gold, but she wasn't focussed on that. She went to the podium, hardly stayed long enough to receive the medal, and generally behaved very inappropriately. Three hours later, in the 800-metre race, she lined up with eight other girls at the starting line, including the "dreaded girl" from B.C., about whom she had talked to us all evening and morning—classic perseveration. When the gun sounded, Catherine took off like a scared rabbit and within 50 metres was looking over her shoulder. When Catherine crossed the finish line, the next runner was just rounding the corner into the stretch. At the podium, when the television cameraman wanted to take her picture, she stuck out her tongue, which provoked more lectures from Charlene, from me, and from her coach about behaving appropriately whether you win or lose. That very same afternoon, she competed in her third event, the high jump, and once again she was the national champion. There was no scene at the podium. The next morning, her fourth event was the 1,500 metres, her favourite. She won in five minutes and 42 seconds, her fourth gold medal. Not only did she behave at the podium, but she even reached out to raise the arms of the other two athletes. We were elated.

Next she led off the Manitoba 4-x-100 relay team. She was ahead after her section and watched as the Manitoba team won the gold, her fifth medal. Her final event was the 4-x-400. Again, she led off and was ahead at the end of her lap. But she was beside herself as one of the other Manitoba runners lost the lead. Catherine ran beside her just off the track, yelling at her to hurry up. Of course, pacing another althlete in that manner was not allowed, so officials ran after Catherine to stop her. The Manitoba team came second. We had to explain to her that Manitoba had in fact been disqualified because of her action and would not even receive the silver medal because Catherine had changed lanes too quickly in her section of the race. This was too complicated for her to understand.

We recall all those successes with a great deal of pride. But I have not forgotten the hours between races when we would take her aside and tried to keep her at peace, focussed, and not worried that others were laughing at her. We would sit on a blanket, usually under the stands, and Charlene would rub her legs or her back.

The morning after the last races, I picked her up at the athletes' residence at Dalhousie University and drove her to our hotel. I tried to impress upon her how much she had achieved. When we entered the hotel and stopped at the little gift shop, the young woman behind the counter looked up and said, "May I see all the medals you're wearing?" Perhaps remembering the B.C. girl, Catherine very quietly said, "I'm the best in Canada, you know." I was overwhelmed with emotion, as I am every time I recall this. It was one of the first occasions in her life that she had ever spoken to a complete stranger in a positive manner.

It was still summer when we returned to Winnipeg, and, as usual, we went to the cottage on weekends. Catherine decided that she could learn her times tables: 2 times 2 equals 4, 6 times 5 equals 30, and so on. For three weekends in a row Charlene and I did nothing but practise times tables with Catherine while we fished for hours in our boat. I think the fish were so in awe that they did not disturb us because, at the end of three weekends, Catherine, who before that could not add 2 plus 2, knew the entire times table! She, who had always hated school, told us she could hardly wait to get back! Her self-confidence grew by leaps and bounds that summer.

After careful consideration, we agreed that Catherine could train for the 1995 World Special Olympic games to be held in New Haven, Connecticut. The coach, a woman from Edmonton, was to accompany her to New Haven. We made arrangements for her to come to Winnipeg and spend a weekend at our home so that Catherine could meet her before travelling with her to the meet. Charlene and I made plans to drive to New Haven, while Catherine flew with the team. This was to be a huge event. An article in *U.S.A. Today* listed Catherine as one of the favourites in her events.

When we arrived in New Haven, we were greeted very warmly by Steve and Mary Lou Mayo, friends from our graduate school days in New York. We have kept in close touch with them since graduate school. Steve and Mary Lou invited us to stay at their summer house, about an hour north of New Haven, during the games. We laughed and shared stories as if graduate school days had been just the previous year, not 13 years earlier. Their offer to share their cottage with us turned out to be a lifesaver.

We also saw Grant Walker and his wife, Jean, while we were in New Haven. Back in 1968, the week after both of us had completed our master's degrees at Fordham University, Grant and I hitchhiked together from New York to New Orleans. Among the people who gave us rides along the way were a man drinking while he was driving his Cadillac, a man with a loaded gun who was trying to explain to Grant what the term *calibre* meant, and two women who wanted us to sleep with them because they were mad at their boyfriends. At that time, I was still in the Franciscans, and before I could open my mouth Grant gleefully informed the women of that fact. They behaved appropriately after that, and we had some hilarious discussions, as well as some serious ones, along the way. That ride came about an hour after we had been unceremoniously dropped off on a freeway in the middle of nowhere in Georgia because Grant had told the driver that he was opposed to the war in Vietnam. It was the last time in my life I ever hitchhiked. A little over a year later, I presided at Grant and Jean's wedding Mass on Long Island. Grant had been at another wedding the year before our hitchhiking trip, had seen Jean for the first time across the room and stated to his friend that she was the woman he was going to marry. Indeed she was.

These two wonderful couples came to the Special Olympic opening ceremonies with us and supported us through our anxieties about what was coming. The opening ceremonies were held in the Yale Bowl; it was the largest sporting event in the world that year and attracted over 70,000 people, including

President Clinton. With our binoculars, we could see Catherine enter the stadium along with the 7,200 other athletes from 149 countries. We could not believe that she was holding up.

Her team had not got to bed until almost 2:00 a.m., yet she was on the track at 9:00 a.m. for her first heat. Over the next five days, she ran in three heats and three final races. Her success on the track was extraordinary; she came third in the world in three events: the 3,000-, the 1,500- and the 800-metre races. The Special Olympics has a respectful, humane way of classifying athletes. Once they have passed the preliminaries, they are classed by ability and so are never required to compete against others who have widely different abilities. In all three of Catherine's events, she was classified in the top group. The two women who beat her were from Ukraine and Greece, and both were over 25, while Catherine was only 17. She did not see it that way, however. In her mind, you either win or lose and nothing we said could convince her otherwise. Her behaviour off the track was certainly problematic. She would run away, create a scene on the podium, and be generally uncooperative. Instead of accepting her behaviour as evidence of her autism, the two Team Canada coaches viewed it as the bad behaviour of a spoilt child. They wanted to send her home in the middle of the meet but compromised when we suggested that she stay with us at Steve and Mary Lou's cottage rather than at the athlete's compound. We, not the coaches, would care for her every minute that she was not racing. It was a week of hell. After our return to Winnipeg, we wrote a letter to the national office outlining the poor treatment to which Catherine, Charlene, and I were subjected. The Manitoba committee fought for us, and the national office eventually made some changes in the procedures for choosing coaches, such as that choaches would know the disabilities of their athletes better and be able to adjust to the disabilities.

Should Catherine have gone to New Haven? It certainly was

my input more than Charlene's that led us to support the idea. We certainly could not go through the tension again. But should we have done it in the first place?

Global Television in Winnipeg sent a producer and cameraman to New Haven to film the four Manitoba athletes who were competing in the games, including Catherine. Their half-hour production was a thoughtful, understanding, and accurate portrayal of how these four young women approached the games in such different ways. The film captured the tensions and the dilemma perfectly. By contrasting the perfectly coordinated but angry Catherine with another Manitoba athlete who was not as well coordinated but simply thrilled to be there, they showed not only how difficult it is for people with disabilities to live active lives but also how inspiring their efforts can be to others. I thought it was a powerful educational film.

In the 1995–1996 school year, Catherine was asked to train with the "regular" Grant Park Senior High School girls' track and field team; they were the same girls whom she was always afraid were laughing at her. But these girls soon began to realize that Catherine was a great asset to their team, and they started giving her special attention, which helped a great deal in enhancing Catherine's confidence. The transition to running against stronger competition from across the whole city—that is, outside the "shelter" of the Special Olympics structure—did not come easily for her. She did not always win, and she had to learn not to run away and create a scene when she did not. Her coach was Jeff Collins, a man of immense patience and insight, and a true friend to Catherine. Once, she came second in the whole city, other times she came fifth, and other times she was farther behind. But she was proud to be running with the "regular" girls. Near the end of the track season in the 1995–1996 year, she came third in the provincial cross-country race, was once named Female High School Athlete of the Week for the whole city, and helped her track team secure a place as one of the top schools in the city. To cap off the year, she was voted by all the coaches at Grant Park as Female Athlete of the Year. When she was coming back to her seat after receiving the award, I watched some of the other students and was touched by the many who seemed pleased that she had won. As we headed for the car after the ceremony, she opened her envelope and found a cheque for $100. "I could buy a car now, Dad!" she exclaimed.

She now felt that it was better to come third in "regular" competition than to be first in a Special Olympics competition. She liked to feel "normal." Recently she told me how hard things were for her. "I'm in-between, Dad. Sometimes people think I am so smart that I should be able to do everything. Sometimes, they think I'm retarded. If I was really, really low functioning, people would not have expectations of me. But now they expect too much. I can be high functioning in some things, but not in others. It's really hard."

I was, of course, extremely proud of her accomplishments. At first, when I told family and friends how proud of her I was, she would get annoyed and tell me to stop. I made a scrapbook of her successes, but she didn't ever show interest in it or in the pictures of her that appeared in various publications. A number of times I found that she had garbaged her medals after moments of anger, so I took to hiding them from her. What we would see as an organized list of her accomplishments in the scrapbook she probably saw as a cluttered page. No pictures, even of herself, had survived on a wall through the whole house more than a couple of weeks. She is much more comfortable with the clean, uncluttered look than she is with pictures on walls.

One of the joys that Special Olympic coaches can experience is witnessing the sheer excitement and satisfaction that some of the athletes express from simply being in the race. Catherine never gave them that joy. Hard as we all tried to help her understand the

Special Olympics pledge, we had uneven success. But Jeff Collins and the other Manitoba Special Olympics coaches never gave up on her, in spite of what would look to uninformed people like sheer rudeness. They understood her disability, worked with her, and accepted her as she is. It would be impossible to put a price on the dedicated and unselfish work of these people, who work as unpaid volunteers week after week, year after year.

The Special Olympics experience (1992 to 1996) was invaluable for Catherine. Without it, she would never have had those many evenings of training to which she so looked forward. The training sessions were for years the highlight of her week. She would never have gone on to make friends with the "regular" Grant Park girls, whom she began to believe when they told her that they needed her on their team in order to win. She probably would not own a treadmill, which she now uses regularly. She probably would not use running as a way to work off her high levels of stress. Exercise is a key component of her life, as is her concern for eating nutritious food. Over time, she has slowly begun to understand and appreciate her athletic accomplishments. Several years ago, when we met a new couple, Catherine whispered to me, "Dad, tell them about my running." And, just recently, as I walked through the front door of our home, to my great surprise, hanging in place of one of our paintings was a picture of Catherine doing warm-ups in her track suit. It had appeared in *The Winnipeg Free Press* in 1995, and we had had it framed. But she had not wanted it taken out of her drawer. Of course we have left the picture of her there. Indeed, her experience in the Special Olympics gave her a sense of achievement and confidence that nothing else in her life has.

Although Catherine is not competing any more, I continue to attend as many Special Olympic functions as I can and serve on the honorary board. I have told Catherine's story at a number of functions, including golf tournaments, the Law Enforcement

Torch Run Kick-Off, and at the annual dinners of corporations that sponsor the Special Olympics. At these dinners I always seek out sponsors, coaches, and the prominent athletes who attract people to these events and talk to them about Catherine. I stress the value of the Special Olympics, and, as a parent, I thank them for their contributions. I have also been working to set up an endowment fund for the Special Olympics. In order to run the programs in Manitoba alone, the organization has to raise over a million dollars a year.

The first time we watched the video that we took of Catherine's races in New Haven, I could hear myself on the tape, yelling out to her as she passed us, telling her that she was doing really well and to keep it up. Charlene told me she loved those taped sounds, and Catherine, rather reluctantly, admitted that she did hear me. So I have ceased to be embarrassed about it.

Catherine's Special Olympics experience did not consume all of her thoughts or energies, nor does it explain all of her successes and setbacks. But her achievements there were the first major successes in her life, and the benefits will be with her for the rest of her life.

Two events in early 1996 profoundly affected Catherine: Charlene suffered a stroke in February, and just a month later, Catherine turned 18 and had to change residences. It took us two days to recognize the severity of Charlene's symptoms. She has always downplayed any illnesses that she suffered. She would never miss classes, even when she was miserable with the flu, for example, on the grounds that one day she "might *really* be sick." Her mother was with us when the stroke occurred. It happened after dinner on a Friday evening, but not knowing what it was, and not wanting to worry her mother, she *ordered* me not to say anything and simply lay down to rest. The symptoms got worse, however, and on Saturday morning we called a doctor. He thought, as did we, that the medicine he had prescribed earlier for another reason was causing a reaction and prescribed a different one. By Sunday morning she was even more ill, and I took her to the St. Boniface Hospital emergency ward, where she was admitted and where she stayed for 12 days. The paralysis in her face disappeared quickly, but a number of other symptoms lingered. One of the most serious was the loss of her short-term memory. Dr. Choptiany explained that her "starter" was malfunctioning. She still cannot remember what she did yesterday, but if her memory is "triggered," often by me, she can recall events quite clearly. Without doubt, however, the most serious consequence is her inability to organize her thoughts or her day. This has been a source of deep and lasting frustration for her. Preparing a meal for guests is out of the question. "Even if I write things down," she says, "I can't keep them organized in my mind." "I don't know what to do next, anxiety sets in, and I become unable to proceed." This is a woman who was a very fine teacher and an excellent listener; she was loved by her students. She could quickly grasp the meaning of their questions and respond appropriately. She carried out her research, chaired the honours program, and was elected by the University Senate to serve on the Board of Regents. She was also a key contributor on a committee in the city composed primarily of psychiatrists, psychologists, and social workers dealing with adolescent mental health, where she was invited to give the keynote address at one of their annual meetings. She handled all these responsibilities while at the same time dealing every day with the serious disabilities of our two children. The stroke clearly was not as severe as it might have been, but it was severe enough to profoundly affect her and our whole family.

When the stroke occurred, I had little time to reflect upon what was happening. Charlene's mother, Kitty, stayed with us for almost two months to help out. I was still dean, having just begun my second term and trying to rebuild the Faculty of Arts in the aftermath of an academic strike that had lasted 23 days. Catherine was still coming home every weekend. Vincent was in and out of jail or the remand centre. When he was incarcerated, he would call us every day. When he was out, most of the time we did not know where he was. Charlene was incredibly tired.

By June, Charlene agreed with me that a three-week holiday on the west coast would be beneficial, so off we went. We stopped at Robin and Irene's home on Salt Spring Island for three days, then headed up Vancouver Island to Tofino, Qualicum Beach, and Campbell River. The first two weeks were marvellous, but, as we headed toward Campbell River, our lives were shattered again. While we were at an art gallery near Comox, Charlene told me that suddenly she could not see and felt terribly confused. I rushed her to the hospital there and found that she had suffered a transient ischemic attack, an event with all the symptoms of a stroke but without the long-term consequences. We were advised to return to Vancouver, closer to a large hospital, and so we spent a quiet, but somewhat tense week there with my cousin Kathie and husband, Merv, who were very supportive. When we returned to Winnipeg, we spent as much time at the cottage as we could. Charlene felt terribly weak and ill. Later she told me that she thought she was going to die and had come to terms with it.

But Catherine's life was also progressing. She was now 18, and, as soon as new space could be found, she was expected to leave the Hydra House location in the North End (which was geared for adolescents) and enter an adult facility. Hydra House had decided to open a new home closer to our area that would accommodate several young adults, and Catherine was to be one of them. She could hardly wait. I helped interview some of the potential staff members. But the result was not at all satisfactory. The staff members who were hired knew nothing about autism and had to learn on the job. The first house director quit within a couple of months, and her replacement knew no more than she. Catherine lasted less than a year there, and it was a terribly unhappy time for her. We decided to move her to a non-profit agency called New Directions. It was a wise decision.† Charlene had been on the New Directions board of directors but had had to leave after her stroke. I then joined for a six-year term and found the agency to be rigorous in its staff training, transparent in its finances, and highly committed to cultural competency. The agency found a home for Catherine with a family who had a two-year-old daughter, a grandfather, and a young man with autism. Things were looking up.

In early August of the year of Charlene's stroke, 1996, we faced two more crises. My brother John, who the year before had been diagnosed with pulmonary fibrosis and had had to retire from the ministry, could no longer look after himself in his apartment. He had moved in with us for the summer. He was on oxygen permanently and was going back and forth to Riverview, a palliative-care facility, where he had taken up residency in September. He died in December.

In that meantime, Charlene was still recuperating from the stroke that she'd had in February. She was depressed, a common occurrence following a stroke. The nature of the blood clots in her leg suggested the possibility of cancer, and by mid-August she had seen Dr. Ian Maxwell, a haematologist, who had sent her for a CAT scan and other tests for cancer. The tests revealed a possible ovarian tumour, and Charlene now faced surgery, which was to be performed by an obstetrician-gynaecologist. She was put on a waiting list and informed that it might be October before she could have the surgery. I decided on a second opinion and consulted Dr. Haywood, a cancer specialist. We went to see him on a

---

† *In 2006, Hydra House was shut down by the provincial government for financial irregularities.*

Thursday, and he operated the following Monday, when he removed a malignant tumour the size of a grapefruit. We discovered later just how serious ovarian cancer can be and how low the survival rate is if not diagnosed early. We were among the fortunate. Charlene has not had a recurrence of cancer for 12 years. There are still some concerns, however. I'd like to believe that all the pains in her leg from the clots would disappear and that the potential for a further stroke would be reduced. But I cannot get such assurances from her doctors.

John's funeral was held on the 23rd of December. I felt at the peak of emotional exhaustion. But I was not to be relieved. Early in the following year, 1997, Catherine's supportive environment collapsed. The couple that she lived with found out that their little daughter had leukemia, the grandfather had suddenly had a stroke, and the situation was too much for them. So Catherine had to move again, and this time it was with absolutely no notice. She was placed in an apartment with a single woman in her 30s who worked for New Directions and has an excellent understanding of autism.

Even at the best of times, small changes require difficult adjustments for people with autism. I truly felt sorry for Catherine. Adults in our society tend to move frequently; separation, divorce, or a breakup with a live-in partner are common events as we strive to find loving or at least compatible relationships. How hard it must be for those who have little or no say in the living arrangements that are imposed on them. In fact, the term often heard in social work circles is *placement*. What would it be like to be "placed" in a living situation? And with virtually no notice? Catherine lived in this new situation for a little over two years. Her crises became less frequent than they had been, but she remained almost perpetually angry. Nevertheless, she was developing good life skills and a sense of independence. By the middle of 2001, when she was 23, by mutual agreement among Catherine, her caregiver, and the social worker at New Directions, Catherine moved again. This time, we had time to plan the move and to involve Catherine in the decision. She had several preliminary visits with one prospective couple and amazed us with her no-nonsense interviewing skills. She would ask, for example, "Are you so strict you won't be able to accept my disability?" and "How do I know you're not serial killers?" Catherine felt that she was somewhat in charge of the decision and that her social worker at New Directions would look elsewhere if Catherine herself did not feel comfortable with a prospective home. The outcome was beyond our wildest expectations: she enjoyed her new home. I think it was after only the second week living with them that Catherine came for the weekend wearing some of her caregiver's clothes.

We were stunned when about a year later we were suddenly informed that Catherine would have to leave. Having a person with autism in their midst was becoming too stressful for the family. We were told on a Friday evening that the family would not take her back after her normal weekend with us. Monday, when we had to give her this information in the social worker's office, was one of the hardest days of our lives. Here was another abrupt change with no notice. Catherine kicked and screamed: "Nobody wants me. You don't want me, and now they don't. Why can't I go back? What did I do wrong? I'll change." She stayed with us for close to a month while her social worker looked for another place for her, and we all agreed that it was inhumane to allow her to be uprooted so suddenly. We vowed to do everything we could never to let it happen again. One suitable and eager couple was found, but, after several preliminary interviews, Catherine decided that she could not go there. We agreed with her decision.

And so, the search began again. After several weeks, another living situation was found. This one worked well for close to two years, but, once again, the caregiver suffered burnout, and we had to find another place. Catherine was once again distraught, blamed herself, and felt abandoned. She has been in her current foster home for over two years now, and we are cautiously optimistic. But she does not like the fact that we get along very well with her caregivers. She seems to want to create a wedge between us, while what we want is to create a mutually reinforcing network of support for her.

She continues to come to us every weekend, for several weeks in the summers, and at Christmastime. Recently, after Catherine had been staying with us for a few extra days after a weekend because she was feeling ill, Charlene asked her if she was feeling any better. She was quiet for a moment and then said, "Mom, the love in this house heals me." On her birthday in March of 2005, rather than go out to a restaurant, she wanted me to cook all the dishes she loves. As we sat at dinner and talked about her adoption, her birth mother, and other such topics, she said, "I'm sure glad I met you guys." I can find no words to express my gratitude.

Catherine has made remarkable progress over the last few years. There is no single factor to account for the change, but several are important. One was the arrival of Jolaine MacDougall into our lives. In February of 1997, I put an ad in *The Manitoban*, the University of Manitoba student newspaper, looking for a student who would go out from time to time with "a high-functioning autistic 19-year-old woman who loves running, skating, skiing, and movies." Jolaine was a first-year student in human ecology when she saw the ad and responded. The first time she came back to our home after going out with Catherine, I knew we had struck gold. She did not ask Katie (the name Catherine now prefers) if she'd had a good time. She simply said, "Thanks, Katie. I had a really good time." Her values were very close to ours. When Jolaine began accompanying

Katie on outings, Katie, though almost 20, was in some turmoil about teenage issues, and Jolaine's grasp of the problems and her advice were remarkably insightful. Thanks to Jolaine, who had majored in human ecology, good nutrition has become an important part of Katie's thinking. Throughout her four years at university, Jolaine was faithful in taking Katie out somewhere almost every weekend. Even when she began working in Banff in the summers, she would call, write, and send pictures. Katie had found a true friend.

Sometimes, however, Katie is unable to appreciate friendship and behaves ungraciously. But this has never influenced Jolaine's attitude or behaviour. Jolaine would sometimes take Katie to her own home, where to this day she is warmly welcomed. Often they would just "hang out" there. Jolaine's mother and father, Joe and Elaine, have also been good friends. Jolaine's sister, Colleen, who was in Grade 11 when Jolaine responded to my ad, also took to Katie and shares activities with her to this day, even though she has finished university and is working in the community. The consistency of her attention to Katie, her good humour, and her friendship merit the term *extraordinary*. When Colleen travelled to Asia last year, she called Katie from Vietnam to wish her a happy birthday. Recently I tried to thank Joe for all he and his family have done for Katie. "Not at all," he responded. "Katie has taught our whole family so much. We love her."

"When you volunteer," John Ralston Saul has said, "you are at your best as a human being." Jolaine and Colleen have often gone out together with Katie, and sometimes they have invited their own girlfriends and boyfriends along. Not only was the actual time they spent with Katie precious, but also the expectation of the visit (they always call a day or two ahead) and the period of peace after their outing was beneficial to Katie and a blessing for us. Jolaine moved to Alberta in 2004 with her husband, and Colleen followed suit in 2007. This has been a devastating loss for Katie.

Charlene, Katie, and I travelled to Alberta in the summer of 2007 to visit Jolaine, her husband, Kevin, and their two children. Jolaine's response to my letter thanking them for their hospitality was: "It was so wonderful for you to make the trip out and I loved spending all that time with Katie as it hasn't been frequent enough. She is such a playful, hilarious and beautiful woman. I love spending time with her." How could we have been so fortunate! "One of the good things about being in need," Charlene said one day, "is that you meet such wonderful people."

Another factor relating to Katie's progress was the medication she has been taking. Temple Grandin, the accomplished author and university professor with autism, told a group of parents with children with autism that she was 28 before she found the right combination of medicines. Katie has tried probably a dozen different combinations to control the depression, anxiety, and perseveration, trying to find an effective one that doesn't have medical side effects. While we are not yet totally satisfied (the side effects include weight gain), the combination of medicines that she is taking right now is the best she has yet experienced.

Yet another factor in Katie's progress was the autism program at Grant Park, where she had some wonderful, caring teachers, including Barb Ivans, Ruth Lee Tesky, and Bruce Barkwell. Shirley Anderson, a teacher's aide, also loved Katie and was wonderfully good to her. When I say that she loved Katie, I truly mean the term *love*. Our daughter can spot immediately whether someone is simply doing a job or really cares for her, and her response is easy to read. Special-education teachers have a special vocation to carry out the work that they do, and I am not sure that the general public has a sense of how dedicated, competent, and loving they are.

There are long periods of time when Katie can best be described as an angry young woman. There are other significant periods when she simply has angry spells. Nothing we do seems the right thing to break these spells. When she is upset now, she runs away from a situation far less frequently than she did in the past. However, Charlene feels that Katie's life has been difficult, particularly her years at Hydra House, and that it is important for her to be able to verbalize her anger.

Katie graduated from Grant Park High School at 21 and remains under the care of New Directions. She is part of a program that is geared to help her eventually hold a job. She has had job experience at Petland, washing cars at Mid-Town Ford, and cleaning at Value Village, usually with a young man in the program and a supervisor for the two of them. She has delivered flyers to homes, and the directors of her program say she is better at it than anyone else. Other possibilities for the future include working with the Humane Society or perhaps doing lawn maintenance.

After more than a year of support and encouragement in her mid-20s, she learned to take the bus by herself, in spite of her fear that anyone looking in her direction is really staring and laughing at her. "I look out the window, Dad, and just ignore them." A huge accomplishment, I like to think, not unlike that of getting a college degree is for "normal" people. Learning to ride the bus has given her great independence, but, to our constant worry, she sometimes doesn't behave safely or responsibly. She also has learned how to manage her bank account and use a bank machine.

She now loves to shop on her own, especially in the ubiquitous "dollar" stores. In many ways, Katie's disability might be called a "hidden disability." Those who first meet her might not realize that she has a disability. However, her behaviour eventually gives her away. When she is shopping, Katie will pick things up, examine them for long periods of time and even sniff them, and spend time watching the people around her. (A very common characteristic for people with autism is a tendency to want to know what everything smells like.) An hour or two looking around in one store is not an unusually long period of time for her. These behaviours draw attention to herself and cause suspicion. On several occasions she has been accused of stealing or asked to leave. Recently, she called us on her cell phone from a bathroom in a mall, terribly upset because a clerk thought she'd been acting suspiciously. "I don't steal, Dad. I would never do that. I always put my bags at the front of the store when I enter." The clerk did not accuse Katie but told her that her behaviour was causing her (the clerk) concern because it looked as if she was about to steal. To her credit, the clerk did not ask Katie to leave the store. Instead, she suggested that Katie change her behaviour so that she didn't look suspicious. Katie said to me, "Dad, I can't just change my behaviour like that. It would change my personality."

Katie's slowness to make a decision is pervasive. She has her own rhythm, which I, for one, find extremely frusrating. If we go to a Tim Hortons, for example, I encourage Katie to decide what she wants to buy before we even enter. All to no avail. It always takes her an excessive amount of time to order, and line-ups grow long behind us. I sense the frustration and sometimes hear the murmurs of the people in the lineups. If I try to speed her up, or if anyone else does, she becomes emotionally paralyzed, and the decision is delayed even more.

One of the characteristics of Asperger syndrome is developmental delay. Katie at 29 is still developing, and we still see enormous growth in her abilities. Thank God she is not locked away. We are happy that she can now function on her own in the community, as do many others who have relatively hidden disabilities. We expect that she will continue learning how to manage. I just wish that more clerks and others who serve customers, as well as those who wait in line, would be a little less quick to judge and understand that those who are slower may not be just dawdling; they may simply be unable to move more quickly. When I wrote some of these thoughts in a recent article published by *The Globe and Mail,* the editor chose a most appropriate headline:

"To take your time is not a crime." I am constantly having to remind myself of that very view!

I didn't have the privilege of giving Katie a hug until she was almost 19. In fact, it seemed that the person who mattered most in her life was Charlene. I was able to live with that, hard as it was, because I knew that Charlene had profound insights into Katie's life and has always been an incredible listener, indeed the best listener I have ever met. Almost all young children seem to gravitate to her as if she were a magnet. Katie will allow Charlene to rub her back and her legs by the hour. The massage is soothing, and one can almost see Katie's anxiety dissipate as she and Charlene discuss all kinds of issues at the same time.

I am now, thankfully, much more a part of the equation. Perhaps it was simply a result of maturation on Katie's part, perhaps it was a consequence of Charlene's stroke, or perhaps it was because Charlene had had to spend a good deal of time in Kentucky to care for her dying mother in 2000. Katie continues to astound me with her special insights and her newly learned thoughtfulness; thoughtfulness is so difficult for those with autism. One year, when we "bargained" that I could watch the second half of a Super Bowl game, she sat down with me to watch it and said, "You know, I should learn something about football so that I could enjoy it with you. I can't always watch just what I want." This was a step forward, indeed. But the struggle is constant, nevertheless. It is compounded by her stated view that I just don't understand her. I am too fast, too impatient, and too loud, and that's why she is much closer to Charlene than to me. Besides, I'm a terrible tease, and teasing is hard for Katie to understand. It's true that our personalities often do not mesh with those of our children, and it's possible that adopted children feel this more profoundly than biological children do. I may not be the best father, but I am the only one she has, adoptive or not!

The absence of a mental filter in people with autism can lead them to say things that others would not say; it can also have a positive effect. Katie's first experience with death was my mother's, when Katie was 12. At the funeral, Katie walked around the casket several times but said little. Several years later, Ruth Lee Tesky, her wonderful teacher at Grant Park High School, suddenly died of a brain tumour. About the same time, we had taken Katie to see Kitty in Kentucky before her terminal illness became too advanced, and again for her funeral in 2003. In this context, Katie fears that Charlene will have another stroke and die. When we were talking about what would happen to the cottage after Charlene and I died, Catherine looked me in the eye. "Dad," she said very deliberately, "please don't die soon. I would much rather have you than the cottage."

Vincent: Heartbreaks and Hope

The parable of the prodigal son is one of the most touching stories of the Christian Scriptures (Luke 15:6–32; for those not familiar with the details of the parable, I have reprinted it in the appendix). In June of 2000, as we were preparing for a cruise to the capitals of northern Europe, including St. Petersburg, we were looking forward to seeing Rembrandt's painting *The Return of the Prodigal Son,* which is in the Hermitage Museum. My sister, Maureen, brought to our attention the book by the same title written by theologian Henri Nouwen.[4] Nouwen had spent four hours on two separate days observing the painting, and subtitled his reflections *A Meditation on Fathers, Brothers, and Sons.* The book had brought alive for me both the painting and the parable itself. Our level of anticipation was high, as, in addition to reading Nouwen's book, we had looked at a number of Rembrandt's reproductions in our books on art and had read a brief story of his tragic life, filled as it was with the death of many of his children and his wife. As well, on board ship prior to arriving in St. Petersburg, we had gone to an illustrated lecture on Rembrandt's paintings by a medical doctor from Palm Springs, Florida, Dr. Leonard Girsh, who has spent his free time during his medical career fascinated by the 200 of Rembrandt's 700 paintings that are on biblical themes.

Our encounter with the painting was sudden. As we moved from room to room in the museum, we came upon a magnificent stairway that our guide wanted to comment upon. Charlene and I both turned around to get a sense of the setting, and there, through the doorway, we saw Rembrandt's masterpiece. It is situated at one end of a room, which we later realized contained 29 of his paintings. The canvas is larger than life and is mounted on one of four panels that each protrude from an exterior wall and extend more than half way across the room. The result is that, upon first entering the room, one can see only the first panel, which is the painting of *The Return of the Prodigal Son.* A guided tour allows only fleeting moments to view each painting, but we managed to sneak back twice to observe it again. But even our brief encounter with it has left a lasting impression. On our return to London, we visited the National Gallery and spent most of our time in the room dedicated to the 19 paintings by Rembrandt. When we returned home, I began Nouwen's book again, this time reading it aloud to Charlene. Never have I had the experience of a painting and a book together bringing alive a parable of the gospel.

The ending of the parable is so perfect that all the suffering and patience of the father seems like nothing in light of the outcome. But I wonder whether that father, were the parable a modern-day parable, would have talked to others about his son while he was still in the "far-away country." Would he have spoken to his extended family, to his friends, even to a counsellor, for advice and support for himself? This is the question I ask myself as I think about the expectations we had, the dashed hopes, the sadness, the anxiety—and, yes, the anger and fear—but, above all, the uncertainty about how to communicate the love that characterizes my relationship with our son, Vincent.

I have just referred to the prodigal son, whose father welcomed him home after his absence, and I would have wanted to act as the father in the parable did. But our story with Vincent (so far, at least) hasn't turned out the way the parable did. Several years ago we had to ask for and received from the court a protection order, which forbade any direct or indirect contact among the four of us. Our goal is certainly not to disown Vincent, and we don't for a moment want him to think so. The order was necessary for our protection. Yet the law seems to be crafted for situations in which the desired outcome is indeed the end of the relationship. In fact, we found that we could not live with the first court order and went back to court to have it modified so that we can now see him and hug him, but our interactions are restricted to places other than our home, cottage, or workplace.

It was excruciatingly painful to have to provide the judge with all the reasons supporting our plea for such an order. Ours was not a petition coming out of revenge or vindication. In fact, the first time we appeared, I felt that the judge was trying to pry out of me things that I would have to manufacture, things that would make her think that the relationship was worse than it really was. She seemed to wonder why, if I would not describe our relationship as all bad, we needed a protection order. The bottom line was that we did not feel safe in our own home, probably the reason for most protection orders.

How could things have gone so wrong? What could we, should we, have done differently? I ask these questions not because I am ridden with guilt but because I am not at peace with having acted in a way that seems so different from how the father in the parabale did. Was the father ever at peace while the prodigal son was still in the "far-away country"? Was he powerless to help his son, and did he simply have to wait, to be available for the son when he finally came to the realization on his own that he needed to change? My answer is that I am prepared to wait, and with the inspiration of the parable in my mind, to live in hope.

One of the most remarkable aspects of Henri Nouwen's book is that at first he sees himself as the prodigal son, then as the elder son, and finally as the father. As I recount the events in our own family, I realize that I had been perceiving Vincent to be the prodigal son. Much as his behaviour has hurt me, however, I now feel that designating him as the prodigal son is not accurate. In fact, I think it violates the message of the parable to look at him as the guilty son and myself as the suffering father. The perception assumes intentional misbehaviour on the part of the son, and judgements and an expectation of a request for forgiveness on the part of the father. It ignores the pervasiveness of Vincent's disability.

It is astounding to us how much assistance is available for Katie now that she has been diagnosed with Asperger syndrome. However, in Vincent's case, there has been little societal support. He suffers from attention-deficit and hyperactivity disorder (ADHD) and foetal alcohol spectrum disorder (FASD).† FASD is the most frequent source of disability at birth in our society, yet substantial research in the area has begun even more recently than in the case of autism; it dates only from the 1990s. Societies come only gradually to an understanding of their members' disabilities, and it takes even more time when discrimination is a factor. FASD crosses the boundaries of ethnic groups and social-class categories. However, I think that the public perception is that it is more prevalent in Aboriginal communities. Poverty erodes privacy, but it also marginalizes the diseases of those living in that state. I think this is a partial explanation for the slow uptake of

† *Foetal alcohol spectrum disorder (FASD) "is an umbrella term describing the range of effects that can occur in an individual whose mother drank alcohol during pregnancy. These effects may include physical, mental, behavioural, and learning disabilities with lifelong implications" [Albert E. Chudley, Julianne Conry, Jocelynn L. Cook, Christine Loock, Ted Rosales, and Nicole LeBlanc, "Fetal Alcohol Spectrum Disorder: Canadian Guidelines for Diagnosis,"* Canadian Medical Association Journal, *1 March 2005: 172 (5 suppl).] These are the first Canadian guidelines for the diagnosis of FASD and its related disabilities.*

research in this area. Yet, the social implications of this disability are far reaching and all the more tragic because the disability is preventable. On one of numerous occasions while sitting in a court room, I was stunned by Vincent's arrival, not only in handcuffs but also with shackles on his feet. His small steps and unavoidable shuffle, with guards at each side, is symbolic of the constraints of his whole life, imposed both because he is Aboriginal and has FASD.

Vincent to this day has the most wonderful smile and contagious laugh, and has always been extremely active. In fact, during our year in Berkeley when Vincent was two years old, a neighbour whose six-year-old son had ADHD suggested to us that Vincent had many of the classic symptoms. We did not see it, nor did we follow up on the suggestion. Later we realized that Vincent had also had most of the symptoms of FASD, but we were unaware of them at the time.

Once we were back in Winnipeg after my research/study leave, Charlene thoroughly enjoyed taking Vincent back and forth to daycare at the University of Winnipeg when she went there to work. When Vincent began school in French immersion, he did not seem to find the situation overwhelming, though he did require constant attention so that he would get his homework done, which didn't seem all that unusual to us. While he was in daycare, preschool, and during the first few years in elementary school, he seemed to have few problems, and he made friends easily. The symptoms of his ADHD and FASD advanced slowly, but because we were dealing with the issues every day we were less conscious of the real progression in gravity.

In my mind, the serious manifestations began in 1986, when he was in Grade 4. One day at 3:30 in the afternoon, just as his school was letting out, I got an emergency call at the University. I was due to start a meeting at 4:00, when a group of academics would be arriving from the Bannatyne campus downtown to continue the review of the School of Medical Rehabilitation. I had been asked by the vice-president to chair the meeting. I was informed on the telephone that the principal was having to physically restrain Vincent because he wanted to hit another boy and that I was to go to the school immediately. When I picked Vincent up, he was sufficiently embarrassed by the commotion that he remained subdued, and I was able to leave him with Mary Vollrath, who was home with Catherine. I returned to the University in time to start my meeting about 15 minutes late. Charlene rushed home from the University of Winnipeg and took over from Mary. The inconvenience to me is not the main point of this story. It simply illustrates the high level of stress that was now permeating our family on a regular basis. We simply could not predict, day or night, when a crisis would occur. This event marked a new level in Vincent's inability to control his own impulses.

Up until Vincent was in Grade 6, we offered him any number of opportunities to become involved in activities appropriate to his age, which we hoped would expend his enormous bank of energy. Swimming, skating, and skiing were the first. I then took lessons in coaching soccer and had great fun trying to teach Vincent and his teammates not to chase the ball like a swarm of bees. He was particularly good at baseball and water-skiing. Water-skiing, however, presented a particular challenge. One Christmas, we felt he was almost far enough along in his swimming to be able to try water-skiing. We were prepared to buy skis for him as long as he completed one more set of lessons, in which he was already enrolled. But, one evening at the very beginning of December, just three weeks before the end of the course, he decided that he did not want to go to his lesson. He wanted instead to just hang out with a friend. Sitting on the side of Vincent's bed, where he was sobbing uncontrollably, I tried to convince him that he would not get water skis for Christmas if he did not pass the course. All to no avail. I went down to the basement, brought up the brand-new water skis that we had purchased, and told him that if he did not go to the class, I would return the skis to the store the next day. He knew that I meant what I'd said, and he was so taken by the colourful skis that we went off to the swimming lesson without further incident. He passed the course three weeks later. For several summers, every weekend we went up and down Netley Creek in our boat while he did all kinds of tricks and fancy skiing behind us. This story illustrates his difficulty in delaying gratification and highlights the impulsive behaviour typically associated with his set of disabilities.

One evening, while watching a movie at a friend's home, he called to ask permission to come in fifteen minutes late because the movie they had rented was not yet over. "That's just fine," I said, and praised him for calling to ask permission. An hour later he still was not home. I headed out in the car and found him walking to the video store with his friends to return the movie. They had asked him to come along, and he simply was not able to say no; his wish to be with his friends was at the moment more important than his responsibility to be home on time. This may not sound like an unusual occurrence for a young boy, but when such incidents are multiplied to include almost every situation, there is clearly a big problem.

This occurred about the same time as the incident at school when the principal phoned to say that Vincent was out of control. One evening later in the same week, Vincent got extremely angry at the dinner table and was about to hit Catherine. I quickly restrained him, and Charlene called an ambulance to take him to the hospital. By now, this was a scenario that we were prepared for, and we made the decision quickly. Dr. Margolis, our family doctor, met us at the hospital and referred us to Dr. Raymond Atkinson, a child psychiatrist, who quickly diagnosed Vincent with ADHD. As a family we saw Dr. Atkinson almost every Friday afternoon for close to two years. We tried giving Vincent Ritilin, the standard treatment for ADHD, but he had a negative reaction to it, so we tried restricting his sugar intake. We made a concerted effort to eliminate all sugar from his diet, with considerable success for two years. It was a very difficult diet for Vincent to follow, so we rewarded him by allowing him to go to a movie with one of his friends once a week. After two years, however, he refused to follow the diet.

Vincent was now 11. He surprised us one day by announcing that the following Saturday he wanted to take a girl from his school to the movie. The next Saturday afternoon he and I went to the girl's home to pick her up. I waited in the living room for her and was astounded to see this 11-year-old girl come downstairs wearing a beautiful dress, high heels, and lipstick. When we got to our car, Vincent was already in the front seat, so I opened the back door for her. We parked on Donald Street and headed toward the old Metropolitan Theatre. Vincent, as active as ever on our walk to the theatre, walked alternately on the sidewalk and the top of the stone fence in front of Holy Trinity Anglican church, while his "date" walked calmly beside me. It seemed as if he arrived at the theatre a good five minutes before we did. At the booth, I caught myself just in time, before ordering tickets for "two adults and a child." I was flustered and embarrassed, but I had a good laugh later describing the situation to Charlene.

The period when Vincent was in Grade 4 to Grade 7 was extremely tense, but we felt most of the time that we had the situation under control. Vincent still had his endearing, contagious laugh, but we were concerned about the unpredictability of his behaviour and his attraction to heavy metal with its violent lyrics and association with vandalism. We could not seem to help him respect others or their property. On one occasion, we sat down with him to read out the violent lyrics of the songs on a disc that he had just purchased. We told him that he could not keep the album but, for this time only, we would give him money to replace it with one that was acceptable. His subsequent behaviour indicated that he did not learn a thing from this incident.

However, there were some positive events. In Grade 5, he was voted best artist by the teachers in his school and won a series of free lessons at the Winnipeg Art Gallery. After that, we asked him if he would like more lessons, and he completed a second program. He was interested in the guitar and drums, so I drove him to lessons, stipulating only that if he began a set of lessons he had to finish them. This became an enormous struggle for him and for me. Getting him to practise his instruments became impossible. I worked with him on his homework every night and, by the time that was finished, we usually had no energy left to struggle with practising

La Verendrye School offered only up to Grade 6, and we decided to send Vincent to Laureate Academy, a new private school in the St. James area of Winnipeg, for Grade 7. It was set up especially to address the problems of children with ADHD. Before making our decision to invest $8,000 for Vincent's Grade 7 year, we obtained several references from parents of children who were attending the school. At first, everything seemed to work well. There were behavioural problems, of course, but we felt that there was a spirit of cooperation between us and the school. In February, however, Vincent was expelled, unfairly we felt, and with little warning. In spite of their commitment to children with ADHD, they heaped more and more demands upon him, until he went over the edge and simply rebelled. Vincent always found it hard to foresee the consequences of his actions, whether it was his behaviour on the playground or getting his homework done. We felt that the school staff should have been more sensitive to Vincent's limits, his breaking points, and establish a better balance between demands and encouragement.

Vincent finished the year at a special-education program at

Churchill High, where his teacher, Mr. Hamilton, showed a great deal of care, compassion, and skill. Vincent arrived at the school academically quite far ahead of the other boys in his class, revealing just how much he had learned at the Laureate Academy. This made us all the more upset that the Academy had "broken the bended reed," to borrow the phrase from Isaiah. During his time at Churchill, we received assistance from MacDonald Youth Services for a counsellor to take Vincent out in the evenings, again in an attempt to channel his extraordinary levels of activity.

During Vincent's grades 8 and 9 years, we moved into a new level of problems. Any consequences we imposed upon inappropriate behaviour simply had no effect, and we were stretched to the limit. Late one evening, I drove to a downtown mall, where I had reason to believe that he was "hanging out" with his friends. He was surprised when I found him in one of the stairwells, but he refused to come home. After about an hour following him and his friends, pleading with him to come home, I could not change his mind. "That's fine," I said, "I'm prepared to stay the night with you here." He was understandably annoyed. Finally, one of his friends piped up, "Vincent, go on home with your dad. You're gonna freeze if you stay here. These stairs are real cold at night. Go on home! I wish I had a dad that would come to get me." About ten minutes later we left together.

By this time, Vincent was becoming physically aggressive. I learned from a social worker that if I needed to restrain him, I should turn him around and almost hug him as I held him, rather than hold him facing me, where eye contact was in itself a confrontation. After calling the police several times to deal with various of his outbursts and thefts in our home, it was with great sorrow that we came to the decision that he could no longer live at home. He told us later that he wanted to get out badly because he knew he could not live by our standards. "I realize it was not your fault," he often said. He stayed for a short time in a foster home, where it appears that the foster parents had more dope than Vincent had ever seen, then he was transferred to Neechiwam, a half-way house in the West End run by Aboriginals for Aboriginal youth. This was the most successful setting Vincent ever had after he left our home. He was there for over a year. We took him out for meals and talked to him on a regular basis. We had great respect for the staff, many of whom told us that they had been through difficult times themselves earlier in their lives, and we truly worked together in trying to help Vincent take responsibility for his life. We had made a point to teach him respect for and love of his Aboriginal tradition. At Neechiwam, he now had positive Aboriginal role models.

We filled our home with Aboriginal art, not only because we love it, but also because we wanted to help Vincent appreciate his heritage. We read him stories about Aboriginal children. We did not feel welcome at the Aboriginal events that we attended, however, and Vincent behaved as if he were totally uninterested. I truly wish we had done much more. Only in 2000, when I agreed to join the board of directors of New Directions, did I hear of Project Opikihiwawin,† which began at the time that Vincent was a child and is geared precisely to help families who have adopted Aboriginal children. I don't know if it would have made a difference, but I think we would have taken advantage of the opportunity. We lived on Grosvenor Avenue, a middle-class, older area of the city, and Vincent saw few Aboriginals. He grew up not knowing the smell of sweet-grass, nor did he know about the cleansing experience of the sweat lodge or the power of the healing circle to build a community.

On one occasion, Vincent told us how hard it had been for him to grow up in a middle-class, white neighbourhood. "People thought I was going to steal from them. One parent even patted

† *Opikihiwawin is a Cree word meaning "to nurture; to help grow."*

me down before I left his home. So I did steal from them." On several occasions, I tried to talk to the parents of some of Vincent's friends after he felt he'd been treated unfairly. But, in spite of my non-accusatory approach, I never did achieve success. "We respect Aboriginals," one parent told me. "My son would not have done that."

While he was at Neechiwam, life on the street was becoming an irresistible attraction for Vincent. He stole merchandise from stores, he committed break-and-enter crimes, and often threatened to assault people, on occasion even doing so. Not surprisingly, soon he was incarcerated in the Youth Correctional Centre. It was the beginning of a series of incarcerations that have continued periodically since then. From the Youth Centre, he "graduated" to the Remand Centre, then Headingley Jail, and back to the Remand Centre. We visited him regularly in the Youth Centre, and it became clear that he was sitting in confinement with access to absolutely no programs to assist in rehabilitation. This was particularly frustrating for us; we felt that some effective intervention might have made a real difference. While waiting for him to come to the visiting area one day, I was chatting with one of the guards. When I mentioned that Vincent was ADHD, his response was quick: "Well, that may well be. He's just like all the others here. He just needs to take responsibility and behave."

The attitude of that particular guard in the Youth Centre was one of several frustrations we experienced with the justice system. Another was his treatment by the courts. My strong feeling is that he has never had to face the consequences of his behaviour within an appropriate time frame. He would appear in court and be released on bail. Then, for months on end, nothing would happen. By the time he appeared for trial, he had probably forgotten what charges had led to his last arrest because in the meantime he had become involved in even more serious offences. The result was that the earlier charges now seemed to him almost petty. It is significant that, now, whenever we bring up past events, even things that occurred in the very recent past, perhaps, just a few weeks previously, his response is always the same: "Oh, that was a long time ago." It is as if the elapsed time in itself means that the previous behaviour was now insignificant, inconsequential.

The raft of crimes and incarcerations that began when Vincent was about 17 has been a terrible cycle that has let up only in the last two years. Whether he was in the Remand Centre or out on bail, he was required to appear in court time after time because the charges were often remanded to a later date so that he was always facing outstanding charges. Any time he appeared in court, he knew that he would have to return and possibly go to jail at a later date. He began to tell us that it would never be possible for him to have a clean slate. In fact, he believes that the police don't want him to have a clean slate; by keeping him constantly in and out of court, they can keep an eye on him.

In the meantime, our relationship with him became entangled in a complex interaction with the police. At one very tragic moment, we received an urgent call from Vincent at a pay phone. He told us that he had intentionally cut his wrists and asked us to come and get him. I rushed him to the emergency ward. In all such circumstances, the hospital staff are required to call the police. We waited for close to two hours for medical attention, and the police arrived during our wait. I was speechless as I listened to the officer and Vincent talking. It was a lively, joking conversation about a number of boys that Vincent and the officer both knew. It was a world unknown to me, and the camaraderie between them was unexpected, yet heartening. I've since realized that police officers often perform a crucial role in keeping street kids alive until they can get their lives together.

More recently, Vincent has been extremely critical of the police. He tells us constantly that we don't understand how disrespectfully they treat him simply because he is Aboriginal. He tells us that he has been framed, that the charges are fabricated. He will always admit to one or two misdemeanours but argues that most of the charges are totally unfounded and that the police are simply out to get him. "Once you have been a member of a gang," he has said, "they will never leave you alone." (This, of course, is the main premise of the theory of *labelling*.) At the same time, however, he has shown little respect for any authority or for the property of others. (So he fits the label.) We ourselves don't have enough information to make a judgement one way or the other, and we have to leave that to his lawyer and the court. He has never told us enough of any one story, let alone the whole picture, to enable us to take action. Our task is not to judge him as innocent or guilty but to assure him of our love and support in any constructive way that we can.

I was introduced to the term *confabulation* by Dr. Jennifer Frain, now executive director of New Directions. It describes the often elaborate fabrications that individuals can construct to describe situations or events that occurred in their past. Apparently, it is a fairly common behaviour for people with FASD. I don't think Vincent lies about that past, but I do think that he engages in a series of explanations about his behaviour that are not true but that he has come to believe are true. Whether dealing with us, the police, his lawyer, or the courts, he is unable, I believe, to reconstruct the past accurately.

The police have had to come to our home more times that we can count, asking us questions and taking statements. They have always been polite and thorough in writing down what we have said. They have always shown us our statements before asking us to sign them. However (and thankfully this is a very small percentage), there are still a few police officers who, the moment they hear that our son is Aboriginal, feel that they have now found the explanation for his behaviour. This is deeply offensive to us. It is the essence of racism. When we challenge this interpretation, they immediately back down, but the original expression of the attitude is not lost on us and has been troubling. It also makes us wonder whether at least some of what Vincent says about his treatment is true. There were enough instances in his early life when we intervened because other children or parents were treating him unfairly that we do not doubt the pervasiveness of prejudice, and at times real discrimination, against Aboriginals in our society. We had a sobering experience one evening when Vincent was quite young. As Charlene was giving him a bath, he burst into tears: "One of the kids at school told me I had slanted eyes and called me a Chinaman." Even at that young age, Vincent knew it was meant as a slur.

When Vincent was just 17, he and his girlfriend at the time became parents of a beautiful baby boy. Charlene held a shower for the mother, and we kept in touch with her long after Vincent had lost interest. But our relationship with her was fraught. On several occasions when Vincent was back in jail, we parked our car in the Canadian Pacific Railway parking lot on Higgins Avenue late at night and waited unsuccessfully for an opportunity to rescue the mother of our grandchild from what is known in Winnipeg as "the low track." She was working as a prostitute to support her drug habit. Within a year, the little boy was apprehended by Child and Family Services and later placed for adoption.

As Vincent reached adulthood, he spent more and more time in jail. In a call from jail in 2005, he informed me that this was the eighth time he had been in jail at Christmastime. Much of it has been at the Remand Centre, that is, waiting for trial. It is called "dead time" because there are no rehabilitative programs of any sort there, even though prisoners might spend many months there. He developed a pattern of calling us almost every day, often several times a day, while he was incarcerated. For years, both Charlene and I have concluded every conversation by saying "I love you." A good deal of the conversations revolved around his jockeying, indeed pressuring us, for financial support when he was released. We set him up several times with an apartment, furnishings, and food, as well as money, but these positive situations never lasted.

He spent some time at Headingley Jail in 1998, which was by far the most positive of all his incarcerations. There he seemed to be making significant progress in dealing with his issues. He took anger management courses and treatment programs for drug and alcohol abuse. He asked to be separated from gang members, and we arranged to have a gang tattoo removed from his body. He had a job there and was for a time spokesperson for his jail "range." One of the key staff members at the jail told us that Vincent was a leader and meant that in a very positive sense. He continued calling us and one time asked me for some advice on a fine letter he was writing to the warden asking for educational opportunities for inmates. We arranged to have a psychologist visit him regularly, and for a short time he was getting some schooling assistance from the John Howard Society. We supplied him with many books over the years of his incarcerations, and his reading skills were assessed at university level. His drawing improved dramatically too. I suggested that he begin a portfolio of drawings that I promised to forward to a comic book publishing house and asking if he could get contract work with them. We thought he might be able to do that from jail. He liked the idea but did not want to do it from jail because he was using his artistic talents there as barter for cigarettes.

The first time he asked us for bail when he was in Headingley, we refused, as we felt he needed more time to truly assimilate new attitudes. I regret now that three months later we did put up bail. When Vincent appeared in court, the judge accepted from me, through Vincent's lawyer, a written application for bail that Charlene and I, and our niece, Andrea, had put together with Vincent's agreement. Andrea, Vincent's godmother, has been close to us since she was a child, but especially since she lived with us for a year after our return from Berkeley in 1979. She was living in Halifax at the time of this application for bail. She has a master's degree in educational counselling and had been executive director of Stepping Stone, an agency whose mandate was to help sexually exploited young women get off the streets of Halifax and to help adult prostitutes who would not leave the street to find a safer environment. Vincent had always wanted to get out of Winnipeg and go to Halifax to get a new start. Andrea arranged counselling for Vincent in Halifax, as well as job training and housing. The judge said that the proposal we prepared was the best alternative sentencing application he had ever received. After a stern lecture to Vincent, he released him. The day after we put Vincent on the bus for Halifax, we flew to Salt Spring Island for the funeral of my brother, Robin, Andrea's father. It was February of 1998. The day before the funeral, we got a phone call from the person who was to pick Vincent up in Halifax with the news that he had not arrived by bus as expected. It was one of the most disappointing moments in our lives, a missed opportunity that we felt would never come again. Two months later, he called to say that he had made a mistake, that he should have gone to Halifax after all. He had got off the bus around the corner from the terminal in Winnipeg and never left the city.

Andrea was still willing to help him resettle in Halifax, so we took him to the airport, thinking that he would be less likely to change his mind if he went by plane. We watched him go through security. Charlene suggested that we wait until the plane actually left, but I could not get out of the airport fast enough. Her intuition turned out to be accurate. When he did not arrive at the airport in Halifax where Andrea was waiting, we made inquiries back in Winnipeg and found out that he had got off the plane before it left Winnipeg, claimed his baggage, and disappeared in the anonymity of the city. It was months before we heard from him again.

On a recent flight to Toronto, I met a woman who had graduated from the Harvard School of Business, having written her thesis on intergenerational trauma. She noted that alcoholism, depression, and mental illness can be transferred from one generation to another. This made me reflect on how the general trauma of a wounded, unappreciated culture is passed on. Perhaps Vincent will really be able to "come home" only when the richness and respect for the Aboriginal cultures so permeate our society that it renders the grieving and the anger of these communities no longer necessary. C. Wright Mills[5] writes about the difference between private problems and public issues. If there is one Aboriginal in jail, one can consider the misdeeds of the one person. However, when a disproportionate number of those in jail are Aboriginal, and while Aboriginals comprise less than 10 percent of the population, then that is a public issue. When the life expectancy of Aboriginals remains some 15 years less than that of Caucasians, that is a social problem. When the suicide rate is triple that of Caucasians, that is not a private problem but a public issue. We have lived out in our home the tragedy of many of these public issues. The comprehensive poverty of Vincent's birth family had a huge effect on his prenatal and early postnatal care and affected his early childhood development. While we do not pretend to have been perfect parents and indeed admit that we made many mistakes in our approaches to parenting, our home was a haven of love, respect, non-violence, and opportunities not available to everyone. Vincent has been more *unable* rather than *unwilling* to take advantage of the home situation we provided. I don't think he, himself, realizes the impact of his disabilities.

We've put up bail more than once. Our reasoning was never so much to get him out of jail but rather to get him into programs in the community that might help him. And we did it only when Vincent appeared to be making significant progress.

For the last number of years, Vincent has established a relationship with an Aboriginal woman his own age. We love Sherri very much. Together they have two children—Bishop, now six, and Phoenix, five. The exciting thing is that Vincent is a loving and caring father. We often take them to the park or the museum, and Vincent's behaviour is always beyond reproach. He is obviously proud of the children and at ease disciplining them, and he loves them deeply. When he is living with Sherri and the children, he keeps the apartment spotless, cooks, does dishes and his share of child care. In fact, he took on full child-care responsibilities recently while Sherri took a diploma course in medical terminology. Since 2004, Vincent has had several jobs for short periods of time and clearly enjoys having a paycheque. He has taken up tattooing in a serious way and is pleased both with his expertise and with the money he is earning. His relationship with Sherri has been through rocky times, however, and Vincent comes and goes. In late 2006, just as we were becoming cautiously hopeful for a secure and stable future for him, we found out that Vincent is now the father of another child, this one with another young woman. Although he is once again living with Sherri, this has complicated matters substantially, and we currently just don't know what our role should be or how to deal with all the complex relationships that have emerged.

In January of 1996, I attended a meeting of the National Association of Deans of Arts in Washington, D.C. I was having a late dinner, by myself, in a restaurant in the luxurious hotel where the conference was being held. I was feeling pensive, sad, and unable to face yet another academic discussion or the noise of The Grand Slam sports bar, and I didn't want to walk the streets of Washington. I had just finished an hour-long phone conversation with Charlie and Diane Keely, great friends from graduate-school days in New York.

During our phone conversation, we went through the usual: How are you? How are the kids? My turn, their turn, telling our stories, getting caught up. I got off the phone feeling worse than when I had called, and finally, at dinner, the reason hit me. I just felt weary, having to face all the inevitable questions about the family. Now I truly understood why Charlene did not like attending social gatherings and facing questions about the children. Our lives have been surrounded by, indeed dictated by, the disabilities of our children. In my years as dean of the Faculty of Arts in the 1990s, we were reminded of this practically every evening as we unplugged the phone in search of a quiet night, knowing that Vincent's calls always came late, after we had gone to bed. Twice we rented a hotel room in the city for the night because we fully expected to get a late-night visit, and I needed a good night's sleep for work the next day. Charlene's days seemed filled with meetings, either with service agencies or government agencies about Catherine's needs, and she thus had to spend too many evenings and weekends working on her academic responsibilities. This pattern prevailed until she had her stroke in February of 1996. In the year before the stroke, she had shifted her research interests to disability studies, and she proceeded with more conviction, more sense of purpose, and more sense that this work might make more of a difference than her previous research activities had. Ironically, she did this with the worry that the reality of the disabilities in our family would again make the research impossible to complete. Vincent's escapades were draining, to say the least, and the frustration of finding solutions for Catherine's disabilities were intense. Our lives were surrounded by chaos. The inexorable, unrelenting weekly bouts of Catherine's perseveration were taking their toll. And no amount of calm, cool discussion, no amount of reasoning, expressed frustration, or even anger (always followed immediately by guilt) could seem to turn Vincent's life from that of crime to that of a responsible citizen and reasonable family member.

As I ate my solitary dinner that evening in Washington, I wondered how I could continue to talk about our kids. What was worse, I didn't think I had anything else to talk about! So I sat there quietly. Had Charlene been with me, I would have cherished this moment of escape, even if were only temporary.

Did my doubts mean that we had not *accepted* the disabilities of our children? That word is just too easy to say. It sounds like a situation when an evangelist asks me if I have accepted Christ, and if so, to please come forward. Too simple for me. Of course we have not accepted our children's disabilities. I doubt that we ever will. Are we angry about the disabilities? Not at all. *Permanently saddened* would be a better descriptor. We have much for which to be thankful, so, certainly, we are not always in a state of sadness. Our marriage has survived, even grown, over the years of our struggles with the children. I am in awe of Charlene's insights and her patience; her stroke has not robbed her of these gems. Of course we have had to make sacrifices. We have both suffered lost career opportunities—for example, offers of jobs in other universities in Canada that we did not pursue because it would have meant uprooting Catherine. (I am not sure, though, even without the impediments that the children presented, that I could ever have accepted an offer to go elsewhere, given my commitment to the University of Manitoba.) Charlene had to forego the opportunity of a professional trip to China in 1984 because being away from Catherine for an extended period when she was only six would have been detrimental to our daughter's progress. We have also made sacrifices of the day-to-day type, both for our children and for each other. We have found ourselves becoming more and more isolated. We have friends, of course, but we have so little time to see them, and we are saddened. More often than not, we have shielded family members and friends from our constant ups and downs, not to burden them. When we occasionally poured out our hearts, we often felt a sense of guilt because of the implication that we were indifferent to the importance of their lives.

Recently I wrote to the archbishop of Winnipeg suggesting that there be a special ritual at baptism, and perhaps as part of confirmation, for children suffering from learning, cognitive, or physical disabilities. Often parents know about such disabilities when the children are born, and an appropriate prayer—and perhaps even an anointing—would provide support for both the child and the parents. It could also alert the community to the fact that the family will require special support. Instead of seeing these children as misfits and the parents as incompetent, people might offer understanding and encouragement. In fact, neither of our children have been confirmed (a reaffirmation of one's faith early in his or her teens). We were not able to impart the significance of the event to them in such a way that they would want to affirm their faith in that manner.

In 2004, when my sister was dying of pulmonary fibrosis, she said that she was offering her suffering for our children. I told her I thought her prayers were answered in a certain way: I still had good health enough to cope with the needs of Charlene and the children.

Katie's achievements continue to astound us. They are gradual, but every so often we stop, look back, and reflect with her on how much she has grown in independence. It would be easier if she herself could see this progress, but she remains angry much of the time. She has developed a way of moving quickly on to new issues as if she is making up for years and years of lost time, more angry that the next goal has not yet been achieved than happy about her recent accomplishments. After learning to ride the bus, she wanted control over her own social allowance.

After she was able to control her bank account and bank card, she then focussed on having control of her own medicines, not having to rely on her caregivers. This, too, is a fait accompli. In early 2008, after much preparation, including a detailed reconnaissance of the airport, she took her first plane trip on her own to visit Colleen and Jolaine and Kevin in Alberta. As she came down the escalator to the baggage area on her return, we were so proud. She headed for the carousel, picked up her luggage, and headed for the parking lot, leaving us in her dust. Given this success, she constantly reminds us and her caregivers that she is certainly ready to be left alone in the house for longer and longer periods of time. We include Katie in almost all family events, even if she might occasionally behave unpredictably.

These family events are beginning to include Vincent and his family. For the last two years, they have come to our Easter brunch at the Viscount Gort Hotel, where Charlene and I host about 25 family members each year. Katie loves to come with me and spend time with Vincent and Sherri's children when I go over to their place, virtually every weekend. Recently I had the most extraordinary, simple human experience. While Katie played with the children, Vincent, Sherri, and I tore down a shed together. A simple activity, common to many fathers and sons, but the first time in 31 years for me. The normality of it thrilled me.

Henri Nouwen points out that the parable of the return of the prodigal son could easily have been entitled "The Welcome by the Father" because it is more about the father than about the son. Nouwen's reflections on the parable have helped me understand that my task, my responsibility, is above all to be tender, merciful, forgiving. In fact, I have not found any of these responsibilities to be difficult. But I have been made aware of another, much more daunting, challenge, and that is to be trusting. The father does not ask the son why he has returned. He does not try to exhort a promise that his son will behave from now on. He simply accepts him. Vincent's life is characterized by times of progress invariably followed by setbacks. In fact, he is now less frequently in trouble with the law, and when he is, the charges are less serious. And this represents progess.

Nevertheless, each new disappointment leaves its mark. I want to trust. But I am resigned to the fact that the "return" of this prodigal son will be gradual. But how will I know which step forward will be real and lasting and which will be only fleeting? I have decided that, in any case, this is not a relevant question. Instead of dwelling on it, what I need to do is learn to trust him. I wonder if Vincent can understand that I love and forgive him but that I am struggling to trust him. I fervently hope so. For all the years of his life that it takes for him to become worthy of trust, Vincent will know that he is my child. He and I have talked about rebuilding trust and the fact that this trust must be earned. It is Vincent's responsibility to earn it. And he is gradually doing just that. And what is my responsibility? As much as it hurts, I must bear the pain of another possible disappointment. I must be willing to be vulnerable and to support him. I must keep on telling him that together we can always start again. I know that it hurts him to know that I do not trust him completely. And I am not sure that he understands just how hard a thing it is to do.

What the future holds, we do not know. We live in hope. In the meantime, we continue to suffer with our children.

CHAPTER 9

Living with the Dying of Others

Maureen, Gatineau Hills, 1997

During my years in the priesthood, I often had occasion to tend to a family in grief, both at the moment of the loss and in the weeks that followed. In one particularly poignant situation, the responsibility fell to me to inform a woman that her husband had just died. I stood to one side at the hospital as she cried out to God at the top of her voice to bring her husband back. She was bartering with God for just one more year, but she did not get the answer she was desperate for. In another incident, during my graduate school days, I attended the burial of a 25-year-old man from the church in the Bronx where I used to celebrate Mass on Sundays. It was seen by all present to have been a preventable death. The young man had arrived to serve in Vietnam just a week before his death, when the war was almost over. The continued fighting was simply a means of bargaining on the part of the United States for a better position at the end. In the predominantly Irish parish where the church was located, the war had been supported by the majority, but that now turned to a palpable sense of bitterness. The grief I experienced in these two circumstances was focussed on the survivors. In neither case did I know the person who died, so my emotional response was directed at the family's loss.

My mother's death in 1990 filled me with an immediate sense of profound grief. Losing that personal relationship was unlike anything that I had ever experienced in my ministry. When my father died in 1954, I was young at 19, filled with my own dreams and plans, and it was only over time that I recognized the enormity of my loss.

Frequently in the months that followed Mom's death, without warning, I would sense what I can describe only as a dark cloud of sadness over me. Sometimes it took careful thought before I could identify the sudden change of mood and the root of it. I think it was at least a year before the image in my mind changed from that of a frail, brittle, and breakable person of her last years to that of the vibrant person she had been most of her life. Even in her final year, however, she continued her mothering and her gift of support for everything I undertook.

In death as well as in life, she was an inspiration. When she was 87, about two years before her death, I remember having to tell her that one of her closest friends had died. I thought she would be devastated. I can only describe her reaction as that of a person who knew and accepted that dying is a part of life. It is not that her strong faith had given her all the answers to suffering and death. She did not torture herself to find or know all the answers. Rather, I think, she accepted the human condition in its full cycle, including living with the mystery of dying.

Mom's death began what turned out to be more than a decade of uninterrupted illness and deaths of a dozen loved ones. The deaths were sequential, but the illnesses overlapped one another. I should not of course have been surprised by the deaths of so many loved ones. I was in my 60s and had become part of the oldest surviving generation of our family. There were complicating issues; in addition to emotional support and sometimes even a caregiving role that we were asked to provide, and very willing to play, these were the very years when the most serious consequences of the disabilities of our children were manifesting themselves. There were times when we felt overwhelmed. Each death required that we take a leap into the unknown and face our own mortality. Each death taught me in different ways.

Charlene's dad, Mose, died in 1993. (He got the nickname *Mose*, by the way, as a teenager, when his friends joked that he was so small he must have been hidden in the bull rushes in the same way that Moses had. Even after he married, his wife, Kitty, could not get his friends to call him by his real name—Charles.) Every year of our married life, Charlene and I had taken a summer holiday with her parents. A tour of Europe, three weeks in Portugal, time in San Francisco, and camping trips in the Canadian Rockies, through Kentucky, and down to Florida—all these were times of easy companionship. Mose was a pro at telling jokes. These were not one-liners but, rather, stories that you would want to hear repeated because he always timed the punch line perfectly. Although he had little education, he knew the geography of the world and a great deal of history. I don't know how often I would say to some who expressed amazement that I'd spend my holidays with my in-laws, "But you don't understand, my in-laws are my best friends."

Our favourite times with Kitty and Mose were at our cottage at Netley Creek, where we would fish, or Mose would give me advice on how to build or repair things, or we would just sit quietly by the lake. We'd joke that the cottage was their northern investment, as it was thanks to their generosity that we were able to finance a good part of it. Mose took his fishing very seriously, so it was all the more fun one time when I caught a large silver bass, which we then mounted for display at the cottage. He'd had a huge fish on his line the previous evening, but it had got away, and we went back to try to get it the next day. I swore that the fish I had caught was a different one, because it had no hook and line in its mouth from the previous evening. But he always claimed that it was the original fish and that he had just softened it up for me to catch.

It was obvious for about a year and a half before Mose's death in April of 1993 in Louisville, Kentucky, that his health was declining. In fact, he and Kitty both had cancer. As soon as classes were over in April of that year, Charlene headed for Kentucky, and she was there for the last 11 days of his illness. During those final days, he suffered so much that he said he just wanted to die. I was attending a meeting in Montreal when he did die. Charlene called when she knew that death was imminent, but I was unable to make it there to see him before he died.

As the funeral arrangements were being made, I was filled with a sense of dread about the plan; I thought it would be too taxing on the family. There was to be a viewing of the body for two and a half days at a funeral parlour, and the family was to be present at all times. As I quickly learned, this was a tradition in parts of the South. It turned out to be an extraordinarily touching experience for me—one that I shall never forget.

As is usual, the funeral parlour provided a number of viewing rooms, so that several families could view their deceased loved ones at the same time. But this particular funeral parlour had a feature that I had never seen before: a separate large room off from the viewing rooms that was divided by panels into private "resting" rooms. The number of these resting rooms equalled the number of viewing rooms. Each resting room had a large table that could seat about eight people, a kitchen sink, a microwave oven, and a large fridge. Families could take a break from the viewing rooms for a snack or simply a bit of quiet time. I remember urging Kitty to come into our resting room occasionally, but she and Charlene stayed in the viewing area for the whole time that the funeral palour was open. There were clusters of comfortable chairs and sofas in the viewing rooms. People came and went as they wished. They offered condolences to Kitty, Charlene, and Charlene's brother, John, and then stood or sat and talked in small groups and would pause in front of the open casket before leaving. Family, relatives, friends, co-workers, members of St. Ignatius Parish in Louisville, and members of AA, to which Mose had belonged for 20 years, all came. The stories told were of his honesty, his compassion, his great joke-telling ability, and his friendship and support for others in need, especially in AA. In the end, because of the informality that the funeral palour had provided, I felt I knew him better than ever. I realized that we had all grieved and supported one another in the best manner possible. Funerals are indeed for the living.

Dot (Aunt Dot) Schuler died in Kentucky in December of 1996. Dot and Elmer Schuler were friends of Kitty and Mose even before they were married in 1937. Dot had three children: Dotty Beth, Rosemary, and Fred. Dotty Beth was Charlene's lifelong closest friend, and Fred is her godchild (Charlene was 15 when he was born). Whenever we visited Kentucky during the early years of our marriage, Aunt Dot and Elmer would come over every Saturday evening, and we would always join them for their weekly dinner out. These were two couples whose lives were entirely focussed on their families and their work, but their work was simply a means to care for their families. When they arrived home in the late afternoon, job worries and responsibilities were put aside until the next day. This was an approach to work and a balance in life that was certainly unlike my own. Both in the priesthood and the academic world, there is a strong sense of never-ending work to be done, and I learned a valuable lesson from their approach.

The story of the friendship between the two families is one of those rare ones in which the ties are so deep that they go into the third generation. Charlene's lifelong friendship with Dotty Beth was the first extension. Now that Dotty Beth has also died (in 1998), Charlene's friendship with her brother, Fred, and his wife, Joyce, as well as with Dotty Beth's four daughters and their spouses, has continued. I had come to know Dotty Beth when Charlene and I were preparing to be married. Because I was in Winnipeg, Charlene took care of all the wedding arrangements, and I planned our honeymoon in South America. Dotty Beth was, among other things, a bridal consultant. Ironically, she was going through a difficult divorce at the time we were married, leaving her a single mom with four small children. The friendship between Charlene and Dotty Beth was a great support to them both at that time. After our honeymoon, Dotty Beth showed up at Charlene's home as we were pulling out to drive to Canada with a U-Haul truck and Charlene's car in tow. On the day that Charlene's dad died, Dotty Beth arrived and sat on the porch, not wishing to interfere with the sacred, last moments Charlene was sharing with her dad. Dotty Beth was keeping her own vigil in support of her lifelong friend.

Just before Aunt Dot died, Dotty Beth herself learned that she had cancer. She suffered terribly for the next two years and died in December of 1998. Again, it was for us a long period of living with the dying of others. Dotty Beth had asked Charlene to give a eulogy, a task that was very difficult for Charlene after her stroke. Dotty Beth had lived an interesting and flamboyant life. As a single mom of four daughters under the age of four, including a set of twins, she often did not have enough money even to buy milk for the children. In spite of her overwhelming parenting responsibilties, however, she took a job-training course and, while doing other jobs, blossomed as a wedding planner. Just before she died, she was recognized as a Master Wedding Planner, one of 10 in the world at the time. Her own daughters' weddings were featured in a major bridal magazine. When her own 25th wedding anniversary date arrived, well after her divorce, she hosted a party for all her female friends. The table had a black table cloth, black candles and black napkins. In the bathroom there was only one towel, and it was inscribed with "hers." There was even half a wedding cake. Her ultimate organizational task was to plan her own funeral service, much to the chagrin of her daughters. She did it beautifully, and the day after her funeral, Charlene, Kitty, and several other of her close friends each received a beautiful ceramic angel with a thank-you note that Dotty Beth had written and arranged to have delivered after she died. In 2007, nine years after her death, Charlene and I attended the wedding of Andrea, the only one of her daughters not married when she died. At the wedding rehearsal, the eldest daughter, Beth, handed Andrea two beautiful letters that Dotty Beth had written to Andrea and whoever would be her future husband. It was a touching moment. In spite of her own suffering and impending death, she had the courage, forethought, and selflessness to think of her daughter's future happiness.

After Aunt Dot's death, the only surviving member of our parents' generation left in our family was Charlene's mother. We were experiencing the deaths of relatives in our own generation, however. My cousin Bill died in Flin Flon, in northern Manitoba, on the 4th of January, 1995. At 69, he was the oldest of the eight of us who had grown up with each other. I'll never forget the weather in Flin Flon when we went to his funeral. It was at least 40 below, no matter how you calculate it. The day before the service, we drove downtown for coffee in one of the small cafes. The whole town seemed to be in the coffee shop, and all the half-ton trucks and the few cars on the street were running and belching exhaust fumes; no one worried about a vehicle being stolen. The weather was bitterly cold, but there was warmth in the family. Still, I had a sense that his death shattered the fragile wholeness of the eight of us and our spouses.

About a year before Bill died, my brother John called to say that he had informed Archbishop Wall that he had to retire because of his ill health. He was diagnosed with pulmonary fibrosis, a relatively rare type of lung disease. We eventually became very familiar with this disease; both Robin and Maureen, my two other siblings, were later diagnosed with it, and all three died from it. Charlene was in Kentucky at the time of John's decision to retire, and I suggested that he and I go out to dinner that evening at Rae and Jerry's, one of his favourite restaurants. We spent the whole evening talking about all the parishes where he had been posted since his ordination in 1955. He lived by the principle that every seven years he would ask the archbishop to move him. He felt that in seven years he had done the best he could, and it would be good for the parish to have a different pastor.

His ministry was filled with the same sorrows and joys one could expect in any career. In his first years as an assistant pastor, he found himself stationed with a priest who suffered from alcoholism and who later took his own life. As was customary in the seminary where John trained for the priesthood, all the seminarians were encouraged to make a promise not to drink socially for the first ten years of their priesthood. John kept that pledge, and it certainly helped him through those particularly difficult years.

During the year I lived with him after I left the Franciscans, I was able to see first-hand how he conducted his ministry. We shared many values. He loved to study and often set up a small group with whom he prepared his Sunday sermons. He actively sought the views of parishioners, especially through parish councils, and he was respectful of other Christian denominations. In fact, one of his appointments was as pastor of John Twenty-Third Parish in Assiniboia, which was a joint parish with Anglicans. He used to laugh about the occasion he walked down the aisle with the Anglican priest who was pregnant at the time. He introduced the practice of women distributing communion, long after he had appointed the first altar girls in the diocese. He spoke with great respect about the faith of his parishioners, and their generosity, and made many friends in his various parishes. He told me that he never felt lonely in any parish where he'd served. In his obituary, I stated that the family wanted to thank parishioners throughout the diocese for their support for him in his ministry. After his retirement, he stayed in Dauphin because he had loved that parish so much, but his health deteriorated very quickly and he had to resettle in Winnipeg where he could get better access to his particular health-care needs.

For six months he rented an apartment and went back and forth to the Riverview Health Centre. Soon he could not care for himself any longer and came to live with us for the summer. In the early fall, he was admitted to Riverview as a permanent patient. I visited with him almost every day for the last six weeks of his life. He was a remarkable man and a true inspiration to me. During that time, I had the opportunity to thank him for his unquestioning support of me when I resigned from the ministry. He never showed the slightest embarrassment over my resignation, nor did he try to change my mind.

As the end approached, we discussed with a social worker what treatment he wanted near his death, and he signed a living will. During the last two weeks, over three or four evenings, we prepared his funeral liturgy. He chose the readings and asked our cousin Sheila Sturley if she would read the epistle. For the gospel, he wanted the text that we had read at Mom's funeral: "Consider the lilies of the field" (Matthew 6:28). He selected the hymns, the priest he wanted to give the homily, as well as who would read the prayer of the faithful, bring up the gifts, and serve as pallbearers. We talked about death openly. He said he felt lucky that, even though he was having more difficulty breathing each day, he was not in a great deal of pain. When Maureen and I asked him if he was afraid, he responded, "It's like when I sailed from Vancouver to Hawaii: I wanted to be brave, but I was not sure I could be." In the same context, he told me, "I have tried to console and support so many parishioners when they were dying: I guess it's time I lived what I preached." When Maureen asked him if he could pray, he said, "No, not any more. Now it is just a matter of trust." The evening before he died, I assured him that he had been a very good priest. "I never doubted my vocation," he said quietly.

After John's death on the early morning of the 20th of December 1996, I organized prayer services at the funeral home for the Sunday, two days later, at 1:00 p.m. and at 7:00 p.m. The announcement in the newspaper said that the family would be present between the two services to receive mourners. This was quite unusual in Winnipeg, where, at most Catholic funerals, the prayers are held only the evening before the funeral at the funeral home and last only about 20 minutes. People then file past the family to offer five seconds of condolences and leave. I find this a most unsatisfactory ceremony. Its inadequacy is accentuated by the fact that the bishops want a homily on the Gospel at the funeral Mass instead of a eulogy. I had been hoping to recapture some of the experience of Mose's funeral where we grieved together and supported one another. But people in Winnipeg are used to local customs, and, while many came for one of the two prayer services, the number who came in between or who stayed for any length of time was small.

I was emotionally exhausted after John died, yet I felt I had been privileged to help him prepare for death. Never were we closer as brothers.

After the funeral and burial, the family and a number of friends came back to our home. I remember Robin joking that, if we were to put on a funeral like that for him, he would consider coming back to Winnipeg to die. Little did we know that exactly 14 months later he would die of the same disease. He found out that he had the disease in the summer of 1997, six months after John's death. He had been ill for about eight years, ever since he'd had a heart attack at Red Lake while on a business trip. In fact, his heart attack was followed by a multitude of illnesses. He and Irene had moved to Salt Spring Island seven years before he died because he could not stand the cold weather and the wind in Winnipeg.

On his 60th birthday, the year he and Irene moved west, I called him on the phone and told him that my birthday present was a list that I wanted to read to him: 20 reasons showing that I loved him. This was long before he was diagnosed with pulmonary fibrosis, but his other serious illnesses had given me time to reflect on how much he meant to me. Who has not wished he had said something to a loved one before that person died? I am sure my mother's recognition of all my efforts and achievements inspired this call. I wanted to do the same for Robin. I sensed that he was embarrassed when I started; men just don't say these things to each other. But it was important to me to tell him how grateful I was to have such a wonderful brother. When I finished, he struggled to find words, and I could tell he was deeply moved and appreciative.

One of Robin's loveable traits that I listed was his sense of humour. He relished telling a good, long joke or story; he loved to make outrageous comments to shock people; he was a great tease, but he never made others the butt of his jokes. He even joked when facing death. In his last week, his daughter Andrea commented on the marvelous support group of friends he and Irene had in those hard days. "Ah," he said, "and I suppose you've noticed they're mostly women." We laughed together when I told him a joke on the phone the week before he died, about Machiavelli, who, on his deathbed was asked by a priest if he renounced Satan. "Father," Machiavelli replied, "this is no time to make new enemies."

Robin knew he was dying and bore his illnesses and prepared for death in a matter-of-fact way. Of course, I did not see all the times he and Irene cried together as they faced their imminent loss of one another. The Saturday before he died, friends came to move a hospital bed into the family room. After they had finished setting it up, he invited them into the living room for a drink and said, "Well, I was always hoping to have an Irish wake, but I didn't know I would be part of it."

Living with the dying of others is both painful and depressing. The sense of impending loss is aggravated by the feeling that, already in life, one is losing contact with the dying person. Charlene was the first to bring this to my attention. Some of the moments I had together with John just before he died were the most profound in our relationship, but I sensed the beginnings of his withdrawal as his death approached. It was partly because he was too tired to talk, which was not in itself a problem, as we both appreciated silent time together. But this sense of loss went deeper than that. Every time I have been seriously ill, or thought I was, the illness has been accompanied by panic and fear. I saw the same fear and panic in family members who were dying but also saw it replaced by peace after a certain point. I've sought to find the source of this peace but can only speculate that there is some inner sense in humans that allows us to know when we are dying and directs us to prepare for it. And one way to prepare is to distance ourselves from life, to start withdrawing from the temporal.

"The night before he died, a death he freely accepted, he took bread, and gave you thanks . . . " These words of the Eucharistic prayer at Mass reflect an incredible peace. Yet the Scripture tells that, the next day, Christ called out from the cross, "Father, why have you abandoned me?" I wanted to hear from Mom, from John, and from Robin some confirmation that their faith, their sense of the presence of God, was sustaining them during the final weeks of their lives, when I noticed that a peace had come over them. I sensed this peace in them, but they simply could not express it verbally. Perhaps their faith did not give them answers or a vision of the future, but it may have given them hope, hope that there is a future beyond death, unknown though it may be.

It has been instructive for me to observe Charlene's family members, who have been far less verbal about their faith and about life events in general than mine have been. Their philosophy is that things are the way they are and that talking about them does not change matters. But we have not been so taciturn in our family, perhaps because three of us were in the ministry and were expected to interpret the reality of faith to others. But now I am resigned to the fact that my expectation for clear, inspiring answers is naïve. Perhaps John did give me the answer when he told me in the weeks before his death that he could no longer pray but only trust. Individuals have to face death alone, and, whenever I have suffered the death of a loved one, I have always felt very much on the sidelines—helpless and unable to console adequately, to understand, to share. I know that I, too, would barter with God for more time, as did the woman I knew in New York, except that I know it would be a fruitless exercise.

Reading Joseph Cardinal Bernardin's small book entitled *A Gift of Peace*[1] was rewarding. Cardinal Bernardin died less than two months before John, and he finished writing his book just 13 days before he died. The book is about the last three years of his life, when he was falsely accused of sexual misconduct, diagnosed with cancer, and then faced imminent death following a return of the cancer after 15 months of remission. In the final pages of his reflections, he writes:

> What I would like to leave behind is a simple prayer that each of you may find what I have found—God's special gift to us all: the gift of peace. When we are at peace, we find the freedom to be most fully who we are, even in the worst of times. We let go of what is nonessential and embrace what is essential. We empty ourselves so that God may more fully work within us. And we become instruments in the hands of the Lord.[2]

There is, of course, a difference between being ill and facing death, both for the person experiencing it and for family members. Mom was not even really ill before she died; she just died of old age—a natural death. John's illnesses came rather quickly, but at that time we did not know the effect of pulmonary fibrosis and were unprepared for the day-to-day deterioration of his abilities. Robin appeared to have serious illnesses for seven or eight years, but, once the fibrosis was diagnosed after John had died from it, it seemed as if he were living with a death sentence after a long trial, with no chance for appeal. Then, when we were told that Maureen, too, had pulmonary fibrosis, we were devastated.†

I experienced another kind of living with the dying of others: "the untimely death." Bruce, Esmé's youngest child, was dying,

---

† *Because my three siblings had the same disease, my own doctor recommended annual tests for me. The news so far is that I have escaped this genetic legacy.*

and we were unaware of it. When he started not showing up at family events, even Christmas festivities, it became clear to us that he was isolating himself, and, in spite of efforts by almost everyone, we could not enter his world. When Bruce took his own life in the summer of 1999 in his early 30s, we all sensed not only a terrible loss but also a terrible sense of guilt. We knew about his problems with alcohol, and we had family meetings with the Addictions Foundation of Manitoba to plan an intervention, according to their recommended procedures. We arranged a date, but, at the last minute it seemed, the leaders told us that they were uncomfortable and did not want to proceed. Nevertheless, Esmé went ahead with her children Margaret, Thom, and Diane and staged a kind of mini-intervention. But Bruce simply denied that there was a problem. After that, when they failed to hear from him, Esmé sent him a letter. Her only answer, three months after the intervention, was a visit from the police to inform her that he had taken his own life. He truly died alone, in the most tragic manner. The death was so heartbreaking for Esmé not only because she was his mother but also because she had lost another child. (Her son Paul had choked on a hotdog at the age of two on the very day that she had given birth to her daughter Diane.) That was in 1963. She endured all this, after having lost her mother when she was 10. The tragedies of life are not spread out evenly. Father Michael Koryluk, their parish priest, was as compassionate as anyone could be. He reflected the current thinking of the Church: who are we to judge the heart and mind of an individual tortured by depression or other illness that could lead that person to end life in such a tragic manner?

On the day that Princess Diana died in a car accident in a Paris tunnel, the media brought a good deal of the English-speaking world into a period of mourning. Diana was beautiful and cared deeply for the sick and less fortunate around the world. She was the archetypal princess. That same day, another young "princess" had a similar accident in Michigan, which went unnoticed by the media. The victim was one of four daughters of Charlene's first cousin, Mary Lee Barry: Maureen, the second oldest, who was in her 30s. Her car was hit from the side with such impact that her husband was thrown into her. He was killed instantly, and she went into a coma. While she has come out of the coma, her body, especially her brain, was so damaged in so many ways that to this day, 10 years later, she lies in bed, unable to communicate. Their two children, aged nine months and three years, who were in the back seat, survived without physical injury. Her sister Theresa and Theresa's husband, Steve, immediately took in the two children and are raising them with their own two, who are slightly older. Maureen Barry's tragedy reminds me of the death of my mother's sister, Mary, and our cousins, who became part of our family. I wrote Theresa and Steve, at their requst, a long letter describing how our two families became so tightly integrated. Maureen was as physically beautiful as Diana. She had a master's degree in political science and had held very responsible jobs, including the directorship of private funding at the University of Louisville. She was especially caring about people with disabilities. Over the years, she was unusually attentive to our daughter, Catherine, and would often write letters to her. Nothing is harder to come to terms with than the tragedy of a young mother living her life in such a state of helplessness.

If there is one thing I learned in my years in the Franciscans, it is the centrality of the Passover in Catholic theology, the link between death and resurrection. Francis of Assisi is considered the originator of the custom of setting up a crib at Christmastime to help people reflect upon the birth of Christ. But in his writings he emphasized that the completion of the incarnation occurred at the resurrection of Christ. Christ did not simply come on earth, live, and die, but he also passed through death to the resurrection when his humanness was perfected. This is the essence of Christian faith. In one sense, this theology sounds reasonable, rational, comprehensive, and reassuring. However, in another sense, we must understand that knowledge and faith are not the same thing. It is not incompatible with faith to feel the tragedy of dying and death—the mental and emotional pain of losing the physical presence of those we love.

Many obituaries in the *Winnipeg Free Press* are beautiful social and religious commentaries. They often speak of those who have died "after a courageous battle" with one disease or another or, sometimes more graphically, of "succumbing to the violent ravages of cancer." More often, obituaries speak of people dying "peacefully." All three of these comments fit Kitty, Charlene's mother, who died on the 8th of April 2000. She bore her cancer for seven years—first breast cancer, then cancer of the stem of her brain and of the lower spine, and finally a general cancer of the bone. Kitty was ravaged by cancer, and she was indeed courageous, with never a word of complaint. During her life, she was a peacemaker; at the end, she attained personal peace.

I was fortunate to have such a wonderful mother-in-law. She was a big, strong, quiet woman. She was beautiful, with traces of the regal features of her Cherokee grandmother. She never did achieve Andy Wharhol's hope that everyone enjoy 15 minutes of fame, but she was the person who for decades drew the whole family together in Kentucky. She did not achieve fame, but she was loved and respected by all who knew her.

After her two children, Charlene and John, started school, she went to work at Woolworth's and quickly rose to the position of personnel manager. In order to remain close to her extended family, she refused a promotion that meant moving out of Louisville. When she died, she had been retired for over 20 years, yet at her funeral two middle-aged men, who did not know each other, when they paid their respects said that she had given them their first jobs. The number of people in their 20s and 30s who attended her wake was remarkable. Diane, her niece's youngest daughter (and sister to Maureen Barry) was one of those present. She reminded us that, one day when she was in her teens, she had appeared with her hair dyed green and cut outlandishly, much to the chagrin of her parents. "Diane," Kitty simply remarked, "I love how you always find a way to express your individuality."

For a number of years, Kitty had cared for her own mother and then her mother-in-law, both of whom lived into their 90s. Earlier, she and Mose had driven two spinster aunts to Mass every Sunday. "I'll never get any rewards for doing that," Mose used to say, "because I hated every minute of it." Kitty would simply carry on, "because those are the things you just do for family." She had a way of making the most mundane events of life seem significant, important, and satisfying. Caring for her family was the focus of her life, and she was rewarded at the end of her life by the intense devotion of her family.

Charlene and her mother enjoyed a remarkable friendship. They were comfortable just sitting and talking, about family or world events. There was a communion of values, interests, and love. After our marriage, Charlene would make sure to see her family at least three times a year. As a family, we would always get together for a summer visits, they would come for Canadian Thanksgiving, and Charlene would go there during the one-week February break at the University. In between, we were in constant touch by telephone.

My family has benefited enormously from the values that Charlene's family has always lived by. Charlene simply has never allowed personality differences, misunderstandings, or minor annoyances to distract her from her commitment to the bonds we share as a family. Like her mother, she has won respect from others without seeking it. If the world is divided into talkers and listeners, Charlene, like her mother, is definitely a listener. Children, even from outside the family, take to her immediately, because she listens to them so carefully. I am constantly amazed at the insights that come to her because she truly hears and reflects upon what is said to her.

In September of 1999, two days before Charlene and I were about to return to Winnipeg after a brief visit to Kentucky, Kitty received news of another malignant growth. We quickly decided that Charlene should stay to help Kitty get through the radiation treatments. The treatments were ultimately not very helpful, and her health gradually deteriorated until she died in April. Except for two brief periods at home, Charlene stayed the year. With the excellent guidance, assistance, and emotional support of Hospice Services of Louisville, Charlene helped Kitty die at home as she had wished. Charlene was the epitome of the dutiful daughter, one who honoured her father and mother to the end. This gave Charlene not only a great deal of peace but also a tremendous sense of accomplishment, as it was the first sustained activity she was able to perform after her stroke.

Because I was on administrative leave at the time of Kitty's illness and death, I was able to go to Kentucky several times during the year, and I did a great deal of writing there. My last visit began three weeks before Kitty died. I had visited John at the Riverview Health Centre every day during his last weeks, but living in the house with Kitty as she gradually, yet irrevocably, neared death was different. Not only was it more physically exhausting because Charlene needed me to help change Kitty, but it was also filled with moments of intense emotion when we erroneously thought the end had come. Never has the word *vigil* taken on such a profound meaning for me. I prayed a decade of the rosary each day with her: "Holy Mary, Mother of God, pray for us sinners now and at the hour of our death." A week before she died, she asked us to call in her son, John, from work, and, as the three of us surrounded her bed, she asked us to take her hand

and told us, "I think it's time." She looked at Charlene and said, "You know, Charlene, this is not so bad." In a sense, it seemed quite matter of fact. It reminded me of her last visit to Winnipeg, in 1998. We had asked Pamela, her granddaughter and Charlene's niece, to come for a visit at that particular time so that she could fly home with Kitty. On their way home, the plane suddenly dropped about 10,000 feet and then levelled off. Several people screamed, some bled from their ears, and most, including Pamela, were terrified. "I thought I was going to die," said Pamela, recounting the event. Kitty simply said, "Well, I was waiting to see what would happen next." And this is how she approached death in her final weeks. The day she asked us to call John from work, she spoke tenderly to us all and then fell into a deep sleep. We thought that this was the end, but, about two hours later, she awoke, looked at us, and asked, "Who told me I had to die today?" We laughed with her over that. Only the morphine that we administered with increasing frequency kept her from intense pain. She fell into a coma that night, and six days later her heart gave out.

Much grieving occurred even before Kitty died. It is not trite to remember that the more intense the love, the greater the sense of loss. Charlene's loss in particular is almost unspeakable.

When Charlene returned to Winnipeg in late May after settling the major portion of Kitty's estate, we were faced with the imminent departure of my sister, Maureen, from Winnipeg. As her own case of pulmonary fibrosis took hold, she found herself less and less able to get around and care for herself, and she decided to move to a convent in Halifax where the sisters in her community who are ill are cared for. She made the move in August of 2000. Between June and August, Charlene focussed on helping Maureen organize her move, running errands for her and simply caring for her as best she could. It is hard to articulate the significance of Maureen's move. "Going away to die" was the most stark way of describing her departure, and the grief had already set in; we knew our time with her was short.

We were blessed, however, as Maureen lived for almost five more years—until the 7th of July 2005. We were able to visit her several times a year until she died, and we had a regular Wednesday-afternoon telephone conversation. During the years of her suffering, she never lost her sense of humour and love of life. One day in April, about a month before she was finally confined to bed, she was walking back to her room, very slowly, slightly bent over. Laurie, the nurse, was to come behind her, pushing the oxygen cart. Maureen arrived at her room ahead of Laurie, and when a couple of minutes had passed and no oxygen cart had yet arrived, she lay down on the floor with a mischievous grin on her face. When the nurse opened the door, Maureen threw up her arms, crying "Oxygen, oxygen." I don't think the nurses thought it was as funny as Maureen did.

In early May of 2005, I went to Halifax and remained with Maureen for the last six weeks of her life. Charlene arrived two weeks after I. Just before leaving Winnipeg, I told Maureen on the phone, with some trepidation, that I had found what I thought was a great birthday card for her. On the front of the card was a picture of a setting sun, surrounded by yellow, pink, and white clouds. The text read, "On this your birthday I have a special message for you from God." The inside of the card read, "See you soon!" Maureen thought it was hilarious. She ask me to repeat it on the phone three times. When a nurse came into her room, she insisted that I read it to her. "Send it to me now," she said, "I don't think I'll be around for my birthday" (which was the 16th of July).

Maureen and I talked openly about her death. After we had decided upon the readings and the songs for her funeral liturgy she said to Charlene, "I have to decide what I will wear for my funeral." Charlene went to her closet and picked out an outfit.

"Now I need a second outfit," Maureen added. "I can't possibly wear the same thing for the viewing of the body and the funeral."

"But, Maureen," Charlene responded tentatively, "I don't

think you can do that. The beautician and the mortician would have to return." Maureen was immensely pleased with herself that she had tricked Charlene into thinking she was serious.

As far back as I can remember, Maureen had wanted to join a religious community. She always had a distinct sense of spirituality about her and, as a child, could hardly wait until she was old enough to go to school at the Convent of the Sacred Heart. Once she was a nun, it was clear that she could speak eloquently about God. But I, and a number of others, had a sense that she also spoke *to* God. Yet her life was not all consolation. She suffered a deep depression for several years and, even after that passed, she continued to be plagued with some anxiety. She talked about these states of mind and felt she became a better counsellor because of these experiences.

I don't remember a time when I could not share my thoughts and feelings with Maureen. We were kindred souls. For the last six weeks of her life, while I was with her in Halifax, I read to her daily, especially from the Scriptures. It was wonderfully satisfying for me to read a text, pause, reflect upon it, and then talk about it with her.

I have heard over and over again from people, not only Catholics, that Maureen was a wonderful spiritual director. In a way, she was a paradox; while little things bothered her, big things did not. She didn't judge people, and she displayed enormous empathy for others. Furthermore, the depth and the authenticity of her own spiritual life inspired people, as did her contagious simplicity in the way she addressed and coped with the balance between secular and Church events. I think she was both naïve and wise. These traits made people comfortable speaking to her and laying open the complications of their lives. She had an abundance of friends in many cities across Canada. Sister Anne Marie Conn, Maureen's superior in her community, told us at her funeral that Maureen always wanted to plan time for fun as part of community activities.

Maureen was always proud of the Religious of the Sacred Heart. She was proud of their mission, their gifts, their educational goals, and their foundress, Madeleine Sophie Barat. Once, during the last few years of her life, as her illness became more prominent, Maureen told me that she had received her "hundredfold here below," a reference to the biblical text in which Christ promises that those who leave family for his sake will receive a hundredfold in the hereafter.

Maureen suffered terribly in her last months. While she was at peace in the depths of her soul, the surface waters at times churned as she battled storms of doubt and faced panic as she sought the most simple thing in life: air to breathe.

She had been receiving excellent nursing care in the convent, which was a designated facility for the sisters in her community who were dying. The nurses there were marvellous. They fulfilled their tasks with obvious love, attention, compassion, and skill. As she approached death, her needs changed. She was dying and she knew it, and she needed palliative care. She no longer needed to go through the excruciating pain of getting out of bed to go to the bathroom, simply to keep active. She didn't need outside efforts to prolong her life. I don't know what led her to ask her doctor for palliative care; it may have been the very positive experience with palliative care that our brother John had had at the Riverview Health Centre in Winnipeg. As soon as the Halifax palliative care team started looking after her, there was a change in Maureen's disposition. She could now rest in bed without feeling guilty about "giving up." She could receive carefully regulated doses of morphine that cut her panic; she could be assured, over and over, that she would not suddenly suffocate at the end. The change seemed subtle in a way, but it was real and dramatic in its consequences. What she needed and wanted, and what they provided, was for her to be physically comfortable, to prepare for death in as much peace as was possible.

She was courageous. And, as my brother John had said eight years before, as he was dying of the same disease, Maureen told me, "I can't pray any more; now it is a matter of trust." But she was happy that I was able to lead her in prayer. We prayed Lamentations together:

> It is good to put one's face in the dust and wait. The mercies of the Lord last forever. My portion is Yahweh says my soul, and so I will hope in him. (Lamentations 3)

We prayed the Psalms:

> In your loving kindness, answer me, Yahweh. In your great tenderness turn to me; do not hide your face from your servant, quick, I am in trouble, answer me. (Psalms 69)

But in her last two weeks, we focussed more on the glories of God. Several times I read to her a text from St. Paul, one of many that she had underlined in her Bible, and that mirrored her own ministry.

> I want you to be happy, always happy in the Lord. I repeat, what I want is your happiness. Let your tolerance be evident to everyone. The Lord is very near. There is no need to worry, but if there is anything you need, pray for it, asking God for it with prayer and thanksgiving, and that peace of God, which is so much greater than we can understand, will guard your hearts and your thoughts in Christ Jesus. (Philippians 4:4–7)

Despite the privilege of these profound religious moments with my sister, Maureen's death was the most difficult I have ever experienced. She possessed a degree of faith and spiritual strength that I lack. Yet I was the one consoling her! It remains a mystery to me that, the night before she died, she told me she was experiencing terrifying fear and an intense sense of abandonment by God. Was this the dark night of the soul that the mystics spoke about? I simply spoke the words of Scripture that I knew were special to her. She turned her face toward me and quietly said, "You'll never know, Raymond, how helpful you have been." Those were her last words to me.

Within a month of Maureen's departure, the losses Charlene and I had suffered in the previous decade seemed to weigh down upon us all at once. We had lost Charlene's father and mother, her lifelong friend Dotty Beth as well as Dotty Beth's mother; Maureen Barry is close to death; we had lost my mother, my two brothers, as well as Bill and Bruce, and now my sister, Maureen. While the pain of these losses is intense, I remain blessed by the presence of my three cousins, the Sturleys, who are like sisters to me.

Recently, Charlene and I spent an evening reading all the texts about the resurrection in the Gospels and Epistles. I remain struck by Paul's prayer for the Philippians, "that the faithful will experience God's peace which surpasses human understanding" (4:7). I have had serious discussions with a friend who does not believe there is life after death. There is obviously not enough human "evidence" to adequately understand the meaning of death or the possibility of life after death. Paul suggests that God's peace can compensate for that lack of human understanding. I have not achieved that peace in the face of death. Does it mean I don't have faith? I don't know. Lord, help my unbelief. In the meantime, I live with the dying of others.

CHAPTER 10

My Life as a Dean (1991–1999)

As dean handing Arts degree to Renata Neufeld, 1998

In 1987, I had been asked by several colleagues to let my name stand for the position of dean of the Faculty of Arts. I was somewhat flattered, but in my mind it was not the next, or even a sought-after, future step in my career at the University of Manitoba. Furthermore, I was not a full professor at the time. I felt that I was close to getting that promotion, and I did not want to be distracted. My scholarly achievements had already been delayed by my years as head of the Department of Sociology because I had taken it on so early in my academic career. Furthermore, I felt strongly that without the promotion I would be missing one of the highly desirable components of the credibility needed to be an effective dean. Nor did the prospect of applying for promotion to full professor during a term as dean have any appeal at all. For these reasons, I refused to give the matter any serious consideration. However, the seed had been sown.

The incumbent dean, John Finlay, was reappointed for a three-year term, and in 1990 the search for a new dean was again undertaken. I received my promotion to full professor in 1989, and so this obstacle was now removed. Charlene suggested that I now consider the matter because, as she pointed out, I was already taking on responsibilities in the University well beyond those in the Faculty of Arts, even though I was no longer head of the Department of Sociology. I remember taking stock of my academic career at the time. I always seemed to end up as chair of committees, to be the person who was asked to get things done. I began to sense that perhaps my greatest contribution might lie in creating an environment that would allow others to make more significant contributions. I therefore allowed my name to stand, with a clear sense that if I were not selected I could quite happily continue to work as hard as ever for the good of the students and the University.

The search for a new dean was a five-month process. Four candidates, including me, were shortlisted, and we each prepared a public lecture. I knew that the lecture played a prominent role in the final decision. I prepared for it by carefully reviewing the financial and personnel situation of the Faculty of Arts. The main messages I wanted to impart were my strong belief in the value of a liberal-arts education that included both the humanities and social sciences; my resolve to inform the rest of the University of the academic strength of the Faculty; my desire to support the development of faculty members and staff, especially at a time of serious financial cutbacks; and, perhaps most important, my commitment to transparency in decision-making. Because there were several competent candidates whom I felt could lead the Faculty, I was at peace as I awaited the decision. I was offered the position in February of 1991 and began my term on the 1st of June.

Several criticisms of my leadership style emerged both before I began and early in my term. One was a simple remark by a colleague in my own department. We were discussing whether or not I should let my name stand. "Frankly," he said, "I am not sure you are tough enough to make the hard decisions." While I like to think that I appreciated his honest assessment, I was hurt by the comment. It came back to me in a number of situations over the years, but, interestingly enough, I usually recalled it after I had made a difficult decision. Nevertheless, I was worried that, if selected, I might be taking on a task at a level beyond my competency.

Another colleague, also in my department, told me within a week of my appointment that he would give me six months in the job before I would quit. Over the years, within my own dean's office, occasionally I would get the comment, "You'll just have to be tougher," or "You'll just have to tell them that's the way it will have to be." I know that I was considered "too soft." Indeed, while I was dean there were numerous insinuations that I let heads of departments and other faculty members pull the wool over my eyes.

I received the same criticism about my style of dealing with students. My response, which I did not tire of repeating, was a modification of a statement that I had heard years earlier regarding welfare: you can set up a system to make sure that no one gets a break who does not deserve it, or you can set up a system to make sure that all those who need help will receive it. I wanted students to feel that we were there to solve their problems and make their educational experience positive. To that end, I asked my associate dean, Bob O'Kell, to create a student's code of responsibility, which, as its main thrust, invited students to become members of the community of scholars, which is the heart of a university. Of course, it is always possible that one can be deceived by others, and when I encountered dishonesty it was indeed hard to take. I think I know why. As a child, when Dad told me that he "was disappointed in me" for having done something or other, he could not have punished me more.

When I erred, I agree that it was usually on the lenient side. The same issue has dogged me in our family life, particularly when making decisions about our children. Some members of our extended family certainly think that we have been too lenient. Professional counsellors have sometimes agreed. Try as I did to be loving yet firm, I don't feel I have ever achieved the right balance.

I have certainly been accused of letting faculty members talk forever. That is a variation of the criticism of lack of administrative toughness. It is ironic to me that, near the end of my first term as dean, Vice-President Jim Gardner wrote me a most complimentary letter about the Faculty Development Policy, suggesting that it could be a model for other faculties. It was my real passion to sustain a climate in which departments and individuals would flourish. I had to consider carefully how quickly I could achieve that. I came to know that if I pushed too fast, be it individuals, departments, or the Faculty of Arts, I would stir up nothing but opposition.

I have come to think that my major strength was simply to address important issues in higher education. My constant reading of the literature, the conferences I attended, and the lively debates with my associate deans and some faculty members inspired me to get the issues out into the open for discussion by proposing policies. The corollary is that I was committed to providing time for careful feedback, to being flexible and open to revisions, and to returning with alternative proposals when the first were not accepted. I made sure that this process occurred for every policy we addressed while I was dean. I was not defensive about my proposed policies, but I was fully committed to the need for clear policies. I came to some peace in concluding that the issue was not a matter of toughness or softness on my part but really about focussing and delivering.

Yet, at the same time, while I was dean, I had been given to understand that the Faculty of Arts was perceived as far too slow to change. In the middle of my term, the dean of each faculty was instructed by Vice-President Jim Gardner to create an accountability policy. Other faculties produced their accountability policies within just a couple of weeks. In my view, accountability often had a "search-and-destroy" edge to it, a presumption that incompetence abounds. I judged that accountability would be best accepted and achieved in a climate of opportunities for professional development. So I decided to start by creating a faculty-development policy. I spent 10 months working with a particularly competent committee chaired by Paul Thomas crafting the Faculty Development Policy, and only after that did we address and complete the Faculty Accountability Policy, which took us only two weeks. By achieving consensus on what constitutes a successful faculty member and how the Faculty of Arts could help individuals achieve that, there was little discussion necessary before consensus was reached on appropriate measures of accountability. Faculty development was the cornerstone of my approach to my tasks as dean.

Like most other deans, I certainly did not take up the position with a solid grasp of the literature on higher education. I must give credit to Ray Perry, a member of our Department of Psychology and the Centre for Higher Education Research and Development, who has received several national and international awards for his research on higher education. He was a wonderful mentor to me. Soon after I entered the dean's office, he began to send me articles on aspects of higher education. I not only read them but also invited him to discuss them with me, much to his surprise. Over the years, he pointed me to the best literature on a large number of issues, such as roles and responsibilities of heads or chairs of departments, approaches to professional development of faculty and support staff, major issues faced by junior faculty members and the importance of mentors for them, and of providing clear, written expectations of performance. I also commissioned some research myself on some of these topics, including a particularly useful survey of mid-career faculty members by Dr. Irene Karpiak. Finally, I read a great deal about what is often called strategic planning and conducted an exercise in strategic planning in the last years of my deanship. I tried to live by a dictum that Arthur Levine, President of Columbia Teacher's College, told us at a dean's conference one year: "Resources follow vision, not the other way around." For example, I believe that, by placing our hiring needs within a framework of a long-term vision of the Faculty, we were often able to secure a few more appointments than would otherwise have been granted to us. I know that a number of faculties of Arts across the country adopted our procedure, or a version of it.

My interest in creating policies was balanced by my efforts to promote the success of individual faculty members and staff. After several years in the position, I developed a pattern of writing an annual letter to all faculty and support staff around Christmastime. The letter was personally addressed to each of the nearly 400 individuals. The first page and a half contained information about developments within the faculty. On the second page I added a personal handwritten note, complimenting the person on some aspect of his or her work: something I had heard about the person's teaching, research, or community or university service. I received more positive feedback from that annual letter than from any other thing I did as dean. One year, when the Faculty Association was at the end of negotiating a new contract with a modest salary increase, a faculty member wrote, "Your positive comments to me about my teaching were worth far more to me than the salary increase."†

In that same spirit I created a number of awards within the Faculty. The first was the Outstanding Teaching Award for students in doctoral programs; it was designed to encourage them to take teaching seriously as they prepared for an academic career. Later I added a Professor of the Year award in the Faculty and an Internationalization Award, the latter to recognize academics who brought an international perspective to their work.

During my first day on the job, however, I was immediately faced with balancing the Faculty budget, which was close to $1 million short of the previous year's. The budget of about $23 million supported over 300 teaching staff and researchers, about 70 support staff, a number of research centres, and close to 8,000 students taking at least one course in the humanities or the social sciences in 17 departments. Just before my term began, Acting Dean Karen Ogden, to her credit, had made the difficult but necessary financial decision to cancel all new appointments, even some previously approved. The University is not allowed, by law, to have a deficit. She did not want me to have to make such decisions during my first week on the job.

---

† *One explanation that I have found particularly useful in understanding why individuals can persist in a situation when they are no longer performing well is the phenomenon of "burnout." Peter Vail (Managing as a* Performing Art, *San Francisco: Jossey-Bass, 1991) describes it as (1) the retention of an abstract commitment to a task, (2) associated with the loss of heart to continue to fulfill it at an excellent level, (3) yet coupled with the decision or lack thereof to remain in the situation, subject to the culture and all the expectations of it.*

This was the start of an era of severe budget cuts that became a protracted exercise every year of my deanship. To say that these exercises clouded the skies underestimates their impact. The constant uncertainty fostered a monumental waste of our time and energy as we tried to plan for scenarios that could, and did, vary every year by several hundreds of thousands of dollars. To this day, I cannot understand why successive Manitoba governments have felt that it is acceptable to inform universities of their budget only days before, or even after, the fiscal year has begun, when academic hiring has to be initiated almost a year before new staff arrive. Rarely were we first on the market to hire the latest and perhaps best graduates looking for employment. Furthermore, often we could hire scholars for only one-, two-, or three-year terms. Near the end of these short terms, they would have to face the difficult decision of staying in Winnipeg in hopes that the budget would allow them another year or to search for a job elsewhere. If it turned out that they could not be rehired here, it was often too late for them to find a position elsewhere. This kind of uncertainly does not foster a creative research climate, where projects can often take years to bring to fruition. Our society spends an enormous amount of money on higher education, yet, because of these uncertain government policies, we often cannot make good use of the graduates by offering them stable positions.

Another serious problem stemming from the cuts and the late announcement of budgets was the lack of trust by faculty members in the administration of the University. The President's Office was frequently unfairly blamed for the financial crises. In these uncertain times, maintaining and developing a healthy morale among heads of departments and throughout the Faculty was a huge challenge. Support staff also lived in constant fear of cutbacks.

I am proud of the fact that in my eight years as dean I always balanced the budget. I recognized that I was dealing with taxpayers' money, and I felt an enormous responsibility to spend it wisely. Early in my term, I was discussing a budget request from a department head with my budget officer, Brent Clark. "I can't afford to support that. I don't have the money," I said. "Oh, you have money," he replied. "You just have to decide your priorities." He was right, and his comment influenced many of my subsequent decisions.

The annual budget crisis at the University of Manitoba of course had more far-reaching consequences. The federal government has recently dramatically increased research funding for universities. Not only have the three major granting councils received larger budgets,† but also, funding for a number of other major research projects has been secured. But funding often has strings attached. As former Industry Minister Allan Rock worded it, "Universities have finally, formally acknowledged that they must make a more direct commercial contribution to industrial development if they expect taxpayers to continue to funnel more dollars into the academy." *Matching grants* is the magic phrase these days. In cases where it applies, government will support research at universities only if matching funds can be found within the community. However, this almost invariably negatively affects a faculty of arts in favour of "applied" programs, such as computer science, medicine, nursing, and management.

To illustrate this effect, I like to draw a comparison between the roles of preventive medicine and applied medicine. Our society has had an astounding ability to address medical problems and conquer them. The treatments for leprosy, tuberculosis, polio, and hepatitis, for example, are all medical triumphs. But there is no question that our society is much more willing to

† The three Councils are CIHR (Canadian Institutes of Health Research, with a budget close to a billion dollars), NSERC (National Science and Engineering Research Council, with a budget close to $600 million), and SSHRC (Social Sciences and Humanities Research Council with a budget slightly under $400 million).

fund efforts to cure illnesses than to fund efforts to prevent illnesses. Funding the humanities and social sciences is like funding the prevention of social illnesses. You can see their importance only when the diseases break out—for example the diseases of illiteracy, of ignorance, of intolerance, and of narrow-mindedness. And the lack of imagination, of curiosity, and of the pursuit of wisdom can best be addressed by a liberal-arts education. One's enjoyment of beauty, truth, and creativity, as well as the importance of ideas in history, are all essential to the vitality of a society. But they are immune to economic indicators and specific job-creation projects.

However, it is not only the arts and humanities faculties that can suffer when directed funding becomes the norm. So too can the professional faculties. Dr. Henry Friesen, a former head of the Medical Research Council of Canada, was interviewed by Shelagh Rogers on CBC in the late 1990s, and he provided a striking example of the centrality of basic research. If we had had the current economy-driven, applied-research focus when the polio epidemic was occurring in the 1950s, he said, perhaps there would have been matching grants from industry to develop a computerized lung-breathing apparatus. In fact, it was basic research on viruses, in its origins totally unrelated to the polio epidemic, that enabled the vaccine for polio.

At the first retreat that I called for heads of departments and program directors, just 20 days after taking up my appointment as dean, I threw out the agenda after an hour and spent the rest of the day answering questions and articulating my approach to administration. Obviously, so early in my term I could not even imagine many of the issues that would arise. Therefore, I tended to focus on my principles of administration. Stanley Fish, whose term as dean of the Faculty of Arts and Science at the University of Illinois, Chicago, overlapped my own term, wrote about "the golden rule of administration." While I read his statement after I finished my term, it resonated with what I said that day about transparency in administration. "It has three components," he wrote. "First, always tell the truth. Second, always tell more of the truth than you have been asked, and third, tell it before you are asked to."[1] While there are some exceptions—particularly on personnel issues when all cannot be revealed—this openness invites reflection on the issues, it invites feedback, often constructive, it fosters fairness, and it facilitates acceptance, or at least tolerance, when there is not agreement.

The annual budget process is a perfect application of Fish's advice. I described the allocations to department heads in great detail, explaining the principles behind each of the components (such as graduate-student support, supplies, new faculty teaching, or research incentives and research centres), and several times the department heads and I decided together to change our priorities.

The most successful example of the openness I worked to achieve was the procedure that I established for the hiring of new faculty members. There is not an issue more important to a department than its ability to attract new, younger, fresh academics to strengthen their unit. Together with the heads, I set up a process that required them to rank all applications for new academic positions (except those submitted by their own departments) according to 13 agreed-upon criteria. Outside the Faculty there were certainly criticisms that this was excessively democratic and time-consuming and limited the flexibility of the dean. However, I believe that this process helped heads to develop a vision of the broad needs of the whole Faculty. It muted their criticism of appointments to other departments over their own needs. In some years, one department might get two or even three positions while others got none. Small and large departments alike, social science and humanities departments alike, cooperated with one other for the common good. Given an opportunity to change this system of hiring new faculty members in a year when there were five new heads, the remaining heads assured the newcomers that the system was fair and in their best interests. I guarded the flexibility I needed by making it clear that I would make some appointments independent of the process as necessary. But the consultative process usually brought consensus on about 70 percent of the proposed appointments. On the remaining 30 percent, the very lack of consensus made it easier for me to make an independent decision.

I confess to being particularly thrilled when, in 1994, the Faculty of Arts received a national award from the Canadian Association of University Business Officers (CAUBO) for innovation in management practices specifically for the hiring procedures that I have just described. In the same year, I also shared the first University of Manitoba Faculty Association Administrator of the Year Award. And I was delighted to be awarded the Peter D. Curry Chancellor's Award offered by The Investor's Group "for individuals who have made distinct contributions to University governance and/or development" when I finished my term as dean.

When I took on the job as dean, it became clear very quickly that I could divide the multiplicity of tasks and issues that would confront me into three types. The first type included the inevitable annual tasks, such as overseeing the assignment of teaching responsibilities. The second type included the tasks thrust upon me by circumstances. The third included the things I chose to tackle because of my values and goals. My plate was always full to overflowing. The members of my own department knew that this would happen, and their gift to me when I assumed the deanship was a pair of roller skates.

All three types of tasks could be either difficult, disappointing, or extremely satisfying. It is remarkable that I rarely felt completely alone in addressing problems. The personal and professional relationships with my three associate deans could not have been better. Our Tuesday morning meetings were crammed with issues, but we made time to address large policy issues and discuss alternative solutions to practical problems. Bob O'Kell, who succeeded me as dean, was astounded when I approached him to become an associate dean. "I have disagreed with you over and over in executive meetings," he pointed out. I told him that I wanted to appoint individuals who viewed matters differently from how I did. It was a very successful strategy. Our debates were often intense, but the respect for one another was palpable, and the loyalty of my associate deans was gratifying. My executive assistants, particularly June Stewart and Harry Sutcliffe, and a staff of about 15 in the General Office, created an environment that made it a pleasure to come to work.

I also had a positive relationship with everyone in the Office of the President, including both President Arnold Naimark and later President Emöke Szathmáry. Of course, we had our differences of opinion, and I certainly did not get everything I wanted or felt the Faculty should have, nor did I believe the right decisions were always made. But I felt that we were working together as a team in trying to solve problems. This is not a flippant statement. A dean is right in the middle, required to defend and promote the faculty and at the same time to help the president promote the development of the whole university. In fact, some of the most intense differences of opinion tended to emerge in Dean's Council meetings. I was not as successful as I would like to have been in convincing the senior administrators that we needed more resources in Arts and Science. Yet, as the years progressed, while we argued more in Dean's Council, we also grew in respect for one another. When I retired, one of the things I missed the most was the interaction with other deans and with senior administrators.

It was important to me to initiate positive interaction with the Faculty Association. I encouraged faculty members to bring a representative with them when I was dealing with a disciplinary matter, and on several occasions working with Eve Finnbogason, a university lawyer, I informed the grievance officer of the Association ahead of time of the issues that I would be addressing. On only one occasion during my two terms was a disciplinary matter not resolved within the Faculty, and the Association grieved a decision at a higher level. On several occasions when preparing drafts of new policies that I felt the Faculty needed, I sent them to the Association for their views before bringing them to Faculty Council for approval.

My relations with the Office of the President, with other deans, and with faculty members were severely put to the test when we had a faculty strike in October of 1995. Recently I reread a paper that I delivered at the meeting of Western Deans of Arts and Science in 1996 called "Anatomy of a Strike." In it I tried to outline the causes and illustrate the myriad of practical problems that had to be faced during and after the 23-day strike. But, most of all, rereading the paper recalled for me the tension, the ambiguity, and the uncertainty of relations that emerged. I was not only dean of the Faculty of Arts but also a member of the Board of Governors elected by members of the University Senate. Ninety-two percent of faculty members of the Faculty of Arts went on strike; this percentage was matched only by the Faculty of Social Work. I knew that I would have to lead the Faculty after the strike. During any strike, there are labour laws that must be obeyed by both sides, and accordingly I was not allowed to communicate information that I had as a member of the Board or as a dean. I could not even correct statements that I knew to be erroneous. Nor could I be involved in the bargaining process in any way. Nevertheless, my associate deans and I worked with Dean Jamieson from the Faculty of Science, and on three occasions we met with President Naimark to suggest resolutions to the dispute. On each day of the strike I would come to the campus by a different one of three entrances. I would stop and talk to those on the picket line, inform them that we were working to help end the strike without going into detail, and listen to their views.

The morning after the strike ended, a faculty member appeared at my door with a petition containing 100 names requesting an emergency meeting of Faculty Council. When I inquired about the agenda, it was made clear to me that I should go prepared to listen, not to speak. It sounded very ominous, but it turned out that there were several conflicting agendas among the faculty members who wanted the meeting. At the appointed time, over 200 faculty members attended. After a few brief opening remarks, I opened the floor for discussion. The first speaker began by stating, "We need a new dean." For the next seven minutes (or was it 70!), he gave his reasons. He alleged that I did not respect academic freedom, that I was a pawn of the administration and "a corporate man" during the strike. This is probably the worst insult a dean of Arts could possibly hear. It reflects the strongly held view in many faculties of Arts across the country that governments are caving in to corporations and corrupting the most basic mission of a university (which is to develop an informed citizenry) in favour of more narrow economic goals. I was taken by complete surprise. I put my head down in order to avoid recognizing another speaker until I could formulate my response. In the moments of complete silence that followed, I somehow found a sense of unusual clarity. The attack was very personal in nature, but I consciously decided to respond only to the erroneous statements while trying to achieve some emotional distance from the rest. But the next three speakers repudiated the first speaker, and their comments were greeted by applause. Thus, an extremely tense situation was diffused. I spent the next hour and a half answering questions, giving my views on academic freedom (which was the defining issue of the strike in the minds of the faculty members), and about my behaviour during the strike. I took advantage of the situation to propose a state-of-the-Faculty address, which I would deliver in a month. In the next few days, I was touched by the numerous supportive phone calls, notes, and e-mails that I received from faculty members. One theme was that my behaviour in response to the first speaker was probably the best way that I could have demonstrated how much I value academic freedom of speech. I deeply appreciated the vote of confidence in my leadership that came out of this especially stressful meeting.

Any who have experienced a strike in their workplaces will know how animosities both within and among levels of authority can be long festering. I was under no illusion that all was settled in the Faculty. For about six months, the aftermath of the strike was intense. In Faculty Council, motions of non-confidence and censure of the president and two vice-presidents were introduced. These motions were well beyond the authority of Council, and I ruled them out of order. While some deans hired replacement teachers during the strike, several of us did not, and there was controversy over reallocation of funds that resulted from their decisions. One tactic that I think helped the Faculty was a meeting I organized immediately after the end of the strike with the representatives of the union in each of the departments in the Faculty. We discussed how we could put the strike behind us and recreate a climate of cooperation in the Faculty.

Earlier in the year of the strike, I was faced with a completely different type of major problem. While it was clearly one thrust upon me by circumstances, I decided that I needed to address it with some unusual decisiveness. In April of 1995, a woman in the Department of Political Studies resigned, citing an "inhospitable environment." Two days after her resignation, after discussing the matter with the vice-president, I decided to establish an ad hoc committee to investigate "the climate" in the

Department. While it was her resignation that prompted my decision to speak with the vice-president, rumours, hearsay, and other factors also were relevant, including a previous resignation by the only other tenured woman in the Department. The issues were extremely complex. Defining a "chilly climate" is difficult, almost as difficult as investigating it.† Alleging that a department has a chilly climate can taint innocent individuals who might be caught in the situation. There are dangers of violation of academic freedom. Where are the dividing lines among sexual harassment, violation of human rights, chilly climate, bullying, incivility, and simple rudeness? What responsibilities do individuals have when others in a department behave in-appropriately? Whenever I was faced with conflict within the Faculty, my guiding principle was to ask myself what would be the consequences if I did nothing? On several occasions, this principle gave me the courage to address very complex issues.

The first issue I needed to tackle was to establish an appropriate committee, and our decision turned out to be among the most important in the whole process. I asked Mary Lou Dietz, from the University of Windsor, to chair the committee. She was a winner of the Sara Shorten National Award for Outstanding Leadership by a Woman in Academic Life. I also chose Judy Anderson from the University of Manitoba's Faculty of Medicine and Wayne Simpson from the Department of Economics within the Faculty of Arts. In addition, I appointed Jon Young, an associate dean in the Faculty of Education and an expert in race and ethnic issues, to act as an assessor of the committee in its investigative work—that is, to ensure that the committee acted reasonably, fairly, and in good faith. I was looking for four qualifications

† *I gave the committee two lengthy definitions of* chilly climate *so that they had a well-conceived and unambiguous mandate to work with. The beginning of the first definition was: "The climate of a campus is its mood, including culture, habits, decisions, practices and policies that make up campus life, as perceived by its members . . ."*

in all these people: to be recognized teachers, to be strong researchers, to be knowledgeable of the issues that women face in universities, and to have a history of involvement in the Faculty Association. I did not want the results to turn into a war between union and management. The appointment of an independent assessor and his positive assessment of the process in his separate report turned out to be critical in having the report of the committee publicly accepted as a fair process by faculty members within the University as well as in the wider public sphere.

I instructed the committee to focus exclusively on issues of climate and to refer any complaints of sexual harassment or violation of human rights, if they were alleged, for investigation by the appropriate university officer. It is only here that such charges could be properly investigated, as, in order to ensure fairness and justice, the individuals involved would need to be able to confront the accusations they were facing. A confidential committee report such as the one I was setting up would not permit that. It is worth noting that a department or any work situation can have a chilly climate without any explicit sexual harassment, just as it can have a case of sexual harassment without having a chilly climate.

In sorting through the chilly-climate issue, I received excellent advice and support from individuals in the Office of the President, particularly Vice-Provost Karen Ogden and Eve Finnbogason, as well as from my associate deans, particularly Karen Grant. President Arnold Naimark made the decision to let the Faculty of Arts address the issue on the grounds that, whenever possible, those closest to a problem should resolve it. I certainly appreciated his confidence in me.

The process began in late April, and the final press conference after I received the report occurred in the middle of June. In that time there were 100 radio, television, and newspaper reports and many letters to the editor that brought local, national, and international attention to the inquiry. The letters to the editor expressing various points of view fanned the flames. Several people who thought the climate was indeed chilly spoke to the press on numerous occasions, but I was unable to respond to their accusations because it would have violated confidentiality. Once I struck the committee, I remained completely at arm's-length and received no communication from them other than the final report. In spite of our numerous efforts to clarify the situation to the media, most of the reporters still seemed unable to recognize that the mandate of the committee was to investigate the issue of chilly climate and not accusations of sexual harassment if they were to arise.

The report contained a large number of recommendations, and I worked hard to implement all of them, though budget limitations caused some delays. Following is part of the conclusion in my statement to the press when the committee's findings were released:

> While we are addressing the issue of climate, we do not want to create an environment that is free from controversy, disagreement or intellectual disputes. The academic community is always filled with controversy, and rightly so; be it over schools of thought, intellectual approaches or policy approaches. Most departments go out of their way to hire individuals with varying theoretical approaches, who have graduated from a variety of universities. But women, members of other designated groups and some perspectives have been at the margins. Equity issues must be understood within this historical context. Collegiality has been carried out predominantly within the context of male cultural sociability. That is no longer acceptable.

Some academics suggest that addressing a chilly climate is a game that one cannot win. I could not disagree more. Our process was not perfect, but I believe that it was fair in its fundamentals. It was not a long, drawn-out affair, nor was the cost exorbitant (it was under $10,000). Our committee was perceived to be legitimate. The Royal Society of Canada later published a report sent to presidents of all universities in Canada outlining how to conduct such inquiries when they are needed, and our procedures were prominent among those recommended in that report. More important, the process led to a number of significant proactive measures to improve the Department, the Faculty, and the University. In fact, at the end of the inquiry, the Department members themselves organized a series of meetings with a facilitator from outside the University of Manitoba.

The investigation into the chilly-climate issue was an extremely difficult period during my deanship. As was the case during the strike, I had to face a plenary meeting of the Faculty to explain the process, the findings, and what I planned to do about the situation. In a sense, it epitomized my efforts to create a positive working and learning environment for all faculty members, support staff, and students.

I had not intended to continue after my five-year term as dean, but a forthcoming change in the presidency of the University, the chaotic budget situation, and some unfinished strategic planning that I had initiated after the strike in 1995 led me to let my name stand. However, I made it clear that if selected I would agree to only a three-year term—1996 to 1999. I wanted to be sure to leave before everyone wanted me to!

Just as my first term as dean began in 1991 a few months after we received Catherine's diagnosis of autism, so did my second term begin in the midst of a family turning point: Charlene had suffered a stroke in February of 1996 and then underwent surgery for cancer in September. The first of these events made the decision to continue as dean that much more difficult. However, Charlene was an incredible support. She encouraged me, and never, ever gave me the sense that I was neglecting her needs or the children's in doing my work. At the same time, her poor health meant that she was not able to accompany me to most of the many University and community evening functions that are part of the responsibility of a dean. Her reluctance in the first year came primarily from physical fatigue and some depression, but, later on, it was the increasing prominence of other effects of the stroke. We were fortunate that the physical effects of the stroke were short-lived, but she has not been able to recapture her short-term memory. At one point, she spent close to four months trying to prepare a single class on a topic that she knew well, hoping to return to teaching at the University of Winnipeg. But organizating the material proved to be beyond her. So also was her ability to engage in conversation that required her to remember events of the recent past or to tell a story. The anxiety associated with these tasks was almost paralyzing. Many times she would tell me she would love to come to a particular event, only to decline at the last minute because the prospect of interacting with others when she felt almost empty was just too daunting.

I began my second term in July of 1996, when my brother John was living with us just prior to his move to Riverview Health Centre and his death four months later. As well at this time, we had to make the decision to move Catherine to a new agency and a new home, and Vincent was in and out of jail. I admit that going to work was sometimes a relief from the stresses that I was experiencing at home.

The three years of my second term were consumed primarily by strategic planning, but it also included the final stages of implementing what became known as University One. University One was extremely exciting and in many ways a model of how change can occur in a university. Many students arrive at university with the idea that they will become doctors, lawyers, or engineers. A large number drop out of those programs during or after their first year for various reasons, but, instead of pursuing options in other faculties where they would be better suited, they often see themselves as failures and leave university altogether. In this context, President Naimark proposed a new program for first-year students. Dean Jamieson and his associate deans in the Faculty of Science, as well as I and my associate deans, felt that we could modify and improve President Naimark's proposal. He supported our efforts. We undertook the task and, after well over a year of work, including individual consultations with every dean in the University to convince them that we were not simply trying to increase enrolments in our own faculties, we introduced the new idea—University One—to the whole University. After establishing the key principles and the goals that we wished to pursue, we asked Dave Burton, Associate Dean of Science, to take the lead; the final outcome was the result of cooperation from a very large number of key administrators across the whole University.

The introduction to university life that University One provides gives students a chance to make more informed decisions about what they want to study. They do not have to make a premature choice for specialization before they have had a basic introduction to the core disciplines (humanities, social sciences, and natural sciences) and an initiation to one or two professional faculties that are of interest to them. The program doesn't lengthen the time they need to spend completing a degree, which is important for those who do know exactly what they want. There are also much improved counselling opportunities for them. A tracking system has been set up to monitor the success of the program, and recent research has confirmed that the new program has significantly reduced the dropout rate of first-year students. It took longer than it should have to get University One up and running, but it was successful in that the process reflected a vision, a sense of trust, good will, and cooperation among deans, as well as a great deal of listening and a good communication strategy. Jim Gardner, Vice-President Academic at the time, was a key supporter of the project.

My second term coincided with the arrival of our new president, Emöke Szathmáry. It takes time to know the leadership style and priorities of a new president. Because the Faculty of Arts is so large, and because I was on major university committees, including the Board of Governors, I had more opportunities than most to interact with her. We had some tense moments at the beginning, but, after a particularly difficult exchange in a planning committee of the Board, I noted that our disagreement did not affect my ability to work with her. It became clear quickly that she would be a fierce and effective promoter of the University of Manitoba. Early in her term, she initiated a University-wide strategic-planning process. I prepared three submissions for her committee at different stages in the process and took part in many discussions and workshops with deans and directors. I very much wanted her to be successful, even if I did not agree with every recommendation. One that I could not support was a proposed merger of the Faculty of Arts and the Faculty of Science.

Meanwhile, our own faculty plan was moving ahead. I think a number of faculty members in Arts would look back on our faculty planning exercise as a waste of time. I am not so harsh in my judgement as to say it was a waste of time, but it is obvious that I made some mistakes. I began the process too late in my term, and it became clear that my last year in office was not the appropriate time to propose even modest changes in the organization of departments. As well, the process was going to be too drawn out. Staff are not prepared to live with uncertainty about possible structural changes for long periods of time. While we already had long-standing criteria to evaluate individuals, we needed to determine criteria by which departments as units should be evaluated, and we spent a great deal of time doing so. Perhaps we spent too much time at this, but the very nature of a faculty of Arts dictates that the criteria will be scrutinized for every possible interpretation. After we achieved agreement on the criteria, I was far too slow in writing an evaluation of every department based on the criteria. In fact, after I finished my term as dean, I spent the first three months of my administrative leave writing the final 100-page report. I was disappointed to learn that the Executive Committee of the Faculty, an elected committee to advise the dean, quickly decided to put the report aside on the grounds that the situation had changed and the evaluations were no longer valid. I have no idea if individual departments found the evaluations of their own units useful. Frankly, I think it was a waste of my time to have written the report, even if in my own mind it brought some closure to the process.

In spite of these setbacks, I believe the process of renewal in the Faculty had significant successes. There were substantial improvements in faculty development, including more support for incoming faculty members, some initiatives regarding student learning, a greater appreciation of the role of the colleges (St. Andrew's, St. John's, St. Paul's, and University College) in relationship to the Faculty of Arts, and, most important of all, a better balance between the reward system for teaching and research responsibilities. I believe that the various departments within the humanities benefited the most. For example, it was through explicit discussion within the Strategic Planning Committee that the Department of Religion was revitalized. Committee members recognized the importance of the study of world religions, and, in spite of a shortage of resources, gave priority in the Faculty to new hires in that area. While some structural changes regarding the organization of language and literature study was defeated in Council, much to my disappointment, their importance in the Faculty was certainly reaffirmed. In all, 50 recommendations were contained in the final report of the Committee to Faculty Council. We debated these over three meetings while I was still dean. Interestingly, a number of recommendations had been implemented long before the final report came to Faculty Council. This was indeed a case in which the process was far more important than the final document. And I would say the same of the president's strategic-planning exercise.

My reflections here recall only a few of the major issues that I faced as dean. Hardly a day went by without the development of some new issue. Interaction with heads of departments, both individually and in our monthly meetings, were often challenging but more often very rewarding. Our faculty members were always excelling, whether their achievements were publications, research grants, national recognition, or teaching awards, and it was Associate Dean Karen Grant's particular responsibility to acknowledge and nurture these. We developed a new student-exchange program for students from Mexico, thanks to the efforts of Associate Dean Jim Dean. And we finalized a new academic agreement with the University of Iceland, which facilitated faculty and student exchange.

The Province of Manitoba has the highest concentration of people of Icelandic descent outside Iceland, and our university has the only Department of Icelandic Studies outside Iceland, as well as the second-largest library collection. The stories of the Icelandic settlers in Canada were inspiring to me. It is sometimes said that when these settlers came to Canada in 1875, they brought their children and their books, and often only the books survived. The donation of many of these books to our University library over the years form the basis of the remarkable collection we now have. Thanks to the extraordinary leadership of Dr. Kenneth Thorlakson and the support of many others, the Western Icelanders (as those of Icelandic origin living in Canada are called) committed themselves to strengthen the Icelandic presence at the University. I was invited, along with Dr. Thorlakson and Carolynne Presser, Director of Libraries, to visit Iceland in 1998, and, as a result of the meetings, we were given very substantial financial support for our Department of Icelandic Studies and its library. We were also able to negotiate a comprehensive exchange agreement between the two universities, an excellent model for the many other such agreements the University has around the world. The fact that the population of the whole of Iceland is less than half the population of Winnipeg (310,000 versus 670,000) only highlights the significant achievements of Icelanders, including their unparalleled commitment to literacy, education, and the arts; it's a lesson for the world.

Icelandic is one of seventeen languages taught in the Faculty of Arts at the University of Manitoba. The academics who teach these languages are highly committed to the link between the literatures and the cultures that these languages express. However, most students want to learn a language for practical, job-oriented reasons; their interest in the literature and culture expressed by the language is usually far less intense than that of their teachers. A teacher's decision to teach literature in the original language or in translation is a complex one, and sometimes the two approaches can be used simultaneously. In addition to language and literature, increasing opportunities are being provided to students to accompany professors to different countries for research, for classes, and for cultural experiences. Within Winnipeg itself, it was a true pleasure for me to attend ethnic events, particularly in the Polish and Italian communities, to thank organizers who often gave us substantial sums of money to support our language and literature programs.

One of the public commitments that I made in my address to the Faculty of Arts before beginning my second term was to strengthen the Aboriginal presence in the Faculty. In spite of intense competition for academics specializing in Native studies across Canada, we did recruit successfully, and the Department of Native Studies began a graduate program. Aboriginal lawyers, doctors, and engineers are also graduating in increasing numbers from the University, not to mention the large number in Arts and Science and other professional faculties, such as Social Work. Former Governor General Adrienne Clarkson and her husband, John Ralston Saul, an independent scholar, each made a point of praising the successes of the access programs for Aboriginals at the University of Manitoba. In addition, there is significant research being accomplished in cooperation with Aboriginals in a large number of disciplines. As the President's strategic plan words it, I think that the University can indeed become the "institution of first choice" for Aboriginal education in Canada, but we still have a long way to go. In fact, I must say that we have moved far too slowly in this area.

I enjoyed myself right up to the end of my term as dean. However, on my last day, I admit that I left early, at 3:30 p.m., to head out for a holiday in Kentucky.

As I reflect upon my years at the University as a dean, I realize that what I loved about them was what I also loved about the ministry. In both situations I was asked to take on leadership roles. I believe that my approach to leadership was nourished in the Franciscans, where there is no superior but, rather, a guardian. It is based on the idea of *service*, but it is service with a vision. I have always possessed an urge to get things done in whatever situation I am in. I hate interminable meetings, and I want action. I have always insisted that any meetings I am part of record action items and that these should be the first things reviewed at the next meeting. However, I don't believe that these actions necessarily have to be based on my ideas. The vision that should be acted upon should be based on consensus—what is best for the organization. In the case of the Church, the vision is one of faith, which nevertheless has to be carried out in a human organization, and this is not an easy task. The vision of a university is equally complex—to promote the best of human knowledge and wisdom. My terms as head of the Department of Sociology and dean of the Faculty of Arts gave me the immense satisfaction of trying to make a difference in the university community and in society.

Chapter 11

My Retirement (2000–2008)

With Charlene on cruise around South America, 2001

I was 66 years of age in 2000 when I retired from the University of Manitoba. I didn't have a clear plan for what I would do with the rest of my life, but I did know what I *didn't* want to do, and I did know what was important to me. I wanted to focus on my passion for learning, my love of teaching, my deep interest in research, my continuing search for spiritual meaning, my service on volunteer boards in the community, and on making as useful a contribution to the community as I could. Much to my genuine surprise, I was given the honorific title of dean emeritus by the Board of Governors.

I am still attached to the University as a dean emeritus and a senior scholar,* but, after retirement, in spite of the possibility of maintaining an office on campus, I began to work at home as much as possible to help Charlene cope with the ongoing consequences of her stroke. I was adjusting nicely to the change. It was good to be away from the stresses of academic life. I was glad to be away from the tension of half-hour regimentation, of entering a meeting without having reviewed the minutes as carefully as I should have and fearing an unpredictable challenge, the frustration of not having read and reflected on everything I should have. I was glad to be away from the difficult personnel decisions of the dean's office. My retirement plan was to retire from stress, not work.

I feel fortunate to be in a position that enables me to continue to make modest contributions to society. Part of the reason for this is that Canada is such a relatively small country. When I lived in New York, when I reflected on the size of the city, the state, and the whole country, I felt overwhelmed and felt that my work and my ideas would never matter. I have never had that sense in the context of Manitoba or Canada.

As retirement approached, my transition was facilitated by the fact that I was already being invited to conduct workshops with deans and department chairs at universities across the country. These exciting new opportunities flowed naturally from the work I had been involved with during my time as dean, such as with the Centre for Higher Education Research and Development (CHERD) at the University. Under the sponsorship of CHERD, I have visited more than a dozen universities in Canada and abroad (in South Africa, for example) giving workshops on such topics as the changing nature of scholarship, faculty development, and conflict resolution. As well, I have evaluated both graduate and undergraduate programs in several of these universities. Whenever I present a case study in one of the workshops and one of the participants responds, "This is exactly what I am facing in my department," I feel highly rewarded. I have also addressed national and regional meetings of deans. At my own university, I was asked by Vice-President Robert Kerr to be an informal advisor for new deans of faculties. To call this activity "mentoring" sounds a bit pretentious to me, but the idea of assigning an experienced dean to new arrivals for both formal and informal discussion is, I believe, a useful activity.

When I'm engaged in these academic activities, I always try to address what I see as the most important changes in academic life, many of which are common to many countries around the world. I believe that these changes have mainly to do with how approaches to scholarship are changing and that they are internal to universities and government alike. I don't for a moment think that all the changes are positive, particularly when the interaction between universities and government is at times difficult, but for the most part I believe that if we manage the changes well they can be extremely fruitful.

I find it refreshing to hear teachers and parents talking about the research their children are conducting in school, even in grades 1 and 2. The high school science fairs seem to be the pinnacle of these early efforts. The pervasive idea that everyone can conduct research is a wonderful development. Just as young children are learning about research, the nature of research in universities is changing, and these changes fit the way children are being taught before they get to university.

Michael Gibbons[1] has described the changing research climate as a shift from Mode 1 to Mode 2.[2] Within the framework of modes 1 and 2, he identifies four major shifts. First, while research by *individuals* (Mode 1) continues, research by *teams of researchers* (Mode 2) is on the rise. Second, while *discipline-based* research remains significant, there is a shift to more *problem-based*, issue-based, and trans-disciplinary research. Third, there is a shift in the organization of research, in which we find a move from a *local-organizational-knowledge* base toward that of *network-based* research. Fourth, the quality of research in Mode 1 is judged by *peer review*, while that in Mode 2 incorporates both *peer review and users* (for economic and social effect). The humanities are probably the least affected by these changes, but the social sciences, health sciences, and the natural sciences are being deeply affected.

Interdisciplinary research is a core component of these changes in approaches toward research. We know that ignorance leads to intolerance, and we need to learn about the contributions of disciplines other than our own, to share knowledge, and to respect that knowledge no matter what its origins. My involvement in the ecumenical movement, when I was active in the ministry, and specifically my participation in the discussions with theologians from different denominations at Dubuque, Iowa, helped me appreciate how much we need to break down the many institutional barriers to cooperation between departments and faculties; this is a difficult process, but it is an important one, and it is gathering momentum.

Another major change that Gibbons describes is the search for a new balance between basic research and applied research. Basic research, driven by the problem under scrutiny, will always be the core academic research enterprise. But there is also an important place for applied research, and to embrace both is a complex issue. The two approaches are not antithetical to each other, and the way one is undertaken can affect the way in which a researcher or a team of researchers undertakes the other. Applied research, of course, addresses how knowledge can be applied responsibly to known, consequential problems and is sometimes referred to as the scholarship of engagement to highlight the interaction of theory and practice. However, discovery followed by application is not always a one-way street. New intellectual understandings can often arise from the very act of application. The process of arriving at knowledge, as it draws upon contexts and relationships, is in itself valuable. It is different from an abstract, analytic approach, and some groups of subjects (Aboriginals, for example, who are tired of being studied without input from their own cultures) appreciate it. They expect the values of their culture to inform the research.

In the late 1990s, the Social Sciences and Humanities Research Council (SSHRC) initiated a category of grants called Community/University Research Alliances (CURA), in which academics can apply for grants only if there are community partners. Because they require building engagement and mutual respect between academics and community members, projects funded by CURA are extremely time-consuming. The participating community members need to be educated in the research process, and the academics need to understand the insights of community members and to share decision-making. This is a further democratization of the research process that can have enormous benefits. Some of the most successful research on domestic violence and abuse, for example, has emerged from collaborative projects between academics and community organizations.

One of the offshoots of seeking a better balance between basic research and applied research is the determination by some governments to require more policy-oriented outcomes from academic research. We often hear that governments are increasingly committed to "evidence-based decision-making." While this is an admirable idea, which I strongly support, I am a bit cynical about its reality. It is rare that a government enacts a social policy directly based on social-science research. Our influence is usually much more indirect. Changes in social policy are more often initiated by interest groups, by members of the public, and by media attention on an issue. These groups can be forces that convince government to change its direction or to take up issues that the groups believe have been ignored. In other words, the first consumers of research are often groups in the community, long before governments. For example, research on the health dangers of smoking were available long before policy changes occurred. Mothers Against Drunk Driving (MADD) has had an enormous effect on legislation to curb drinking and driving. The existing research was invoked by government only once the interest groups had used the research to mount their cases and public pressure convinced government to take notice.

Social policy is carried out in a political context, and there is no guarantee that even the best research will influence the position of any government if the political fallout will be greater than the ruling party is prepared to accept.

These multiple approaches to research have gained prominence in universities and in the work of individual faculty members. However, if scholars are asked, and expected, to undertake more interaction with the community, then this interaction must be acknowledged and rewarded. So far, we have rewarded overwhelmingly only Gibbons's Mode 1 research—that is, the individual, basic, and discipline-based research. At the University of Manitoba, I have seen little evidence that the expectations for tenure and promotion are changing to reflect the changing nature of scholarship, and this distresses me. I see much of the hard and important work done by academics go unacknowledged. Rather than adjusting their responsibilities, we are stretching our faculty members beyond reasonable limits, and I worry about the burnout that is occurring among the junior members especially.

Without question, my most extensive research activity since retirement has been as chair of the national Research Data Centre Network, which I undertook in 2002. The research data centres that make up the network are unique in that they focus on *longitudinal* data analysis, which means that researchers follow the same people over a long period of time. The centres are established in highly secure physical sites in universities and have rigorous rules for access, including RCMP security clearance. The regulations completely protect the privacy of Canadians yet allow us to track important social trends. One of the 100 projects contained in the centres for analysis is the Longitudinal Survey of Immigrants to Canada. Twelve thousand new adult immigrants who arrived in Canada in the one-year period beginning on the 1st of October 2000 were interviewed six months after they arrived, two years later, and again two years after that. Scientific sampling procedures were used, and the interviews were conducted in 15 languages. The immigrants were asked each time, for example, how they are adjusting to Canadian society, whether they are finding work that suits their skills, whether they are able to earn a living wage for their families, whether they are learning English or French, whether their children are doing well in the school system, and whether their health is changing. The results are of great interest to Canadian policy-makers; they are telling us how new immigrants are adjusting to life in Canada over time; and they are providing information on the factors that can facilitate or hinder this adjustment.

The National Longitudinal Survey of Children and Youth is designed to collect information about factors influencing a child's social, emotional and behavioural development, and to monitor the effect of these factors on the child's development over time.

The survey began in 1994 and is now in Wave 6, interviewing the children (or the most knowledgeable adult associated with a child in its very early years) every two years. Through this survey, for example, Lisa Strosheim found that the effect of divorce on children is not as great as the effect of conflict between the parents prior to divorce. A finding of this nature can have far-reaching consequences in the way families, religious groups, and societies deal with divorce. Other researchers have documented the effect of low income on how early or how late children learn to read and write and can predict the long-term consequences of low income on the future educational achievement of these children. These kinds of findings, and hence our ability to see significant social trends, can be discovered only if the same individuals are followed over time. Only longitudinal, comparative studies can allow us to measure the effects of the child-care policies in various provinces, for example. A study of the highly subsidized daycare system in Quebec found, among other things, that 40 percent of the cost of running the system was being recovered by the taxes paid by an increase of women in the labour force.

The Research Data Centres are located at universities throughout Canada, including one at the University of Manitoba. The first of these centres opened at McMaster University in 2001. The network has grown from an initial nine to 24, and researchers from 40 universities carry out the research. Currently, 1,600 researchers are working on over 1,200 different projects. In 2002, I was elected chair of the National Coordinating Committee of Research Data Centres and, in May of 2006, was elected to a third term.

My first task as chair was to start developing polices for all centres, and we have consequently become a true national network. My second task was to spearhead three grant applications, all of which were successful. In 2005, we received $8 million, to be released over five years, from the SSHRC and the Canadian Institutes of Health Research together. In November of 2006, we received $4 million from the Canada Foundation for Innovation, which is being used to dramatically improve the infrastructure and communication network among the centres and to strengthen our ability to make comparisons with European and American research findings on similar topics. Beginning in 2007, the centres began receiving $1 million from the federal Department of Human Resources and Social Development (to be spread over a three-year period). These funds have enabled the research centres to become among the most exciting developments in the social sciences in decades. We are now working with similar international projects, which will allow for important comparisons between the effect of Canadian social policies and those of almost 20 other countries. Charlene tells me that I am attached to a shooting star, one not likely to fade in the near future. I believe that social-science research is hugely important in our society, because it can describe, inform, debunk, and link the attitudes and behaviour of our citizens. I recently served as a member of the External Research Advisory Committee of Human Resources and Social Development Canada, and currently serve on the Social Conditions Committee of Statistics Canada that reviews existing and proposed surveys undertaken by that agency, and I feel sure that these opportunities came because of my work as chair of the Research Data Centre National Coordinating Committee.

These highly satisfying projects are providing me with an ideal way to make my transition to *real* retirement. The workshops and lectures that I present on academic leadership allow me to express ideas about which I am passionate, and they give me a forum in which I can suggest changes in universities that I feel are critical. They keep me focussed on the work and welfare of faculty members, which I always felt was my most important task as a dean. Chairing the Research Data Centre National Coordinating Committee is a culmination of my long-term passion for social-science research. I think of the development of the Research

Data Centres as a quantum leap forward in social-science capabilities in Canada.[3] My academic achievements since retirement have surpassed my wildest expectations but meet my best dreams.

I cannot remember a year throughout my priestly and academic careers when I was not on at least one or two boards of directors of community organizations. Currently I serve on five such boards. One of my most demanding responsibilities since I retired has been associated with the Prairie*action* Foundation, which included a three-year term as president. After the massacre of 14 women at the Ecôle Polytechnic de Montréal in 1991, the federal government awarded $500,000 grants to five universities across the country to research violence and abuse. The University of Manitoba received the grant for the prairie region and set up a research centre called the Centre for Family Violence and Violence against Women. While I was dean, I allocated funding to the research centre, but the constant budget problems in the Faculty of Arts meant that this, as well as several other research centres in the Faculty, faced uncertainty. As the federal-government grant was coming to an end in 1997, long-term stable funding was needed for the continuation of the work on ending domestic and other forms of intimate violence. Thanks in particular to the dedication of Senator Sharon Carstairs, Margaret Newall (both of whom recently received honorary doctorates from the University of Manitoba), and Jane Ursel (who was awarded the Order of Manitoba for her work in ending domestic violence) two initiatives were taken. The research centre was expanded to encompass the three prairie provinces, with centres at the universities of Saskatchewan (now moved to the University of Regina) and Calgary added to the Centre at the university of Manitoba, and was renamed RESOLVE (Research and Education for Solutions to Violence and Abuse).

At the same time, a non-profit body called Prairie*action* Foundation was also established as a funding arm for the RESOLVE centres. I joined the board of the Foundation as I was ending my term as dean of the Faculty of Arts in 1999. Our mandate at the Foundation is threefold: to provide at least $200,000 a year in infrastructure monies to the RESOLVE research centres; $100,000 a year in support of specific research projects that are identified as joint initiatives of communities and universities; and engage in education and awareness activities about violence and abuse with the aim of finding solutions. So that we can succeed in carrying out our mandate, the endowment fund needs to reach $7.5 million. We are just above $6 million now. In addition to well over 100 projects conducted by the RESOLVE network, over 25 projects have been carried out in communities as diverse as Selkirk, Pinewa, North Battleford, Prince Albert, as well as the larger cities on the prairies.

Progress is being made in finding solutions and breaking the destructive cycle that causes violence and abuse. Successive Manitoba governments have been very proactive in this effort. More victims of violence and abuse (mostly women) are willing to come forward and press charges because they know that these charges will now be treated seriously. The courts are handling these cases more efficiently, more perpetrators are receiving sentences that include counselling, and the rates of recidivism for perpetrators are declining. What is most encouraging, however, is that the rates of domestic homicide in Canada have declined from 16 per million to 8 per million over the last two decades. One of reasons for this decline is most likely the fact that, with all the focus on domestic violence, women are now much more likely to report abuse early, thus avoiding being murdered. Winnipeg still has a large number of murders per year relative to other Canadian cities, but the rates of domestic homicide are now among the lowest in Canada. Ever since the opening of a court dedicated to addressing issues of family violence over 12 years ago, the RESOLVE research team has been in the court every day conducting research on the disposition of the cases. The courts have been most willing to hear the results of the research.

While social-science research has been the main focus of RESOLVE and of Prairie*action* Foundation, we have started to develop what I like to call "healing through the arts." We have received funding to establish a major archive of stories of child abuse told by the victims themselves, to be administered by the RESOLVE network. The project was proposed to us by Elly Danaka, herself a remarkable survivor of abuse.[4]

Writing is healing for victims, instructive for researchers, and inspiring for more recent victims, who may not be able to see the possibility of survival or healing. Perhaps we might also invite sculptors, painters, and other artists who have experienced abuse and are able to express their horror of, and their recovery from, abuse. There are already several monuments situated across the country where victims and others can express their grief. The legislative grounds in Manitoba has such a monument: Women's Grove Memorial, which is identified as a sacred place where people can remember the Montreal massacres and participate in candle-lit ceremonies when women are murdered. Michael Irving's Child Abuse Survivor Monument in Toronto is an inspiring testament to the possibility of healing. The expression of the effect of violence and abuse, as well as of ways to survival and healing, through the literary and visual arts has a long history. As Jane Ursel noted when I proposed the idea to her, "unlike the social-science research, art is an unmediated expression of the experience by victims themselves that can be an extremely important contribution in our efforts to find solutions to violence and abuse."

In May of 2006, the Prairie*action* Foundation helped sponsor a play at the Manitoba Theatre for Young people entitled "Boy, Bang, Boy," a portrayal of a teenage boy who did not understand that "no means no" and forced himself upon a young woman. Given that barely more than 1 percent of date rapes are reported to police, we felt that this was an important project. What is unusual about it is that it is presented from the point of view of the perpetrator, not the victim. Over 4,000 Winnipeg students saw the play. When we overheard one young woman leaving the theatre saying to another "You just must report that to the police," we knew that the project was successful. It is hard not to feel compelled to carry forward this work. In November of 2007, with the enormous help of Els Fenton of Siloam Mission and Debbie Goodfellow of the Manitoba Real Estate Association Shelter Foundation, our foundation organized the first Breakfast with the Boys in Winnipeg, an event to which we attracted 325 men and where we considered the role that men can play in ending violence against women. The leaders of all three levels of government were present. And we also sponsored 50 young men from universities and high schools. Feedback from some men who attended the event suggests that it changed the way they view relationships with women and also changed their understanding of violence and its effect.

Charlene and I began our marriage with a honeymoon travelling down the Amazon and in other points in South America. We have continued to travel the world. Following her stroke, our preferred mode of travel has been to take cruises, which allow her to rest. One exception was our trip to South Africa, where I conducted two weeks of academic workshops, after which we undertook three weeks of safaris. Our travels often overlap with my academic work, and generally we extend our trips with four or five days of holiday. One remarkable trip was an 11-day art cruise to Nunavut, where we were privileged to visit Inuit artists in 11 communities.

Rereading this chapter and reflecting on the academic and community projects in which I am involved, I feel intensely rewarded. I am fortunate to have good health and a supportive wife. I work out of my home and work when I wish. The disabilities of our children remain a constant worry. They are also the source of a great deal of the uncertainty in my life. Charlene and I are frequently uncertain about how to respond appropriately to the situations we face with our children. But their successes, while not those we might have hoped for, are nevertheless important and satisfying. In the end, it is the happiness of our children that we as parents desire above all. Currently, that can only be considered "work in progress." The diversity of my interests and activities energizes me. Friends laugh and tell me I am not really retired. I can only respond that I thoroughly enjoy what I am doing because, above all, I believe that the projects are all worthwhile. Whatever the future holds, I hope I will never forget how fortunate I have been. That is a sense that I would not have experienced as intensely as I do, now that I have written these reflections.

A night out with Noranne
Left to right: Rod Banks and date, Noranne, me

Mount St. Francis Retreat House, Cochrane, Alberta

In my Franciscan habit, 1960,
year of ordination to the priesthood

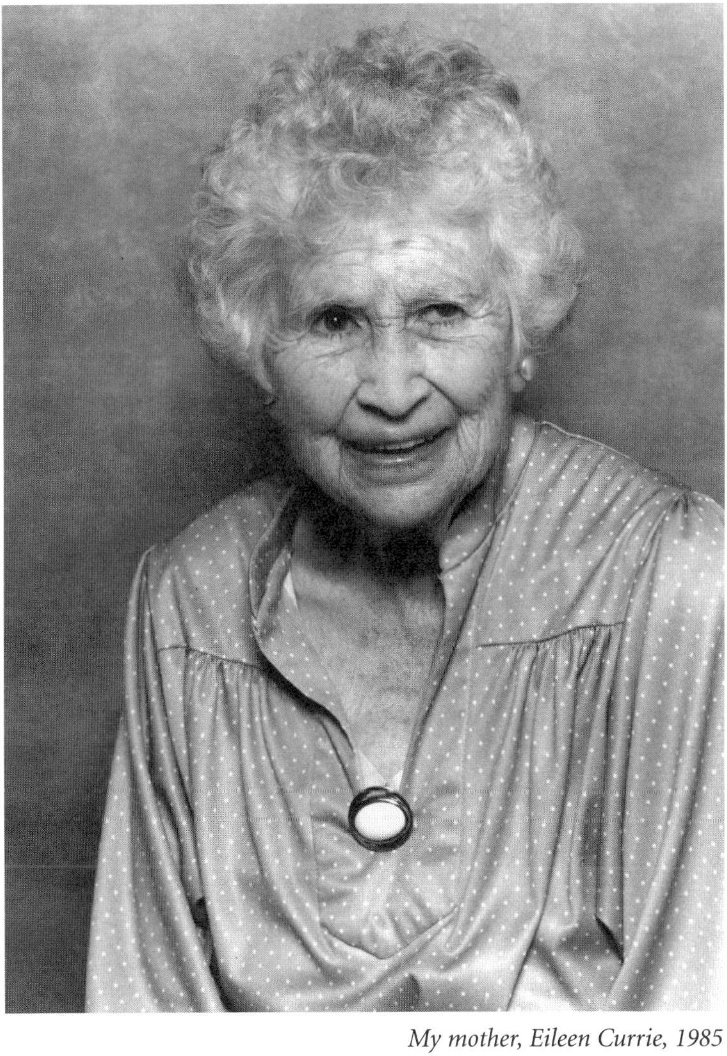

My mother, Eileen Currie, 1985

The Curries and the Sturleys at the cottage, summer, 1995
Back row: John, Robin, Maureen, and me
Front row: Sheila, Kathie, Esmé and Bill

Charlene's parents, Catherine (Kitty) and
Charles John (Mose) Thacker, on their golden wedding anniversary,
May 29, 1987 in Louisville, Kentucky

Reading to the children, 1980

Katie competing in Special Olympics national competition in Halifax, 1994

With Charlene at the cottage, July 1998

Katie makes friends with all animals, especially dogs, 2005

Sherri, Vincent, and daughter Phoenix, 2003

With Vincent in Halifax, 2005

Charlene, 2002

Left to right: Colleen McDougall, Katie, Jolaine Kelly

Sponsor to Lloyd Axworthy when he received his honorary doctorate at the University of Manitoba, 2004 (photograph courtesy of Bob Talbot, University of Manitoba)

Charlene with grandson, Bishop, 2005

Postscript

In 2001 I was asked by our long-time friends Art and Ardelle Martin if I would be a sponsor for their son Tyler at his confirmation. I was given to understand that they had discussed the matter with Tyler at some length. Since the Vatican II Council in the Church in the early 1960s, the rite of Confirmation was restored to its original function as an adult choice, or a reaffirmation of faith by individuals at an age when they could make an informed choice. The average age of the confirmant is now around 15. It is very much like the bar mitzvah and bat mitzvah for Jewish teenagers.

I thought long and hard before accepting the responsibility. A sponsor is a role model, and in matters of faith, as I have already mentioned, I am more a seeker than one who has found answers. Eventually, however, I agreed, and during the several months that Tyler was preparing for the event, I wrote the letter that we as sponsors are asked to give to the confirmand during the ceremony. With Tyler's permission, I have reproduced much of the letter here.

April 27th, 2001
Dear Tyler:
I am very proud to be your sponsor at Confirmation. I want to thank you for the privilege. It has led me to think back on my own confirmation and to reflect on the role of my faith over my lifetime. I have taken a good deal of time to write to you because this

responsibility means a great deal to me. I hope that what I have to say will be of interest to you and benefit you. . . . Perhaps some of it might mean more to you in a couple of years from now when you are older.

The challenges the two of us face are quite different. While you are preparing for a full life ahead, I am reflecting on a full life lived and preparing for death. I don't say that with sadness. Nor do I expect it to be soon. But it is a difficult reality I face just as you are about to face some of your own difficult realities.

The challenges you face at the personal level are the most pressing. Are you going to smoke? Will you use your school and study time well? Are you going to take illegal drugs? If you drink, will you drink responsibly, at the right age, the right amount, at the right time? As your sexual drives become stronger, will you treat yourself and others respectfully? Will you choose to tell the truth even if it is very hard at times? Will you nourish your faith or let it die? I feel sure that you already have the answers in your mind to these questions. But I can assure you that you will be tested over and over again, that some of the decisions have to be made not once in a life, but almost daily.

Another set of issues may seem a bit more distant, but likely they are already beginning to come to your attention. We are social beings, and you will be expected to take a stand on so many issues that I could not begin to list them all. We are lucky to live in Canada, where a number of our laws provide some protection for all people. . . . We cannot legally discriminate in hiring people or in refusing to rent housing to people based on religion, sexual orientation or race. Nor should I neglect to mention our responsibilities to people in other countries, particularly in developing or Third World countries, and our responsibilities to the environment. The list seems endless.

I do have a little advice for you on these matters. First, you cannot personally address all these issues. There are simply too many. On the other hand, you can take courage from the fact that there are so many people in the world trying to make it a better place for everyone. Your own family is one perfect example. The community service component of your preparation for confirmation is a first step to help you get involved in social issues where you can make a difference.

What are the most important things you can do? First, try your best always to be honest with yourself, try your best to be a man of integrity! Above all, you want to be at peace with yourself, respect and love yourself. . . .

When Christ said we should love our neighbours as we love ourselves he really meant it! The more successfully you deal with the personal issues I mentioned above, the more you will be able to face the world and have much to offer.

In dealing with others, let people say of you: "When Tyler gives his word, you can count on it." "Tyler is a man I can trust." "Tyler is a man of integrity, an honest man, a thoughtful and compassionate man." All that may sound like a tall order. But you can do it. You have been blessed with good health, a loving home, good education, a wonderful disposition and it is clear to me from our few conversations that you have very good values.

Of course you will make mistakes of judgement, you will make mistakes of doing and of not doing things. We all do. I think that in those times we embarrass ourselves even more than others. Don't forget that we are a community of sinners!

How does all this relate to confirmation? My faith has been a great source of strength in my life, Tyler. Let me tell you how. First, my faith has taught me that God is a loving God, a forgiving God. The Parable of the Prodigal Son could also be called the Welcome of the Compassionate Father. There is a theme that is repeated frequently in the scriptures that is very comforting to me. It goes like this: "The Lord, the Lord God, slow to anger, rich in kindness and fidelity, forgiving unto a thousand generations, wickedness, crime and sin." When we know we are loved we feel good, really good. We know we will be forgiven mistakes, the sun seems brighter, the trees and flowers prettier, the games we play more fun, our studies easier. "Who can separate us from the love of Christ?" asks Paul in his epistle to the Romans, and then he proceeds to assure us that nothing can do that.

The sacrament of Confirmation is a wonderful time to remember that. It will not only confirm your faith in Christ, but even more important it will confirm Christ's love for you and thus give you new strength.

There is one final thing I do want to say to you. My faith has taught me that what we call the "church" is a very complex reality. It is a community of faith, including individuals, families, children, women as well as men, older people, healthy people, poor as well as rich, those with disabilities, dying people, theologians as well as bishops and priests and sisters. Together we are on a pilgrimage, and this Catholic community provides wonderful signposts on the way. But it does not dispense us from personal responsibility for our lives. Indeed we have the responsibility to be well informed (don't you hate it when kids or adults talk about some things when they don't really know anything about the matter!). But once we have tried to become informed or knowledgeable, we then have to make our own decisions. That is why good people can differ on politics, and yes, even on religious issues. I am suggesting that Confirmation will give you the strength to bring your own understanding, your own intuitions, your own judgement to life situations. Indeed, at times you may even have doubts about your faith. Don't feel guilty about that. Any thinking person will have doubts. Don't be afraid if that happens. Face your doubts, take your time, become better informed, reflect and pray about them, perhaps talk about them with people you respect, and then act with honesty and integrity.

One of the questions I was asked to address in this letter, Tyler, is what kind of relationship we might have after your confirmation. To be honest, right now I am not sure what it will be. And I am not worried about that. Things will work out over time. I do not want to be an "obligation" in your life, someone you have to see. I think we should get together occasionally and let things happen naturally. But one thing I am absolutely sure about: if you ever wish to talk about any issues, I will find time. You can count on it.

In the meantime, I look forward to your confirmation. You can count on my prayers for you now and in the future, as I hope I can count on yours.

Raymond

The Parable of the Prodigal Son

A man had two sons. The younger said to his father, "Father, let me have the share of the estate that would come to me." So the father divided the property between them. A few days later, the younger son got together everything he had and left for a distant country where he squandered his money on a life of debauchery.

When he had spent it all, that country experienced a severe famine, and now he began to feel the pinch, so he hired himself out to one of the local inhabitants who put him on his farm to feed the pigs. And he would willingly have filled his belly with the husks the pigs were eating but no one offered him anything. Then he came to his senses and said, "How many of my father's paid servants have more food than they want, and here am I dying of hunger! I will leave this place and go to my father and say: Father, I have sinned against heaven and against you; I no longer deserve to be called your son; treat me as one of your paid servants." So he left the place and went back to his father.

While he was still a long way off, his father saw him and was moved to pity. He ran to the boy, clasped him in his arms and kissed him tenderly. Then his son said, "Father, I have sinned against heaven and against you. I no longer deserve to be called your son." But the father said to his servants, "Quick! Bring out the best robe and put it on him; put a ring on his finger and sandals on his feet. Bring the calf we have been fattening, and kill it;

we are going to have a feast, a celebration, because this son of mine was dead and has come back to life; he was lost and is found." And they began to celebrate.

Now the elder son was out in the fields, and on his way back, as he drew near the house, he could hear music and dancing. Calling one of the servants he asked what it was all about. "Your brother has come," replied the servant, "and your father has killed the calf we had fattened because he has got him back safe and sound." He was angry then and refused to go in, and his father came out to plead with him; but he answered his father, "Look, all these years I have slaved for you and never once disobeyed your orders, yet you never offered me so much as a kid for me to celebrate with my friends. But for this son of yours, when he comes back after swallowing up your property—he and his women—you kill the calf we had been fattening."

The father said, "My son, you are with me always and all I have is yours. But it was only right we should celebrate and rejoice, because your brother here was dead and has come to life; he was lost and is found."

—Gospel of St. Luke 15:11–32
(trans., *The Jerusalem Bible,* Garden City,
NY: Doubleday, 1966)

GLOSSARY

Asperger syndrome
"A neurodevelopmental disorder on the autism spectrum. It shares many of the same characteristics as autism, including difficulty within the reality of social interaction, communication, and understanding and displaying appropriate emotions. Sometimes people with Asperger syndrome also experience anxiety, depression and various learning disabilities" (from pamphlet entitled "Asperger Manitoba Inc., Celebrating Abilities").

associate professor, full professor
Academics usually begin their university career as assistant professors, are then promoted to associate professors after an average of about seven years, and may later be promoted to full professors, based on their teaching, research and community-service record. At the time I was dean of the Faculty of Arts, approximately 50 percent of the faculty retired having achieved the rank of full professor.

brotherhood
Male members of religious orders can be brothers or priests. Those choosing to be brothers wish to embrace religious life but prefer other responsibilities than those of the priestly ministry. Francis of Assisi was himself a brother.

director of vocations
The person responsible to attract recruits to the religious community.

Divine Office
Seven sets of prayers (Matins, Lauds, Prime, Terse, Sext, None, Vespers, Compline), spaced over five periods of the day, which each priest is expected to recite. Those living in friaries and monasteries normally recite the prayers together, but the responsibility remains with the individual to do so if group prayer is not possible.

ecumenism
While the term need not be restricted to religious matters, in the religious context, an ecumenical approach is an attempt to look for all the positive signs of the Divine in religious traditions other than one's own.

Franciscans
More formally, Franciscans are known in the Catholic Church as the Order of Friars Minor, founded by Francis of Assisi, in Italy in 1209.

friars, friary
Traditionally, friars in a friary go out from their communities "into the world" to preach the gospel. Monks, on the others hand, tend to stay in the monastery and interact with visitors there. Franciscans and Dominicans are examples of friars, while Trappists, Cistercians, and Benedictines are the earliest monks. Jesuits, founded in the 16th century, do not fit either of these classifications.

guardian
The leader of the community in a Franciscan friary is called the guardian. Francis of Assisi did not want anyone called superior because of his desire to avoid a hierarchy.

head of department
At the University of Manitoba, the legal term for the person in charge of an academic department is called a head. In most universities in Canada, that person is designated as the chair. While there are slight differences in legal responsibilities between the two, in this book the terms are used interchangeably.

hierarchy
Bishops, priests, and deacons fill the fundamental positions of authority in the Roman Catholic Church. Archbishops normally oversee several bishops in a geographic area. The pope is the bishop of Rome and the head of the Church. The Vatican II Council (1962–1965) is the most recent council of bishops of the world called by the pope of the time.

laicization
A term used to describe priests who have asked for, and obtained from Rome, permission to resign from the ministry.

laity
In the Catholic Church, those who are not members of the hierarchy or members of religious communities are called the laity. In other words, they form the overwhelming majority of all Catholics.

liturgy
The order of prayers, songs, and actions to be carried out in the celebration of Church events, such as the Mass.

minor seminary
A residential high school for Catholic boys who are thinking of becoming priests. More than a dozen of these schools existed in Canada between the 1940s and the 1960s.

novitiate
The first year of training for those entering religious life. After this first year, those who have decided to stay and have been accepted take vows of poverty, chastity, and obedience.

religious
In the Catholic Church, the religious are those who belong to a community of men or women, dedicating their lives to various ministries and taking vows of poverty, chastity, and obedience. Some men in religious orders, but not all, may be ordained priests.

Religious of the Sacred Heart
A Roman Catholic order of nuns that my sister, Maureen, joined. They are prominent for their work in education and ran a school on Westgate Avenue in Winnipeg for years and then moved their school to the west end of Assiniboine Park before closing.

senior scholar
An academic who retires from the University of Manitoba can request to continue his/her research program at the University in the rank of senior scholar. These are three-year, renewable terms with no salary.

seminarians
Those adults studying for the priesthood, usually four years of theology following several years of studies in philosophy. Currently it is more likely that these students will live together and study at a local university, but there are still seminaries that offer their own courses.

SSHRC
The Social Sciences and Humanities Research Council is the principle source of funding for academics in Canadian universities

who are conducting research in the humanities and social sciences. There are two parallel councils: the Natural Sciences and Engineering Research Council (NSERC) and the Canadian Institute of Health Research (CIHR).

state of mortal sin
In Catholic moral teaching, those who commit a serious offense, known by them to be seriously wrong, but who also have the freedom not to engage in that behaviour and who have not repented, are living in what is called a state of mortal sin.

tenure
A "tenure-track" appointment is the dream of every young academic. Usually in the seventh year after being hired by the University of Manitoba, an individual must apply for tenure. The goal of tenure is to provide academics with some security so that they can carry on their work with "academic freedom"—that is, in an atmosphere where they need not worry that what they say could lead to their dismissal because it has offended government or others in the University or the community. They are still subject to annual reviews, and tenure does not protect them from dismissal because of incompetence or unprofessional behaviour.

Vatican II Council
Periodically throughout history, popes have called all the bishops of the world to come together to discuss matters of Church doctrine and practice. These are considered the most important meetings in the life of the Church. The most recent was called Vatican II Council and was convened in Rome between 1962 and 1965 by Pope John XXIII. There have been 21 ecumenical councils in the history of the Church; the one before Vatican II was convened in 1869.

BIOGRAPHY

Born in 1934 and brought up in Winnipeg, Manitoba, Raymond F. Currie attended high school in Edmonton and then in 1953 entered the Franciscans, a Roman Catholic religious order. After theological studies in Quebec, he was ordained a priest in 1960 and conducted ministry all across western Canada until 1967, when he went to New York to pursue graduate studies in sociology at Fordham University. He received his MA (1969) and his PhD (1973) and returned to Winnipeg to the University of Manitoba, where he was a faculty member until his retirement in 2000. He resigned from the priesthood in 1973, married in 1975 and, with his wife, Charlene, shared in the love and raising of their two children, both of whom have disabilities. At the University he was head of the Department of Sociology and then dean of the Faculty of Arts for two terms. Since his retirement, he leads the Research Data Centre Network, a national network of 24 centres at universities across Canada that conducts research in the social sciences. He also serves on a number of national social-science committees and local volunteer boards and has received numerous awards for his professional contributions, including a Faculty Association Administrator of the Year award, the Peter D. Curry Chancellor's award for "individuals who have made distinct contribution to University governance" and the Queen's Golden Jubilee Medal for public service. He lives in Winnipeg with his wife, Charlene, near their daughter, their son and his partner, and their two grandchildren.

NOTES

Chapter 2: Catholic Family

1. Maureen Daly, *Seventeenth Summer* (New York: Dodd, Mead and Co., 1942).
2. Benen Fahy, trans., *The Writings of St. Francis of Assisi* (Chicago: Franciscan Herald Press, 1963).
3. Graham Greene, *The Power and the Glory* (New York: Penguin, 1940).

Chapter 4: Studies in Philosphy and Theology

1. Karl Marx, *A Contribution to the Critique of Political Economy* (Moscow: Progress Publishers, [1859] 1977).
2. F.X. Durwell, *The Resurrection of Christ* (New York: Sheed and Ward, 1960).
3. Bernard Häring, *Moral Theology: The Law of Christ* (Manwah, NJ: Paulist Press, 1954).
4. Herbert Jone and Urban Adelman, *Moral Theology,* 13th ed. (Westminster, MD: Newman Press, 1953).
5. p. 263.
6. Michael Novak, *The Open Church: Vatican II, Act II* (New York: Macmillan, 1964).
7. John Courtney Murray, *We Hold these Truths: Catholic Reflections on the American Proposition* (Lanham, MD: Rowman and Littlefield, [1960] 2005), p. xiii.
8. Eric Hoffer, *The True Believer: Thoughts on the Nature of Mass Movements* (New York: Harper and Row, 1951).
9. William K. Carroll, Linda Christiansen-Ruffman, Raymond F. Currie, and Deborah Harrison, eds., *Fragile Truths: Twenty-Five Years of Sociology and Anthropology in Canada* (Ottawa: Carleton University Press, 1992).
10. p. 8.
11. Gregory Baum, "Contraception and Holiness: *The Catholic Predicament,*" in *Contraception and Holiness: A Symposium Introduced by Archbishop Thomas D. Roberts* (New York: Herder and Herder, 1964), p. 313.
12. Canadian Bishops' Statement on *Humanae Vitae: Encyclical on The Regulation of Birth,* 28 September 1968.

13. As quoted by the *New York Times,* 14 December 1965, in Dorothy Dohen, *Nationalism and American Catholicism* (New York: Sheed and Ward, 1967), p. 1.
14. p. 144.
15. Raymond F. Currie and Zachary Zimmer, "Supporting the Bruised Reed: A Longitudinal Study of Young, Single Moms, 1985–95" (Winnipeg: Villa Rosa, 784 Wolseley Ave., Winnipeg, MB, R3G 1C6).
16. Geoffrey Curtis, *Paul Couturier and Unity in Christ* (London: SCM Press, 1964), p. 48.

Chapter 5: Early Years in the Ministry

1. Paul Strychman and Bob Gaudet, *Priests in Canada: A Report on English-Speaking Clergy* (Quebec City: Laval University Press, 1971).

Chapter 6: Graduate Studies in New York

1. Hans Küng, *Truthfulness: The Future of the Church* (New York: Sheed and Ward, 1968).
2 p. 70–72.
3. Graham Greene, *The End of the Affair* (Portsmouth, NH: Heinemann, 1951).
4. Reginald Bibby and Merlin Brinkerhoff, "The Circulation of the Saints," *Journal for the Scientific Study of Religion* 12 (1973): pp. 273–283.
5. Ernest L. Boyer, "Ways of Knowing," in *Scholarship Reconsidered: Priorities of the Professoriate* (Princeton, NJ: Carnegie Foundation for the Advancement of Teaching, 1990).
6. Eugene R. Rice, "Making a Place for the New American Scholar," delivered at the AAHE Conference on Faculty Roles and Rewards, Atlanta, Georgia, American Association of Higher Education, 1996.
7. W. Kauffman, *The Future of the Humanities* (New York: Thomas Y. Crowell, 1977), p. 200.
8. Charles Y. Glock and Rodney Stark, *Religion and Society in Tension* (Chicago: Rand McNally, 1965). [This is the first of many studies by these two scholars on the quantitative approach to measuring the various dimensions of religious commitment.]
9. Blaise Pascal, *Pensées,* trans. A.J . Krailsheimer (New York: Penguin Classics, 1995), p. 127.

Chapter 7: Marriage and Begining of Academic Career

1. Raymond F. Currie, "Belonging, Commitment, and Socialization in a Western City," in *Religion in Canadian Society,* ed. Stewart Crysdale and Les Wheatcroft, 462–478 (Toronto: Macmillan of Canada, 1976).
2. Raymond F. Currie, Barry Trute, Bruce Tefft, and Alexander Segall, "Maybe on My Street: The Politics of Community Placement of the Mentally Ill, *Urban Affairs Quarterly* 25:2 (1989).
3. William K. Carroll, Linda Christiansen-Ruffman, Raymond F. Currie, and Deborah Harrison, *Fragile Truths: Twenty-Five Years of Sociology and Anthropology in Canada* (Ottawa: Carleton University Press, 1992).

Chapter 8: Suffering with our Children

1. Oliver Sacks, *An Anthropologist On Mars: Seven Paradoxical Tales* (New York: Vintage, 1996).
2. Temple Grandin, *Thinking in Pictures: Autism and Visual Thought* (New York: Vintage, 1996).
3. From Charles Horton Cooley, *Human Nature and the Social Order* (New York: Scribner's, 1902), pp. 179–185.
4. Henri Nouwen, *The Return of the Prodigal Son: A Mediation on Fathers, Brothers, and Sons* (New York: Random House, 1994).
5. C. Wright Mills, *The Sociological Imagination* (New York: Oxford University Press, 1959).

Chapter 9: Living with the Dying of Others

1. Joseph Cardinal Bernardin, *A Gift of Peace* (Chicago: Loyola Press, 1997).
2. P. 152.

Chapter 10: My Life as a Dean

1. *Chronicle of Higher Education,* October 2001.

Chapter 11: Retirement

1. Michael Gibbons, *Higher Education Relevance in the 21st Century,* UNESCO World Conference on Higher Education, Paris, October 5–9, 1998.
2. Gibbons's insights are discussed in an outstanding article on the future of higher education entitled "Academic Work in the Twenty-

first Century, Changing Roles and Policies," by Peter Coaldrake and Lawrence Stedman, Higher Education Division, Occasional Paper Series 99H, Commonwealth of Australia.
3. Raymond F. Currie and Byron Spencer, "Research Data Centres: A Quantum Leap Forward in Social Science Capabilities," *Policy Research Initiative* 8.1 (2005): pp. 38–41.
4. Elly Danica, *Don't: A Woman's Word* (Toronto: McClelland and Stewart, 1990).